THE BRONTË SISTERS AND GEORGE ELIOT

First published in Great Britain 1988 by
The Macmillan Press Ltd

First published in the USA 1988 by
BARNES & NOBLE BOOKS
81 ADAMS DRIVE
TOTOWA, NEW JERSEY, 07512

ISBN 0–389–20756–X

Library of Congress Cataloging-in-Publication Data

Prentis, Barbara.
  The Brontë sisters and George Eliot.

  Bibliography: p.
  Includes index.
  1. English fiction—Women authors—History and
criticism. 2. English fiction—19th century—History and
criticism. 3. Brontë, Anne, 1820–1849. 4. Brontë,
Charlotte, 1816–1855. 5. Brontë, Emily, 1818–1848.
6. Eliot, George, 1819–1880. 7. Women novelists, English
—19th century—Biography. 8. Women and literature—
Great Britain—History—19th century. I. Title.
PR115.P74 1987   823'.8'099287   87–14528
ISBN 0–389–20756–X

The Brontë Sisters and George Eliot

A Unity of Difference

Barbara Prentis

BARNES & NOBLE BOOKS
TOTOWA, NEW JERSEY

Contents

Contents

Principal Dates

THE BRONTËS

1813	Maria Brontë born at Hartshead, Yorkshire. Baptised 23 April 1814.
1815	8 February. Elizabeth Brontë born at Hartshead.
1816	21 April. Charlotte Brontë born at Thornton, Yorkshire.
1817	26 June. Patrick Branwell Brontë born at Thornton.
1818	30 July. Emily Jane Brontë born at Thornton.
1820	17 January. Anne Brontë born at Thornton.
	25 February. Brontë family move to Haworth.
1821	15 September. Mrs Maria Brontë dies, aged 38.
	Aunt Branwell assumes care of Brontë family at Haworth.
1824–25	The sisters, Maria and Elizabeth and Charlotte and Emily, attend Cowan Bridge School.
1825	6 May. Maria Brontë dies, aged 11.
	15 June. Elizabeth Brontë dies, aged 10.
	Autumn. Charlotte and Emily return home from Cowan Bridge School.
1831	January. Charlotte commences at Roe Head School.
1835	Charlotte becomes assistant to Miss Wooler at Roe Head School.
	Emily commences as pupil, but soon returns home. Anne attends as pupil.
1836	Emily becomes teacher at Law Hill School, Southowram (period uncertain, but possibly only six months).
1838	Charlotte leaves Roe Head School.
1839	April. Anne goes as governess to Ingham family of Blake Hall, Mirfield.
	May–July. Charlotte governess to Sidgwick family, Stonegappe.
	19 August. William Weightman becomes curate to the Reverend Patrick Brontë.
1840	Anne leaves Blake Hall.
1841	March. Charlotte goes as governess to White family, Rawdon.
	Anne becomes governess to family of the Reverend Edmund Robinson, Thorp Green.

1842	February. Charlotte and Emily become pupils at Pensionnat Heger, Brussels.
	6 September. William Weightman dies, aged 27.
	29 October. Aunt Branwell dies.
	November. Charlotte and Emily recalled from Brussels.
	December. Branwell goes as tutor to son of the Reverend Edmund Robinson at Thorp Green.
1843	January. Charlotte returns to Brussels alone.
1844	January. Charlotte comes home for good.
	The Reverend Arthur Nicholls appointed curate at Haworth.
	The Brontë sisters plan to open a school. Issue circulars. No replies.
1845	June. Branwell dismissed from Thorp Green in disgrace. Anne returns home with him.
1846	The sisters publish their poems.
	Charlotte offers *The Professor* to publishers. Rejected.
1847	October. Publication of *JE* under pseudonym of Currer Bell.
	December. Emily and Anne publish *WH* and *AG* respectively under pseudonyms of Ellis and Acton Bell.
1848	Anne publishes *TTWH*.
	24 September. Branwell dies.
	19 December. Emily dies, aged 30.
1849	28 May. Anne dies (at Scarborough), aged 29.
	26 October. Charlotte publishes *Shirley*.
1853	28 January. Publication of *Villette*.
1854	29 June. Charlotte marries the Reverend Arthur Nicholls.
1855	31 March. Charlotte dies, aged nearly 39.
1857	March. Mrs Gaskell's *Life of Charlotte Brontë* published.
	Charlotte's *The Professor* published posthumously.
1861	7 June. The Reverend Patrick Brontë dies, aged 85.

GEORGE ELIOT

1819	22 November. George Eliot born (Mary Ann Evans) at South Farm, Arbury, near Nuneaton.
1824–36	Sent away to boarding schools.
1836	3 February. Death of Mrs Christiana Evans.

1840	GE's first published work (a poem in the *Christian Observer*).
1841	Meets the Brays, and reads Charles Hennell's *An Inquiry Concerning the Origin of Christianity*.
1846	15 June. Publication of translation of Strauss's *Das Leben Jesu*.
1850	Joins John Chapman in the editing of *The Westminster Review*.
	6 October. Meets George Henry Lewes for the first time.
1854	July. Publication of translation of Feuerbach's *Das Wesen des Christentums*.
	20 July. Goes on holiday abroad with Lewes as his wife.
1856	Commences writing of fiction under pseudonym of George Eliot ('Amos Barton').
	Publishes articles 'The Natural History of German Life' and 'Silly Novels by Lady Novelists'.
1858	Publication of *Scenes of Clerical Life*.
1859	Publication of *AB*.
1860	Publication of *The Mill*.
1861	Publication of *SM*.
1863	Publication of *Romola*.
1866	Publication of *FH*.
1868	Publication of poem *The Spanish Gypsy*.
1870	Publication of poem *The Legend of Jubal*.
1871–72	Publication of *Middlemarch*.
1876	Publication of *DD*.
1878	30 November. Death of Lewes.
1879	Publication of *The Impressions of Theophrastus Such*.
1880	6 May GE marries John Cross.
	22 December. GE dies.

Acknowledgements

I owe a special debt of gratitude to those whose initial advice and guidance helped me to consolidate the ideas now brought together in this book. In this respect, I wish to thank Dr Jim Davies, Lecturer in the English Department of the University College of Swansea, for his sustained counsel and support; also Professor Inga-Stina Ewbank of the School of English, University of Leeds, and Mr Graham Holderness, Tutor in Adult and Continuing Education at the University College of Swansea, for their most helpful critical recommendations.

My thanks are also due to all those who were kind enough to read this book in typescript and to give me the benefit of their expert critical comments and suggestions: in particular, Dr Jim Davies, Dr Mary Woodward, Honorary Research Fellow and Senior Lecturer (retired) of the Psychology Department, University College of Swansea, Dr Bernard Harrison, Senior Lecturer in the Division of Education, University of Sheffield, and Mrs Jane James, Head of the English Department, Bishop Gore School, Swansea. Any faults remaining in the work are entirely my responsibility.

I am also especially grateful to the Librarian of the Brontë Society, Haworth, for the unstinting supply of photostats of articles published in the Society's *Transactions*, and to Mrs Mary N. Haight, widow of Professor Gordon S. Haight of Yale University, for so thoughtfully writing to me with her personal permission to quote from her late husband's biography of George Eliot.

Last, but by no means least, I am much indebted to Mrs Rita Williams, Secretary in the English Department, University College of Swansea, for her patient and efficient typing of the final script.

Preface

It has become almost common practice for authors of new books on the Brontës to offer their readers an introductory apology for having produced yet more words upon what is admittedly a much-ventilated subject. The justification usually offered for this implied offence is that some new facet of the lives or works of the sisters has been perceived that has hitherto escaped notice. The same plea is made on behalf of this book, but no apology accompanies it, since it is held that sufficient justification for the continued appearance of books about the Brontës lies within the Brontës themselves. The enigma of their lives and the phenomenon of their genius remain as engrossing as ever, constantly regenerating the supply and demand of literature in this field.

The present book aims to make a new contribution to the discussion by bridging the gap that exists in the comparative literature relevant to the sisters and the only other major English woman novelist born at the same time as themselves. Although the difference of a decade separates the publication of the first Brontë fiction and the emergence of George Eliot as a novelist, the fact is that all four were born in the period between 1816 and 1820, and all grew up under the influence of the same dramatically changing world. It would thus seem reasonable to ask in what ways their responses to that world were similar or different, why these affinities or differences existed and in what distinctive ways they were reflected in the work produced.

To date, most of the comparative work in this area has been confined to particular aspects of Eliot's fiction seen against related elements in that of Charlotte Brontë, and to studies of one Brontë sister with another. In the main, the *dissimilarities* between the Brontës and George Eliot have seemed almost to preclude any close attention to the significance of the links between them.[1]

The argument put forward throughout the present work, however, is that, in fact, the Brontës and George Eliot shared what might be called a necessary intellectual and literary relationship, generated by their mutual historical experience and their united concern regarding many aspects of the general social ethos. The purpose of the work is accordingly to define the nature of this relationship, and to identify and explain similarities and divergences of attitude, as these are revealed in the respective novels. To provide a focus for this, certain of the period's important areas of controversy have been selected for detailed discussion, and these matters form the following chapter headings. These particular subjects were chosen, as against many others that might have been dealt with, because, apart from the obvious restrictions of space, these matters were felt to represent those in which the tensions and anxieties of society overall were most closely matched by those of the four authors.

It should be explained that the designation of 'the Brontës' in apparently unitary terms is purely nominal, and is in no way to be seen as overlooking the very real distinctions between the sisters, either as human beings or as novelists. At the same time, it is hoped to show that the sisters' work as a whole constitutes something of a watershed in the transition that began to take place between the novel as 'romance' and the novel as 'truth'. Similarly, they were the first English writers to present women not simply as tragic, humorous or exaggeratedly virtuous adjuncts to a basically masculine society, but as free-standing individuals with a conscious responsibility for their own moral decisions. Later, in her own rather more oblique way, George Eliot was to do likewise. Of itself alone, this attitude to their own sex is an important reason for examining the four as a group in relation to their age, as well as individuals in relation to each other. Overall, it is hoped to show that the work of these four very different authors cohered to form a unique and distinct 'tradition' within the contemporary literary context, a tradition which was to play a profoundly significant part in the future development of the English novel.

In general, concentration is upon the intellectual and emotional factors which contributed towards the fiction produced by the Brontës and George Eliot. No claim is made to offer any purely literary criticism of a comparative or any other kind, except in so far as matters of theme or style illuminate in some way the artistic or intellectual connections between the novelists. By the same token, no systematic discussion is provided of the Brontë Juvenilia. Except for one or two references to Emily Brontë's earlier poetry, attention is confined in the main to the mature work.

All four authors are looked at individually in relation to the subject forming the respective chapter heading, and each chapter closes with a brief comparative summary. While it may appear that certain of the subjects chosen tend by their nature to overlap – as, for example, death with matters of belief, and love and sexuality with the Woman Question – each subject in isolation yields important differences of focus which render their separate treatment essential.

B. P.
Swansea

Introduction:
Some Connections

At the end of March 1855, after a brief illness, Charlotte Brontë died in her old home at Haworth. She left two solitary survivors: her seventy-eight-year-old father and the husband with whom she had known one brief year of marriage.

Charlotte's death signalled the end of the extraordinary Brontë phenomenon – and the beginning of what might almost be called a legend; today, a hundred and thirty years on, the 'Brontë Story' still fascinates, and looks set to do so well into the foreseeable future. Part of this fascination undeniably stems from the almost unbelievable real-life drama and tragedy of the sisters' lives. But their literary achievement requires no subjective support. Between them, they threw down a challenge to the nineteenth-century literary world – and especially to their fellow women novelists; Romance and Realism had finally been united and the consequences could not be ignored. Within three years, another woman was to pick up the challenge and make it uniquely her own. Mary Ann Evans – or Marianne Evans as she sometimes called herself – produced her first work of fiction, *Scenes of Clerical Life*, taking, under the pseudonym of George Eliot, her first hesitant steps towards becoming the late nineteenth-century's greatest female novelist.

It is the gap between the appearance of the first of the Brontë novels and *Scenes of Clerical Life* – a matter of eleven years – that causes the material distance between the four women to seem greater than it actually was. In fact, Mary Ann Evans was born just two months before Anne Brontë and less than sixteen months after Emily. By the time she emerged as a novelist, however, all three sisters were dead, and we can thus only speculate as to the observations which her work might have generated round the parlour table at Haworth. In the other direction, the situation is happily slightly more illuminating; among the vast numbers of letters which George Eliot left to posterity,[1] several references occur which provide us with a valuable insight into her attitude to the Brontë family in general and to the work of Charlotte in particular, which reached its full recognition in the five years roughly

1

corresponding to the time of George Eliot's achievements as a translator and journal editor.[2] Indeed, when we consider the number of literary figures with whom Charlotte Brontë and George Eliot became acquainted in common – for example, Thackeray, Carlyle, Harriet Martineau, Elizabeth Gaskell, George Henry Lewes – the absence of any actual contact between the two women seems an altogether perverse misfortune from our point of view. Both, for example, visited Miss Martineau at her home in Ambleside, Charlotte in the winter of 1850, George Eliot in the autumn of 1852; Lewes met Charlotte at Mrs Gaskell's home in 1850, just a year before he was introduced to George Eliot, and he was well acquainted with Thackeray, whom Charlotte met on several occasions, the last being in the summer of 1851, only a matter of months before Lewes and George Eliot met for the first time.[3] So far as George Eliot and Charlotte Brontë are concerned, therefore, the picture is one of what we might call 'near misses'.

Nevertheless, despite this absence of any direct personal contact between the four women, a study of their lives reveals a surprising number of factors which all experienced from an early age. It is from the identification of these common influences that there arises the expectation of finding further links or parallels of thought, feeling and literary expression between all four novelists. The following paragraphs are intended to serve only as a brief preliminary clarification of these points, all of which will be dealt with where relevant in the following chapters. The subject of religion, however, is a crucial one and will therefore receive a chapter to itself, where it will be discussed in detail.

Early motherlessness. Effectively, all four girls were deprived of the maternal influence at a very early age. When Mrs Maria Brontë died in 1821, Charlotte was approximately five-and-a-half years old, Emily a little over three and Anne not yet two.[4] The position of Mary Anne Evans differed only to the extent that infant motherlessness was due, not to death, but to what has been described as a psychological problem affecting Mrs Christiana Evans, which led her to send Mary Ann away to boarding school at the age of five and to create what was for all practical purposes a separation between herself and her children.[5]

Environmental and social status. The differences which we might expect to discover between life in a relatively impoverished Yorkshire parsonage on the edge of wild moorland and that in 'a delightful, roomy, red-brick farmhouse'[6] in sheltered Warwickshire tend to disappear in the light of certain basic similarities that come together under this heading: for example, rural environment, class status and political persuasion. As the daughters of a parson – albeit one who had fought his way out of poverty – the Brontë sisters were unquestionably of the cultured class; the influence of their father's politics was 'distinctly Tory'.[7] Robert Evans, too, had come of a lowly background, rising from the occupation of carpenter to hold the reasonably prestigious responsibility of estate management for the distinguished Newdigate family of Arbury Hall. 'My father did not raise himself from being an artisan to be a farmer,' George Eliot once proudly wrote to her friends, the Brays, '. . . he raised himself from being an artisan to be a man whose extensive knowledge in very varied practical departments made his services valued through several counties'.[8] And clearly Robert Evans took care that his relatively superior status should be reflected in his life-style, for we are told he took 'both his politics and his religion from Arbury Hall'.[9]

Early brother-influence. Quoting from George Eliot's 'Brother and Sister' sonnets,[10] Gordon S. Haight describes the young Mary Ann's devotion to her only full brother, Isaac, three-and-a-half years her senior, as 'puppy-like'. From what we know of Brontë family life, it is reasonably certain that a rather more robust relationship existed between the sisters and their brother, Branwell. Nevertheless, the situation in the Brontë household, where typical Victorian hope and veneration centred on a much-valued only son, was not dissimilar. Charlotte in particular appears to have been deeply attached to Branwell when both were young,[11] even though her feelings for him turned to disgusted severity in later life when his dissipations became a blight on all their lives. For the Brontës, as for George Eliot for different reasons, the ideal relationship was to end in disappointment, pain and a sense of betrayal, the effects of which would be identifiable in the novels.

Educational background. This is an area in which a number of similarities can be seen. We might, for example, compare the 'sending away' of the Evans children by their mother with the Reverend Patrick Brontë's decision to despatch his own very small daughters to boarding school. The practical effects were much the same, even if Mr Brontë's probable motives are much more readily understood. Despite the encouragement he seems to have given to his children's varied creative pursuits,[12] the pressures and problems stemming from the daily presence of a large family of motherless girls must have weighed upon him heavily. Equally, as Winifred Gérin points out,[13] he would have realised the urgent desirability of his daughters being in a position to earn their own livings should – as it did – the need arise. What is certain is that the pains of early exposure to boarding-school life, the isolation, homesickness and sheer physical suffering were all experiences which the older Brontë daughters and the young George Eliot shared.

Additionally, there were similarities between the type and standard of education received by Mary Ann Evans and her sister, Chrissey, at Miss Lathom's School at Attleborough and that provided for the Brontës at the Clergy Daughters School at Cowan Bridge. While the latter would seem to have deserved much of the condemnation it received following the outbreaks of disease that claimed the lives of several of its early pupils, including those of the Reverend Patrick Brontë's two daughters, Maria and Elizabeth, nevertheless the school offered a more aspiring kind of education for girls than was generally available at the time. Certainly, at their second school, Roe Head, Mirfield, under the direction of Miss Margaret Wooler and her sisters, Charlotte and Emily enjoyed instruction of a quality that clearly compared by no means unfavourably with Miss Franklin's School at Coventry, where later 'George Eliot was excellently taught'.[14]

Cultural influences. The little that is known of the Brontë sisters' early reading suggests the kind of broad cultural links between them and the young Mary Ann Evans that would be expected of similarly bred and educated female adolescents of the period. Haight refers to Mary Ann reading Shakespeare and Milton, Watts, Pope, Young and Cowper, and such 'moderns' as Southey and Byron, and Byron's biographer, Moore.[15] He also tells us that Wordsworth was the poet whom she was to hold in special reverence for the rest of her life.[16] It is a list that compares in almost all particulars with Charlotte Brontë's own 'catalogue' of recommended reading which, in 1834, while still a pupil at Roe Head, she sent to her close friend, Ellen Nussey. Accompanying the names of Shakespeare and Byron, however, was the salutary injunction: 'Omit the comedies of Shakespeare, and the 'Don Juan', perhaps the 'Cain', of Byron . . . and read the rest fearlessly':[17] an ironic observation from one whose first published novel was to produce a furore of moral indignation among a not inconsiderable section of the English reading public.

For the young Mary Ann Evans, considerable cultural benefit was afforded by her father's position as estate manager to the Newdigate family, who, as her reputation as a promising young scholar increased, invited her to borrow books from Arbury Hall's extensive library.[18] A similar claim has been made for the Brontës in connection with Ponden House, the old Elizabethan manor home of the Heaton family at Stanbury, some two miles across the moors from the Brontë Parsonage.[19] Neither support nor refutation of this notion, however, results from examination of the Heaton papers held at the Bradford City Library; nor is Mrs Gaskell's statement that 'they [the Brontë children] were allowed to get books from the circulating library at Keighley'[20] very helpful. Presumably, Mrs Gaskell was referring to the Keighley Mechanics' Institute Library, which was founded in 1825 'to bring the Arts and Sciences "within the reach of the most humble"',[21] and whose members, we are told, included 'a good sprinkling of gentlemen, professionals and clergymen'. But since the Reverend Patrick Brontë did not become a member of the Institute until some eight years after its foundation, opinion is divided as to the reliance to be placed upon this as a source of the Brontë children's earlier reading.[22] Perhaps the letter which Charlotte wrote many years later to her publisher's reader, W. S. Williams,[23] should be seen as a salutary hint that we should not be over-optimistic in our diligent searches for possible literary sources for the Brontë works. '. . . what seems to you the result of reading and study,' Charlotte wrote, 'is chiefly spontaneous and intuitive . . . .' The position here is ambiguous. We have Mrs Gaskell's word that 'up and down the house [at Haworth] were to be found many standard works of a solid kind. Sir Walter Scott's writings, Wordsworth's and Southey's poems were among the lighter literature'.[24] And we should not forget the family's extensive reading of newspapers and periodicals,[25] among the latter being *Blackwood's* and *Fraser's* magazines, both noted for their trenchant commentary and wide coverage of contemporary events. On the other hand, it has been stated[26] that the Brontës were 'remarkably ignorant' of the work of the fiction writers of their own time, due, it is suggested, partly to Brontë family poverty and partly to the Evangelical influence. The latter suggests yet another affinity between the sisters and George Eliot, going back to a period quite early in their lives – that is, that stemming from the inherent conflict they experienced between inclination and conscience, created by the Evangelical opposition to imaginative literature.

Religious Persuasion. This brings us into the somewhat cryptic area of Brontë/Eliot religious feeling. The individual response to religion is one of the most important single ingredients in each of the four lives, and for this reason, as previously indicated, the subject has been given a chapter to itself. At this point, it is appropriate therefore merely to note that significant links exist in this area, both in the context of inherited faith and in the matter of early religious experience. The Reverend Patrick Brontë has been described as a tolerant orthodox Anglican, 'much more Arminian than Calvinistic',[27] and the Evans's family religion has been defined in similar terms, that is, as being 'of the old-fashioned high-and-dry sort'.[28] A further dimension, however, was added with the introduction from outside sources of Evangelical influences which affected the young Mary Ann Evans and at least two of the Brontë sisters – Charlotte and Anne – in very similar ways. Charlotte Brontë, who became what has been described as 'an Evangelical of the sterner type',[29] was sorely torn between this early religious piety and the lure of imaginative fiction; but what represented a conflict for Charlotte, and also for her sister, Anne, amounted to a crisis of life-long significance for Mary Ann Evans, who, at the height of an Evangelical fervour promoted chiefly by her teacher, Miss Maria Lewis, wrote of her inclinations towards the reading of fiction, 'I shall carry to my grave the mental diseases with which they [novels] have contaminated me'.[30] Like Charlotte, she was able to give qualified approval to certain standard works, but the young Miss Evans found Shakespeare a problem: 'we have need of as nice a power of distillation as the bee to suck nothing but honey from his pages',[31] she wrote.

Youthful writing. As previously stated, it is not intended to take detailed account of the considerable *corpus* of the Brontë Juvenilia – all those tales in prose and verse of Gothic romanticism centred on the imaginary kingdoms of Angria and Gondal, and produced by the sisters and Branwell from childhood until well into young adulthood. It is interesting, however, to note in this context the comparison afforded between the 'apprenticeship' of journalism embarked upon by George Eliot in her twenties, when she became effectively joint editor with John Chapman of the *Westminster Review*, and the intense juvenile creativity which laid the foundations of the mature Brontë output. The mature flowering, when it came, took place in all four cases in ground brought to a fine tilth by much working over beforehand.

The common search for an ideal unity. In each one of the four novelists there took shape the concept of some ideal union of Self with

Another. The differences between the four were of interpretation. For Charlotte Brontë, the ideal would seem relatively quickly to have become defined in terms of human love. Anne Brontë's poems suggest, on the other hand, that, as human hopes failed her, she concentrated increasingly on the notion of spiritual unity with God via the soul's perfectability; while nothing is clearer than that Emily's 'Guide',[32] 'Glad Comforter'[33] and 'God of Visions'[34] were personifications of an intense personal relationship that yet had no connection with anything known in this world. For George Eliot, conversely, as religious belief yielded to humanism, the world was to become everything; her vision was that of the unity of individuals within society. At the same time, we perceive a strange paradox, for in her ultimate concern with the contrast between the isolation of individuals from each other and the ideal of a 'unity of souls' as portrayed in *Daniel Deronda*, it is difficult to avoid mystic inferences. It would seem at least arguable that in the creation of such a concept, as also of such characters as the highly idealised Romola, George Eliot was fictionalising something rather more than a deeply felt social theory, more even, perhaps, than an attempt to objectify the concept of perfect union between one human being and another that had been the continual quest of her early life and that remained her ideal. Exactly how much of herself, knowingly or unknowingly, went into the creation of the mystic elements of these two novels, especially *Deronda*, remains to be conjectured.

Moving from the general connections listed above to factual links of a more specific kind, we see, as would be expected, that it is the longest-lived sister whose life most nearly touches that of George Eliot. Connections between Charlotte Brontë and George Eliot take on an almost personal aspect with the advent into the former's life of George Henry Lewes, the man who was to be George Eliot's husband in all but the legal sense for some twenty-five years; for Lewes it was who was to become Charlotte's principal contemporary literary critic, the acute appraiser to whom she wrote 'at least nine letters'[35] over a period of four years.

George Eliot's critical opinion of Charlotte's work seems to show Lewes's influence. In 1848, there had been more than a hint of exasperation in the letter which she wrote to her friend, Charles Bray, about *Jane Eyre*: 'the book *is* interesting – only I wish the characters would talk a little less like the heroes and heroines of police reports'.[36] In 1851, however, in her capacity as assistant editor of the *Westminster Review*, she was regretfully replying to

John Chapman's suggestion that Charlotte should be invited to become a contributor to the *Review* with the comment that 'there would be the same objection to Miss Bronty [sic] as to Thackeray with regard to the article on Modern Novelists. She would have to leave out Currer Bell, who is perhaps the best of them all'.[37] By 1853, her enthusiasm was unrestrained. *Villette*, she declared, was 'a still more wonderful book than Jane Eyre'.[38] To George Combe she wrote: 'Pray tell Mrs. Combe that I hope she is reading "Villette", and will tell me what she thinks of it',[39] and to the Brays: 'Villette – have you read it?'[40] In one letter, she relayed this first-hand view of Charlotte:

> Lewes was describing Currer Bell to me yesterday as a little, plain, provincial sickly-looking old maid. Yet what passion, what fire in her! Quite as much as in George Sand, only the clothing is less voluptuous.[41]

Meanwhile, for her part, Charlotte Brontë had been forming her own opinion of Lewes. In 1850, after the publication of *Shirley*, he had angered her by flouting the male pseudonym which she had chosen to write under and by emphasising her sex in his note on the novel in the *Edinburgh Review;*[42] nevertheless, in writing to her friend, Ellen Nussey, at this time, she temporised to the extent of declaring that although she believed him to be 'a man with both weaknesses and sins . . . unless I err greatly the foundation of his nature is not bad'.[43] The reason for the compromise was whimsical; she could not, she said, 'feel otherwise to him than half sadly, half tenderly', because his features reminded her of her sister, Emily. A year later, she had changed her opinion again. Mr Lewes, she told her publisher, George Smith, was 'hard', 'insolent', 'coarse' and to be 'distrusted'.[44] Here was no small irony, for Lewes, who had so offended with his disclosure to the world of the sex of 'Currer Bell' was to be a primary influence on George Eliot in her own decision to adopt the male pseudonym. Lewes's advocacy of this course was apparently based on the grounds of the incompatibility of sex-discrimination and good business. 'When Jane Eyre was finally known to be a woman's book,' he wrote, 'the tone noticeably changed'.[45] Thus, fortuitously and unknown to her, did Charlotte Brontë make a significant contribution towards establishing the *modus* for George Eliot's own remarkable literary achievement.

Lacking the valuable impressions which a reciprocal Brontë/Eliot contact would have given us, it becomes doubly interesting to compare contemporary attitudes towards Charlotte Brontë on the one hand and George Eliot on the other. Harriet Martineau, for example, was sympathetically affected by the peculiarly telling combination of frailty and intensity of feeling which she saw in Charlotte: the same combination which had previously been noticed by Thackeray when he met Charlotte in the autumn of 1849 and wrote of 'the trembling little frame, the little hand, the great honest eyes',[46] and by his daughter, Lady Ritchie, who remembered 'a tiny, delicate, serious, little lady, pale, with fair straight hair, and steady eyes'.[47] For Miss Martineau, Charlotte's 'deep mourning dress, and the knowledge that she was the sole survivor of her family' evoked considerable emotion. 'I should have been heartily glad to cry',[48] she said. On the other hand, the relationship between Harriet Martineau and George Eliot, while beginning felicitously enough, with visits exchanged, ended in fluctuations between enthusiasm and antipathy, the latter, as far as Miss Martineau was concerned, often falling little short of malice. Why, asks R. K. Webb, in his biography of Harriet Martineau,[49] 'did Charlotte Brontë escape the condemnation visited on George Eliot?' and he answers by quoting Miss Martineau herself: because 'her moral strength fell not a whit behind the intellectual force manifested in her works'.[50] And here, of course, in the implicit contrast between the brave and much-bereaved Miss Brontë and George Eliot's invidious position as the intimate companion of a man inescapably bound in marriage, lay the nub of the matter: that is, in the force of general social attitudes to morality. George Eliot's position put her outside the sphere of women who, in her own words, were 'invited to dinner'.[51] Even Mrs Gaskell, liberal-minded woman that she was, felt impelled in 1859 to write to George Smith: '*how came she to like Mr. Lewes so much?* . . . somehow he is so soiled for a woman like her to fancy!'[52] Like Miss Martineau, Mrs Gaskell was full of compassion and affection for Charlotte Brontë, and indeed for the whole Brontë family.[53]

After *Villette*, George Eliot's commitment to Charlotte Brontë led her to use aspects of the novel as a kind of light-hearted private code. To her friend, Sara Hennell, in 1854 she wrote that she was 'preparing to go to "Labassecoeur"',[54] and two years later was offering to obtain for Miss Hennell an 'autograph letter' written by Currer Bell.[55] She was filled with pity and sadness when the publication of Mrs Gaskell's *Life of Charlotte Brontë* revealed the tragic details of the Brontë family to the world. Branwell's contribution to them especially upset her. Writing to Sara Hennell, she exclaimed: 'that picture of the old man and the three sisters, trembling day and night in terror at the possible deeds of this drunken brutal son and brother! That is the part . . . which affects me most'.[56] Intriguingly, in his definitive biography of George Eliot, Gordon S. Haight suggests that, although George Eliot could not accept Mrs Gaskell's interpretation of the connection between Branwell Brontë's passion for Mrs Robinson, his employer's wife at Thorp Green Hall, and his subsequent moral disintegration, the story of these events might possibly have influenced the development of George Eliot's finest novel, *Middlemarch*.[57] It was Branwell's belief, wrote Mrs Gaskell, that Lydia Robinson loved him and that the only reason she refused to see him after her husband died was that Robinson's bequest of his property to her was conditional upon her never seeing Branwell again, a situation, says Haight, somewhat similar to Mr Casaubon's 'Dead Hand' attempt to prevent Dorothea after his death from marrying Ladislaw.[58]

Although no evidence exists that connects George Eliot directly with either of the two younger Brontë sisters, we do know that *Wuthering Heights* was among the books which she and Lewes were reading aloud to each other during 1858;[59] it is also suggestive that towards the end of her life, when given a copy of Emily's poem, 'Cold in the earth', she copied all eight stanzas into her Diary.[60] Curiously, these two ostensibly very different personalities shared more than one temperamental attribute. Both had a special love of music and were proficient piano players,[61] and in both the intellectual development of the post-adolescent years was towards a dispassionate but deeply ethical rationalism. This may seem an unlikely definition of the spirit that generated *Wuthering Heights*, but one of the arguments which will be put forward in the following chapters is that Emily Brontë's great novel was neither simply a celebration of primitive natural forces hung upon the framework of the old Gothic drama, nor some kind of catharsis for pent-up personal feeling, but represented the culmination of a long process of philosophical reasoning. Emily's 'powerful reason'[62] and head for logic was first noted by Professor Constantin Heger at the Brussels pensionnat which she attended in company with Charlotte in 1842, and evidence of the qualities of which he spoke is to be found in the remarkable essays which she wrote for him there.[63]

So far, the connections made have been chiefly factual and historical. The final one is psychological. It will be argued that in all four women – with, surprisingly, the possible exception of Anne Brontë – it can be seen that, alternating with the strong pulse of challenge with which they confronted their world, there were recurrent flickerings of a pattern of capitulation that was not only present in their personal lives but was also transmitted to their work in a variety of ways. A minor example of this capitulative impulse is the 'powerful' Emily Brontë's repeated failure to measure up to the impact of the world beyond Haworth Parsonage; another is the near-total collapse of control in George Eliot after the death of Lewes, leading to her panic-stricken retreat into a bizarre marriage with a man twenty years younger than herself.

The ways in which this alternating pattern of challenge and capitulation is from time to time reflected in the novels will be indicated where relevant in the following chapters, which commence, for reasons of appropriate chronology, with the attitudes of the four novelists to one of their society's current and most controversial issues: the nature of, and significance to the world around it, of the Child.

1

The Child and Young Person: in Life and in Literature

Towards the end of the eighteenth century, a new major *persona* began to appear in English literature. The child, hitherto of relatively little interest to the artistic vision, began increasingly to assume the status of a symbol of something very important in current thought. Peter Coveney relates the birth of the Literary Child to 'the revolution in sensibility which we call the "romantic revival"',[1] and places it within the generation of Blake and Wordsworth, and the development of ideas of 'original innocence' which stemmed 'most forcefully from Rousseau'.[2] Coveney writes:

> In a world given increasingly to utilitarian values and the Machine, the child could become a symbol of Imagination and Sensibility, a symbol of Nature set amongst the forces abroad in society actively de-naturing humanity.[3]

But the child of innocence and purity, Wordsworth's child whose 'birth is but a sleep and a forgetting'[4] and who enters the world still 'trailing clouds of glory' was in fact the personification of an idea that went back even further than Rousseau; it derived from the Platonic Soul, for whom the growth of understanding in this world was part of what Plato in the *Meno* called 'Anamnesis',[5] 'the recollection in this life of realities and truths seen and known by the soul before its incarnation'. Blake's dualities of 'innocence' and 'experience' shared the same ancient root. The idea marked a radical movement away from the Church's Augustinian doctrine of 'original sin' – under which the child was seen as part and parcel of a flawed humanity – towards a new meliorist view of man in society. In the novel, it accounted for a new emphasis upon the struggle for individual identity and freedom, seen as imaged by the child and young person. If these were orphans, so much the better. The

12

didactic opportunities in such a case require no stressing, especially in an age in which, as John Reed points out: 'an orphan was already half-engaged to heaven because at least one of his parents supposedly dwelt there in constant expectation of his arrival'.[6]

Treatments varied, however, even in a single author, and the overall pattern was uneven. Dickens, for example, has been charged with 'having succumbed to the Augustinian use of the child figure'[7] with 'enthusiastic conviction', presenting it as a contrast to the world about it and an instrument for redemption. The same critic finds George Eliot's Eppie in *Silas Marner* more 'strikingly similar to Dickens's children'[8] than to her 'counterparts in early Wordsworth'. Wordsworth himself, it is said, finally 'came round to the orthodox position on childhood'.[9] An 'element of neurosis'[10] has also been noted in the literary handling of the theme, especially towards the end of the century, in what has been called 'the seductive shadow of Peter Pan'.[11] Coveney writes: 'It is perhaps not remarkable that through writing of childhood there should be those who wanted to go back to the beginning to begin again and others who wanted just to go back'.[12] But if the cult of childhood was a bastion of defence for Victorians afraid of the future, it was also, in its connection with the Romantic Movement, part of a willingness in individuals to commit themselves to the social good. What Leavis has called 'a distinctive sense of responsibility towards life'[13] marked the romantic revival, and this, combined with a passionate belief in the right of the individual to live according to his own nature and inclination, found its ideal expression in the symbolic use of the child and young person in literature.

This combination of 'responsibility towards life' and commitment to individual expression carries with it strong implications of conflict, an awareness of which was at the heart of the creative vision of all three Brontë sisters and George Eliot. In the essential similarity of theme, for example, between *Jane Eyre* and *The Mill on the Floss* – that is, the painful struggle for maturity of two wayward young girls – we see Charlotte Brontë and George Eliot focusing alike on this potentially tragic clash between duty and compulsion. A noticeable difference here and elsewhere, however, between the authors' treatment of their theme is that of tone. Nowhere do the Brontë sisters write of children with any trace of those adulterations of sentimentality which from time to time notably marred the work of both Dickens and George Eliot. The two most evident reasons for this would seem to have been (a) the austerities of the Brontës' lives, particularly under the regimen of Aunt Branwell, and (b) their own natural attitudes of restraint towards children.[14] Emily, we are told, once informed her charges at Law Hill School that the 'house-dog' was 'dearer to her than they were',[15] while Charlotte's observations on the children in her care included calling one a 'Dolt',[16] presaging attitudes frequently to be seen in her work. In just two paragraphs of *Villette*, for example, she has Lucy Snowe referring to her pupils as 'mutineers', 'this stiff-necked tribe' and 'this swinish multitude'.[17] Yet Emily was not so harsh as to be without her supporters at Law Hill;[18] and Charlotte could be tender, as again seen in *Villette*, where her portrayal of the touchingly precocious little Paulina emerges as a child study of memorable sympathetic insight. We might conclude that much of this Brontë difficulty with children was due more to an unfamiliarity with normal childhood's trivial inconsequence than to any reasoned animus on the subject. One of Charlotte's oldest friends[19] described her, at fifteen years of age, long before her unfortunate experiences as a governess, as looking like 'a little, old woman',[20] her sight ruined by all that intensive juvenile authorship, a girl who 'never played'[21] and who only ever seemed to come alive when talking about 'poetry and drawing'. As a young Sunday School teacher at Haworth she was so shy that one of her scholars recalled 'how she used to wheel round in her nervous fashion till she almost turned her back on them'.[22] It is hardly surprising that the picture which this unchildlike creature drew of childhood in her novels tended to be unaverage, to incline either towards overearnestness and constraint or else to a degree of unpleasantness that, while it reflected accurately enough some of the children whom she had had the misfortune to meet as a governess and teacher, was no more typical of childhood generally than were she and her sisters. To her friend, Mrs Gaskell, she once wrote, 'to what children am I not a stranger?'[23] and she described her attitude towards the latter's own children as that of 'clownish awe'.

Such Brontë gaucheries, together with seemingly unfeminine indifference to children, can indisputably be linked with one marked factor in the sisters' lives: their failure to develop their own full maturity until quite late in their adulthood. As grown women, they retained many of the propensities of childhood: the inability to express themselves freely to strangers, and, in particular, the tendency, which lasted most of their lives, periodically to withdraw into dream-worlds of their own;[24] in Charlotte's case, there was, too, the inability to discern the trend of her own emotions and the obvious inferences to be drawn from them by others, as, of course, transpired so painfully in her unfortunate relations with Professor Heger.

For all this, however, it is not surprising that the sisters shared the contemporary literary preoccupation with the themes of childhood and immaturity, as indicated, for these were for most authors as much, if not more, devices for the expression of moral symbolism as for any personal concern for childhood *per se*. Charlotte's repeated use of orphans, for example, was clearly connected with the desire to make some general statement about both the innocence and vulnerability of childhood – 'Adèle is not answerable for either her mother's faults or yours',[25] Jane Eyre tells Rochester. It also had to do with Charlotte's own personal awareness of such vulnerability, and of the cravings of lonely children for comfort and companionship – 'now that I know she is, in a sense, parentless . . . I shall cling closer to her than before', Jane adds. The fact is that through her series of parentless children, growing to adulthood in their various hostile worlds, Charlotte could explore the furthest reaches of her own pressing needs as the eldest surviving female, the traditional 'mother' figure, in a family bereft. Throughout the childhood years, her closest companion and support, especially in that world of such importance to her, the world of the imagination, had been Branwell.[26] When Branwell betrayed the promise which his life had seemed to hold, he betrayed *her*. Thus, while Emily and Anne could find it in themselves to forgive him, Charlotte could not. That sense, compounded of betrayal, of loss, of disorientation, bewilderment and fear informs in varying degrees every novel she wrote. We might reasonably infer that it accounted for the over-long continuation of that world of intense and often violent imagination that had been the *milieu* of the Juvenilia, and was continued in the passionate novelettes of her early twenties. Bernard J. Paris,[27] drawing upon the psychological theories of Karen Horney,[28] tells us that where a child feels anxious and isolated, 'in a world conceived of as potentially hostile',[29] he becomes 'fearful of spontaneity, and, forsaking his real self, he develops neurotic strategies for coping with his environment'.[30] Such an explanation would certainly fit the curious contrast which we note between Charlotte's agonising social constraints and awkwardness and her passionate freedom of expression in imaginative authorship. With the child's 'basic anxiety',[31] says Paris, goes a fear 'of the self',[32] leading to self-blame and the sense of being 'unworthy of love'.[33] This element of self-loathing and sense of unworthiness were very much a part of Charlotte's early development.

For Charlotte, therefore, the fictional child was the means, which real life denied her, of confronting her sense of loss and of fear on her own terms and of working them out in ways over which she had some personal control. This is why, for her, as for her sisters and later for George Eliot, the portrayal of childhood, as such, was secondary to the more essential task, which was to delineate the process of development in the human being from immaturity to maturity. The basic problem was how the individual might acquire knowledge and experience of life in the world without losing the virtues that stemmed from childhood innocence. Thus, in itself, the child represented merely the first stage in a long struggle whose end was by no means certain. In her own early, immature state, it was necessary for Charlotte that each conclusion should be a happy one; thus the 'idyllic' endings of the first three novels; by the time she came to *Villette*, however, Charlotte had learned to live without the youthful illusion that happiness has necessarily to do with the fulfilment of one's dreams and had begun to perceive the deeper rewards of compromise with life's seemingly autonomous purposes. She could envisage a peace of the soul won through suffering, and was, in other words, in sight at last of her mature self. It was a part of that complex pattern of challenge and capitulation which we see continually recurring in varying ways and degrees in all four novelists; here, via the surrender of the childhood dream, it served Charlotte in a positive rather than negative sense.

The autobiographical function in Charlotte's use of the child theme is, of course, most sharply seen in *Jane Eyre*, her most overtly reminiscent work. Despite arguments against a too-close identification of author and heroine in this novel,[34] we can safely infer that in the writing of it Charlotte looked back long and carefully over her own harrowing experiences of childhood and of other people's children, met within her duties as a governess, and reproduced them with almost photographic fidelity. In *Jane Eyre*'s book-hurling Master Reed of Gateshead, for example, we see the unified model of the little Sidgwick boys who flung stones at the unwelcome Miss Brontë at Stonegappe, the house at Lothersdale, near Skipton, where Charlotte held the post of 'nursery governess' from May to July 1839.[35] Whether Lowood School was a true picture of the Clergy Daughters School at Cowan Bridge, near Tunstall in Lancashire, attended by Charlotte and three of her sisters, became the subject of much controversy following the publication of *Jane Eyre* and the revelation of Charlotte's identity.[36] After her death, her husband, the Reverend Arthur Bell Nicholls, testified publicly[37] to her sincerity in claiming that the picture she had given in *Jane Eyre* was 'on the whole a true picture' of the school at the time that she herself had known it. Evidence more recently adduced,[38] notably an examination of the school's old registers, would seem to confirm beyond any reasonable doubt that conditions at Jane Eyre's Lowood, probably even down to the freezing wash-basin in the bitter pre-dawn dormitory[39] and the sodden shoes in which the girls sat through Sunday service after their two-mile walk to church,[40] constituted a not unfair picture of those that prevailed at Cowan Bridge during Charlotte's time there. Conditions were certainly bad in the school's early days and Charlotte never forgot that it was those conditions that had cost the lives of her two elder sisters, Maria and Elizabeth.

Charlotte's autobiographical motivations as an author, however, went deeper than the mere recording of childhood scenes and events. A more interesting element is the consistent emphasis which she placed upon two distinct aspects of her young heroines' lives: (a) their deprivation, either of an emotional or social kind, or both; (b) their unfailing virtue. All Charlotte's orphans start life lacking the support of a normal, sheltering family background, yet all seem endowed, *a priori*, with a kind of ancient wisdom that keeps their feet unerringly in the path of righteousness no matter what perils arise to confront them. In this, they differ from Emily's 'innocents' in *Wuthering Heights*, from Anne's bibulous little boy, in deadly danger from the snares of loose living in *The Tenant of Wildfell Hall*, and from George Eliot's classic examples of soiled virtue in *Adam Bede* and *The Mill on the Floss*. This is not to say that Charlotte does not give us any 'bad', that is, 'spoiled' children; the Reed family in *Jane Eyre* are striking examples. The difference is that her 'good' children are never in any real danger of falling from their state of pristine virtue; they *suffer* from the badness of others, but beyond the occasional outburst of uncontrolled moral anger, they remain steadfastly uncontaminated as they move on into young womanhood. We do not see in Jane, or Caroline, or even the critical Lucy Snowe, the transformation of character between wilfulness and concern that takes place in the second Cathy in *Wuthering Heights*. We do not see the insidious weakening of will, followed by guilt's fatal catharsis as witnessed in George Eliot's Maggie Tulliver, nor the harrowing organic change of personality foreshadowed for Gwendolen Harleth in the closing pages of *Daniel Deronda*. Where Charlotte Brontë notably differs from her sisters, Emily in particular, and from George Eliot, is in not showing moral status as part of a developing or degenerative process, but rather as constituting fixed parameters – that is, of 'good' or 'bad' – into one or other of which her characters fall. The closest we come to a portrait of a heroine in process of organic change is in Lucy Snowe, but although Lucy's emotional responses are seen to evolve, her moral nature remains basically intact throughout.

For an explanation of this firm line of demarcation between good and bad in Charlotte's work we have to take into account her strong religious bias, the influence of which can be seen both in her narrative style and, in varying degrees of significance, in the ethical and philosophical standpoints of every one of her major heroines. Jane Eyre, for example, holds constantly to the belief that 'God is everywhere';[41] Caroline Helstone, we are told, 'was a Christian',[42] of whom it is observed that 'whom He loveth, He chasteneth', while Shirley Keeldar, whose head was sometimes 'a hash of Scripture and mythology',[43] was nevertheless full of such sturdy virtue that it was her 'bent' to 'admire the great, reverence the good, and be joyous with the genial',[44] and to give away money to the poor.[45] Finally, of course, in Lucy Snowe, we see the staunchest example of all of the 'little English Puritan'[46] who retains her 'pure faith' to the end. These attributes were Charlotte's own, and by the time she came to write her novels she had acquired a good reason for wishing to convey such an impression to her readers. All her novels drew in different ways upon the one great emotional experience of her life – her deep attachment to her Belgian professor, Constantin Heger, happily married and father to a growing brood of children. The details of this one-sided devotion and its effects upon Charlotte's development as a woman and as a novelist belong to a later chapter. It is pertinent, however, to her fictional presentation of childhood and youth generally as symbols of Innocence to note here that this emotional experience which inspired the novels also made it necessary for Charlotte, perhaps for her own sake as much as that of others, to define clearly her moral position. 'I will keep the law given by God; sanctioned by man',[47] she had Jane Eyre say. She now realised that her feelings for Heger had been, as she saw it, falsely construed; she agonised under a sense of rejection and injustice. Thus, in stoking up embers of childhood memory in *Jane Eyre*, it was to do more than simply light a fire under the 'marble'[48] pillars of heartless pedagogy and social 'respectability'; it was to vent her anger against a whole hidebound society that she felt sought to deprive natural human feeling of its innate goodness. In the personification of Jane Eyre, Innocence, at all ages and for all time – and her own, in particular – was in her view vindicated.

In general terms, inasmuch as Charlotte's work is consciously didactic, this can be seen as expressed more in terms of inspiration and illumination than of warning. To a greater extent than either of her sisters, certainly more than George Eliot, she created consistent images of the Romantic, rather than the Augustinian, child. In retaining their innocence, in emerging uncorrupted from the influences of an unjust and victimising society, her young heroines serve as models for the triumph of natural goodness, rather than as evidence of its tragedy. This triumph of Innocence, however, is not to be taken as achieved without effort. In *Jane Eyre*, Charlotte employs an effective literary device to emphasise the threat that surrounds it. In a series of sequences connected with sleep, Jane is made aware of imminent peril. In the first, she falls asleep in the same bed with the saintly child Helen Burns;[49] in the morning, when the two children are found, still locked in each other's arms, Helen is dead. Innocence, it seems, can be lost without our knowing it. The scene is repeated, almost exactly, on the night before what was to have been Jane's wedding day; this time, Jane lies sleepless with her little charge, Adèle, clinging to her,[50] only to face next day another kind of death, in which Rochester is exposed as a purposive bigamist. Linking these two incidents is a third, taking the form of two dreams which Jane has two nights before the planned wedding. In the first of these, she finds herself journeying in search of Rochester on 'a dark and gusty night'[51] down 'an unknown road', 'burdened with the charge of a little child . . . too young and feeble to walk, and which shivered in my cold arms'. In the second dream, which immediately follows, the journey and the search continue and the child is still there, but this time Jane loses it when she climbs a wall to look for Rochester and falls. In these dreams, the child seems to stand not only for an innocence that is threatened with destruction before it has had a chance to take root in the world, but also, specifically perhaps, for the creative love of man and woman, which, in this case, because it is based on a lie, can give birth only to illusion. When Jane falls, the child 'rolled from my knee',[52] and she wakes to find that the mad woman has destroyed her bridal veil.

There can be no doubt that in her novels Charlotte Brontë provided us with a map to the psychological development of her own slowly maturing life. *The Professor*, probably begun within a year or eighteen months of her return from the Pensionnat Heger – and tracing the story of a young girl's love affair and marriage with her teacher – was indisputably an expression of vicarious wish-fulfilment. *Jane Eyre*, following upon two significant failures – the rejection of her first novel and the emotional disillusionment of the Brussels experience – became a vehicle of self-vindication. Into it she poured all her disgust for the closed minds of social hypocrisy and religious callousness, and the strait-jacketing of human feeling. With *Shirley*, the childhood dream was almost over, lost in a hiatus of shock, bewilderment and longing, to which the happy ending seems almost a mechanical literary gesture. *Shirley* is not a 'social' novel, despite its connections with the Yorkshire woollen industry, and the resulting critical speculation on the subject;[53] it is primarily and basically an emotional blood-letting, in the process of which Charlotte gave a sad salute to the memory of childhood and to the two sisters recently dead. Finally, with *Villette*, we have a paradox, for although in this novel Charlotte returned to the scenes and events of childhood and adolescence, her real subject was maturity, the search for the wholly realised self, an entity at one and the same time socially integrated yet capable of independent, objective and creative existence. Lucy Snowe, sitting alone in *l'allée défendue*, watches the new young moon and a voice within her cries, 'oh, my childhood!'[54] And, like Lucy, Charlotte too knew that those days were gone; like Lucy, she stood at the point of self-recognition. It was wholly and almost necessarily fitting that in the same year that this novel was completed Charlotte made the decision to accept the Reverend Arthur Nicholls as her future husband.

It is a salutary and somewhat reassuring exercise to look down from the challenging altitude of *Wuthering Heights* over its author's childhood. So much of Emily Brontë's later life has been represented as being wrapped in a kind of despair, an impression which her solitary novel and a great deal of her mature poetry tends to reinforce. At best, these works have inspired the awe due to what Sydney Dobell called 'a baby god'.[55] At worst, she has been seen as driven by some necrophilic neurosis that hastened her to her untimely end. It is therefore heartening to see her, as it were, on her nursery slopes, through the eyes of those who knew her before 'the dream of horror'[56] closed around her. At school at Cowan Bridge for instance, where she arrived at the age of six years and three months in the care of her sister, Charlotte, she was considered to be 'a darling child',[57] and 'quite the pet nursling of the school'. Those who so designated her were not, of course, aware that this same small child, a year before, had advised her father that if Branwell were naughty he should be reasoned with and if that failed he should be whipped.[58] Given the eccentricity of the father, however, and the modes and practices of contemporary family discipline, we should not perhaps see this as early evidence of an unduly harsh nature. Rather, we may take heart by looking forward a little to the stage of adolescence when Charlotte's friend, Ellen Nussey, visiting Haworth for the first time in 1833, found the fifteen-year-old Emily to be a quiet, kind-eyed girl[59] who, once released from the constraints of the Parsonage to her beloved moors, laughed, talked and joked as freely as any and took a 'gleesome delight'[60] in everything around her. This picture of normal, cheerful, fun-loving adolescence is confirmed by Emily's own diary note of the period. Her entry of 24 November 1834[61] reveals that her interests were, as Laura Hinkley listed them, 'pets, politics, cookery, character, dialect, humour, imaginative play, outdoor play, food, music, mischief, domestic responsibility and domestic co-operation'.[62] As she grew older and sadder, her lightheartedness subsided into 'a quiet, but robust cheerfulness';[63] even in July 1845, with the first, barely assimilated shock of Branwell's moral collapse hanging over the family, she could write in her diary paper:

> I am quite contented for myself . . . having learnt to make the most of the present and long for the future with the fidgetiness that I cannot do all I wish . . . merely desiring that everybody could be as comfortable as myself and as undesponding, and then we should have a very tolerable world of it.[64]

Branwell's dismissal from his post as tutor to the eldest son of the Robinson family at Thorp Green Hall had taken place only a month before; clearly, the full implications had still to be felt. Meanwhile, it is notable that both Emily and Anne, referring to him in their diary papers at this time, write as if of a child, using almost identical words, that is, hoping that he 'will be better and do better hereafter',

or, as Anne put it, 'in future'.[65] This throws an interesting light on
the attitude jointly taken by Emily and Anne towards this
troublesome brother; it was the attitude one would adopt towards
an erring child, an attitude devoid of censure, composed principally
of pity and regret, and its influence is significant in the light of the
subsequent authorial treatment of the young Heathcliff in
Wuthering Heights and of the vulnerable little Arthur Huntingdon in
Anne Brontë's *The Tenant of Wildfell Hall*. As we see from her poems,
Emily's thoughts about youth and innocence derived primarily from
a general, deep-rooted philosophy about life. She had written, for
example, of childhood's pristine goodness in lines such as '. . . holy
child,/Too good for this world's warring wild',[66] and 'Child of
Delight! with sunbright hair',[67] the 'Spirit of Bliss' whose natural
home, she felt, was 'eternal spring'. Again, in the essay, 'A Letter
from One Brother to Another',[68] she had extolled the 'concord of
soul' and 'sweet and calm happiness of childhood', and in another –
'Filial Love'[69] – had seen every individual life on earth created in the
'image' of God. But these objective reflections received added point
from the example she was afforded every day in her own home. As
the 'resident' sister at Haworth during the two years from the
autumn of 1835 to the October of 1837, when Charlotte and Anne
were both at Roe Head School, and before she herself went to teach
at Law Hill, she it was who had spent the most time with Branwell.
Later, in July 1845, it was she again, with Anne's help, who dealt
with Branwell when he was sent home in disgrace from Thorp
Green Hall to embark on his agonising and humiliating three-year
descent into moral and physical dissolution. Branwell never
recovered from his tragic passion for Lydia Robinson, his
employer's wife, and when, after her husband's death, she refused
to support Branwell's claim that a state of mutual attachment had
existed between them, his reliance on alcohol and drugs accelerated
rapidly, resulting in his death. Emily's authorial sources remain
locked in mystery, but in the light of her especially intimate
knowledge of her brother's self-destructive career, the definition of
Wuthering Heights by Irving H. Buchen as 'essentially a novel about
children' and 'childhood'[70] is suggestive. For Buchen, Emily's
depiction of the loss of childhood innocence and unity is meant to be
a symbol of the soul's separation from God – 'once childhood is lost
the remainder of life is largely hellish'.[71] This is a fair description of
what life must have been like for the sisters in the three years
between 1845 and September 1848, when Branwell died: especially

for Emily, the self-appointed 'housekeeper' of the family since the death of Aunt Branwell in 1842. With this in mind, it is easy to conclude with John Hewish that 'it is reasonably certain that *Wuthering Heights* and Heathcliff would hardly have been the same without this example of romantic self-destruction so close to its author'.[72] It is true that every day for those final three years of her brother's life she witnessed the havoc in his soul, watched his increasing dementia. She could not, in pride and pity, reproduce it in its exactitude, but what she did reproduce was in all its basic essentials of tearing pain and violent self-pity precisely what she saw being suffered but a breath away from her in her own home. Like Heathcliff, Branwell was a relatively rough and inexperienced young man, plunged into the heady presence of an exciting and cultured young woman. To what extent Lydia Robinson, like Catherine Earnshaw, responded to this strange and ardent young man we do not know for sure; Charlotte, who by no means excused her brother's conduct, was in no doubt about Mrs Robinson's: 'a worse woman, I believe, hardly exists,' she wrote to Ellen Nussey in July 1848,[73] 'the more I hear of her the more deeply she revolts me'. Whether or not Charlotte was justified in this opinion, the fact remains that Branwell's obsession, like Heathcliff's, blighted the lives of all around him and ended in his death. It can thus reasonably be inferred that in the creation of *Wuthering Heights* Emily fused abstract thought with tragic personal experience, building upon the 'two children' theme,[74] the dark and the fair, also used in her poems, to emphasise human vulnerability in the face of a corruptible world. For Emily, childhood innocence could not be taken for granted; but there was hope in life's law of contraries, the law by which dark was balanced by light, death by life, the worm in the bud by the butterfly.

There have been many interpretations of the 'two children' imagery of the novel. Lord David Cecil divided the Earnshaws, as 'children of storm',[75] from the Lintons as 'children of calm', revealing a further dichotomy represented by Hareton and the second Cathy as 'children of love' and Linton as the 'child of hate'. More controversial is the view[76] of Catherine and Heathcliff as 'children of rock and heath and tempest, striving to identify themselves as human, but disrupting all around them with their monstrous appetite for an inhuman kind of intercourse'. Whatever interpretation we accept, however, the link between the 'two children' of the novel and the 'beautiful dark boy'[77] and 'golden girl'[78] of the poetry is obvious. In the poetry, the imagery is ambivalent; the dark boy and the fair girl seem to be continually changing places:

> And only *he* had locks of light,
> And *she* had raven hair;
> While now, his curls are dark as night,
> And hers as morning fair –[79]

The novel makes the ambivalence clear. The two are one. 'I *am* Heathcliff', Cathy says;[80] and when, mortally ill, she lies for the last time in his arms, *he* declares that her death will make her his murderer,[81] for 'I *cannot* live without my soul!'[82] With *Wuthering Heights*, Emily Brontë's long-standing intellectual struggles with the problems posed by life's dualities and contraries were almost over, in more ways than one. Opposed to these dualities, as she saw it, was the passionately felt human need of union, of the completion of the One in the Other. When this need becomes misplaced, or self-orientated, tragedy results: tragedy such as she had witnessed in her brother. In *Wuthering Heights*, she posed both the problem and, as she saw it, the solution, identifying, on the one hand, the 'dark' form of the Uncontrolled Self, and, on the other, a kind of healing that stemmed from the 'light' of an interrelationship bred of tolerance and compassionate understanding. The eternal dilemma which she pinpointed, both in the novel and in the poems, was the self's fatal irresolution between these two opposing impulses. For her purpose, the 'two children' theme provided the most effective tool, for in the child, developing through adolescence to adulthood, the evolution of human personality is epitomised. As we have seen, the novel's cryptic and complex patterning allows of a number of different interpretations of that evolutionary process. All the indications are, however, that Emily's child-imagery in *Wuthering Heights* and the poems springs from the same mystical notion, that is, that *all mortal life is itself embryonic*. In her celebrated essay, 'The Butterfly', she wrote:

> here is a symbol of the world to come; just as the ugly caterpillar is the beginning of the splendid butterfly, this globe is the embryo of a new heaven and of a new earth whose meagrest beauty infinitely surpasses mortal imagination.[83]

In human life, the same pattern is personified. Thus, Heathcliff becomes the grub in the flower, the dark boy of the poems, 'doomed to be Hell-like in heart and misery'.[84] But he does not bear this guilt alone. As Emily Brontë had written in another of her Belgian essays, 'The Cat',[85] 'if hypocrisy, cruelty and ingratitude are the characteristics exclusively of mean people, this class includes everyone'. The 'singing, laughing'[86] Catherine Earnshaw, like the 'Child of Delight'[87] of the Gondal poems, is the other half of the Uncontrolled Self with which Emily Brontë is so concerned; this child, too, has an 'erring wing';[88] she is 'not from heaven'. But she should not be judged too harshly, says Emily, because she represents an Innocence that from the beginning is confronted by a world made callous and insensitive by pride and self-interest. Even before childhood is over, fear of the future, the 'spectre's call',[89] is sensed:

> Those tiny hands in vain essay
> To thrust the shadowy fiend away;
> There is a horror on his brow,
> An anguish in his bosom now; . . .
> And childhood's flower must waste its bloom
> Beneath the shadow of the tomb.

Later, in 'Lines',[90] Emily wrote of a Heathcliff-like being with 'stern and swarthy brow', and mourned that, somewhere along the way, this time-hardened man had lost the artless world of the child.

> That iron man was born like me,
> And he was once an ardent boy:
> He must have felt, in infancy,
> The glory of a summer sky.

Here, as she was later to do in the novel, she pressed home the point that the canker comes from within; not from life's material processes in themselves, but from the reactions to them of committed self-interest. The poet looks in vain for a sign of 'remorse', of a 'soul redeemed by love'. But 'One glance revealed how little care/He felt for all the beauty there'.

Finally, in *Wuthering Heights*, the 'iron man', the 'accursed man',[91] of the poems emerged fully formed. This was the being presaged by the Dark Child, the ultimate product of the unregenerate self, the being 'shut from his Maker's smile', in whom 'compassion reigns a little while/Revenge eternally'. And in the novel Emily confirmed the lessons that her close and anguished observations of life had taught her: that we must expect brutality to be parent of the brute, and, at the other end of the scale, excessive indulgence to breed the fatal weakness that will drive a passionate nature headlong into destruction. Can we doubt that, as she watched this very tragedy being enacted in her own brother's life, she mourned again the lack of that discipline in his life which she herself had so early advised?

The point has been made[92] that Emily Brontë saw childhood and adolescence 'as a positive force, opposing itself to the strange and hostile world of adults, a force akin to the "revolt and nostalgia for innocence" which she still felt to the end'. To this, one would wish to add that she nevertheless did not absolve the young from the onus of moral choice. Innocence is not a synonym for inexperience of life, and, for Emily, the difference was important. Catherine Earnshaw was not ignorant of the fact that in choosing life with Edgar Linton she was abandoning her true love; '. . . in my soul, and in my heart,' she told Nelly Dean, 'I'm convinced I'm wrong!'[93] And Heathcliff's vengeance on the house of Earnshaw was the result of a deliberate vow,[94] sustained over a period of more than twenty-five years in the face of appalling suffering, much of it inflicted on those who had done little or nothing to deserve it. The point is made most clearly of all, however, at the novel's end, when the second Catherine makes her own, very different, choice. In imposing a new discipline upon her former wayward self, and a caring responsibility towards the education of her neglected cousin, Hareton,[95] she becomes Emily Brontë's model for the transformation of moral choice from the negative to the positive. Like George Eliot after her, Emily was concerned to show that, while human beings were subject to certain basic influences governing their lives, they were nevertheless free to the extent that they could choose the direction which those lives would take.

> I could think in the withered grass
> Spring's budding wreaths we might discern;
> The violet's eye might shyly flash
> And young leaves shoot among the fern.[96]

Like Nature itself, in whose eternal renewals of beauty she saw an Eden-like potential never wholly submerged, so the human being, from childhood on, reflected the material and corruptible image of a spiritual and incorruptible Truth. But human beings had an advantage over Nature; for them, 'Spring's budding wreaths' *could* become 'young leaves' if they chose, and the 'withered grass' be turned into 'fern'.

For almost six indescribably difficult years, Anne Brontë lived and worked in a world of children, earning her living as a governess in what was one of the toughest social *milieux* which a lone, dependent woman could enter – the world of the wealthy, self-made families of the north-country squirearchy. That she acquitted herself with immense fortitude can be taken for granted from the simple fact of her duration of service. During that service, she witnessed for herself that very change in the attitude of parents towards children referred to at the beginning of this chapter: the change towards a new indulgence, which would occasionally go hand in hand with a puritan harshness. This, she captured with perfect fidelity in her first novel, *Agnes Grey*, in which, for example, the small Bloomfields, hopelessly spoilt, are threatened with a horse-whipping by their father.[97] 'It is beautifully authentic,' wrote Margaret Lane,[98] 'a splendid corrective for any persuasion one may have that the Victorian child was always the meek product of repressive discipline'. But, she added, 'the manners of the age, for all their veneer of religion and sensibility, are far harsher and meaner than we should tolerate today'.

Anne Brontë shared with Emily the desire to expose the damage which the adult world was capable of inflicting upon the young, but there were major differences in her approach. Anne had neither Emily's imaginative intensity nor her philosophical nature. She wrote simply and directly of situations seen and known. For her, the children described in *Agnes Grey* and *The Tenant of Wildfell Hall* were not symbols; they were mirror-images of young individuals she had met with during her governess days. *The Tenant of Wildfell Hall* is not an allegory with Platonist undercurrents, like *Wuthering Heights;* it is a strong, brave, telling protest against the treatment of the Woman and the Child by mid-Victorian society. Even to her own near-contemporary readers, the accuracy of her insight was clear. Lady Amberley noted in her diary for 1868:

read *Agnes Grey*, one of the Brontës, and should like to give it to every family with a governess and shall read it through again when I have a governess to remind me to be human.[99]

From Susan Brooke, writing of her childhood memories of her 'grandmother's old home',[100] Blake Hall, has come a valuable confirmation of the connection between the Hall, scene of Anne Brontë's first governess post and her first novel:

> As children . . . our acquaintance with Blake Hall and its former occupants enabled us to appreciate the strange character of Mr. Bloomfield in *Agnes Grey*. In fact, in some curious way we seemed to know more about him than the governess, so that on certain occasions we felt like giving her a desperate warning: 'Look out – don't you see how he'll catch you out next time.'[101]

Anne, said Susan Brooke, was 'meticulously exact in her observations . . . for anyone who knew the background there could be no doubt that her experiences at Blake Hall were woven into this book'. In other words, we can confidently accept that Anne's accounts of child upbringing among certain of the landed families of her time were basically true to prevailing customs, always bearing in mind, of course, that her experience was confined to conditions in rural Yorkshire. Here, the 'blustering, roystering country squire'[102] of Horton Lodge and the besotted, gun-toting 'Uncle Robson' of Wellwood had plenty of originals. Of the more sophisticated societies of such, for example, as metropolitan Manchester, Anne was no doubt as ignorant as Charlotte was to show herself to be in her reactions to the young Gaskells. Anne, however, differed from her sisters in that, for her, the 'bad' families were the exceptions rather than the 'good' ones; 'everybody is not like Mr. and Mrs. Bloomfield,'[103] she has Agnes Grey tell her mother, '. . . I'm sure all children are not like theirs . . .'. And of the eldest Murray child she has Agnes record that he 'might have been a decent lad had he been properly educated . . . .'[104]

For Anne, as for Emily, with whom she had always been especially close, education, in the broadest sense of the word, was the root of the matter. And nowhere in all the Brontë writings is this more straightly put than in Anne's second and last novel, *The Tenant of Wildfell Hall*. 'Oh, Reader!'[105] she wrote in her Preface to the Second Edition, 'if there were less of this delicate concealment of facts – this whispering "Peace, peace," when there is no peace, there would be less of sin and misery to the young of both sexes who are left to wring their bitter knowledge from experience.' Her aim, she said, was 'to tell the truth',[106] and via her heroine, Helen Graham, she confronted not one but three highly sensitive issues head-on: first, the invidious position of the married woman; second, the harmful results of parental indulgence on children, especially young boys; and third, the effects of marital unhappiness on the mother–child relationship. The end product was a book so unequivocal, so frankly critical of contemporary society that its first reviewers were appalled. The *Spectator*[107] in July 1848 called it 'repulsive' and declared its author to have a 'morbid love for the coarse, not to say the brutal'. Even Charlotte was so dismayed by it that, when approached by her publisher concerning a posthumous edition of the novel, she replied, 'it hardly appears to me desirable to preserve'.[108] 'The choice of subject,' she said, was 'a mistake'. Charlotte's censure was no doubt the measure of the anguish and disappointment she felt over Branwell, whose tragic career would be palpably evoked for her in those of the debauched Huntingdon and his cronies. But the book, far from being a 'mistake', had been written for this very reason: to emphasise how desperate was the need for young boys to be more practically educated for life, and for *both* sexes to be so thoroughly prepared for it in advance that they 'require no experimental proofs to teach them the evil of transgression'.[109] Defending herself against charges of over-protectiveness towards her son, Helen Graham says:

> It is all very well to talk about noble resistance, and trials of virtue; but for fifty – or five hundred men that have yielded to temptation, show me one that has had virtue to resist. And why should I take it for granted that my son will be one in a thousand?[110]

By preparing for the 'worst', she says, she hopes to save the boy 'from one degrading vice at least'. We may feel uneasy before such rigid perfectionism, and feel a certain sympathy with its critics, but we take the point which Anne Brontë wishes us to note: that Helen Graham's fears stem from her life with a callous and degenerate husband and he in his turn is the result of that very lack of early discipline and moral education that she now wishes her son to have.

Just where Anne Brontë stands in the Augustinian versus Romantic scale *vis-à-vis* the Literary Child is not easy to determine.

From the examples she gives us in *Agnes Grey* we might infer that
she believed the child's natural will to be corrupt; on the other hand,
the reasoned arguments of *The Tenant of Wildfell Hall* tend to the
conclusion that children are spoilt only by exposure to the 'vices' of
the adult world. In thus placing the blame upon the lack of proper
parental example and instruction, she would seem to have shared
with Charlotte the idea of the child's original innocence. With
Emily, too, she saw the journey to maturity at whatever age as
attended by 'purging fires',[111] and joined with her in the hope of
blessing 'in the end'. Certainly, in the total realism of *The Tenant
of Wildfell Hall* Anne celebrated her own personal break with
childhood as effectively and as finally as had Emily in the triumph of
love over hate in the last pages of *Wuthering Heights* and as
Charlotte, five years later, was to do in *Villette*.

Few novelists have written more felicitously of childhood than
George Eliot. That she *enjoyed* writing about children is clear from
their ubiquitous presence in her novels. We recall, for instance, such
delightful studies as the small Job Tudge in *Felix Holt*, little Chubby
Barton in *Scenes of Clerical Life*, along with the saucy workhouse boy,
Master Fodge, to be followed by a series of examples that culminate
in the splendid brood of Cohens in *Daniel Deronda*. Unfortunately,
this authorial pleasure which George Eliot took in children
sometimes inclined her towards a cloying sentimentality. There are
moments when the picture she paints is *too* delightful, her view is
too limited to the 'apple-cheeked'[112] and 'sweet, fair face'[113] of
childhood, with 'dimpled fist'[114] and 'golden curls'.[115] Maggie
Tulliver, it is true, is often 'naughty', but – George Eliot seems to say
– what delicious naughtiness it is! It is tempting to imagine the
sardonic humour which this view of the unruly child would have
provoked in Charlotte and Emily Brontë; even the gentle Anne
would surely have sighed.

Given the young Mary Ann Evans's unsatisfactory relationship
with her mother, it seems reasonable to believe that this tendency in
her as an author to create 'idyllic' childhood portraits was part of a
sub-conscious effort towards self-compensation. Ruby V. Redinger
has argued convincingly for a connection between Christiana
Evans's invalidism and symptoms of deep emotional need in the
young Mary Ann.

It would seem that Christiana did not languish on the couch or otherwise withdraw herself in a physical sense. Rather, she effected an exodus of the children, so that one by one they were sent away from home, the reason always being the irreproachable one of their mother's enfeebled health . . . .[116]

While, however, George Eliot's indulgent, at times almost mawkish, treatment of children in her novels may well have owed something to her need to create a warmer, more satisfying childhood world than her own had been, it would be a gross underestimation of her rational powers and penetrating psychological insights to suggest that this represented her basic attitude towards the role of the child *vis-à-vis* the world. In an article which she wrote in 1847, called 'The Wisdom of the Child',[117] she again described the attributes of childhood in terms which would have raised quiet smiles round the fireplace at Haworth, but these terms are more equivocal than they at first appear. 'Self-renunciation, submission to law, trust, benignity, ingenuousness, rectitude, – these are the qualities we delight most to witness in the child', she wrote, and declared that 'true wisdom, which implies a moral as well as an intellectual result, consists in a return to that purity and simplicity which characterise early youth, when its intuitions have not been perverted'. This would appear to be pure Rousseauism; indeed, Rousseau is mentioned at the beginning of the article, which also, at the end, indicates Wordsworthian inclinations with the familiar quotation, 'the child is father of the man'. George Eliot then, however, appears to modify this view, defining the parallel between the wise man and the child as that of 'a similarity with a difference'.

the wonder of a child at the material world is the effect of novelty, its simplicity and purity of ignorance; while the wonder of the wise man is the result of knowledge disclosing mystery, the simplicity and purity of his moral principles, the result of wide experience and hardly-attained self-conflict.

Thus, for Eliot, the child's simplicity and innocence is merely an unacquaintance with complexity. Her position, therefore, in the Augustinian *versus* Romantic scale seems somewhat ambivalent, for the Eliot child – as seen, for example, in Eppie in *Silas Marner* – would seem to be a regenerative force, yet at the same time rationally it constitutes for Eliot a mere *tabula rasa*. This would appear to justify the criticism of Eppie mentioned at the beginning of this chapter – that is, that rather than existing as a character in her own right, she functions more as the Dickens child does, as 'a contrast to the fallen world and a means of its redemption'.[118] From this standpoint, Eppie is created primarily to serve an idea and therefore has no personal, evolving sense of consciousness. Maggie and Tom Tulliver in *The Mill on the Floss* are claimed to be the exceptions to this tendency in George Eliot because they appear as 'minutely detailed and psychological character studies'.[119] It is certainly true that, of all George Eliot's characters, they are the most drawn from personal memory and experience. The novel undoubtedly became for her a means of giving release to instinctive feelings of guilt over her own moral vulnerability in the eyes of society; there was, too, the sense of resentment, of loss and of betrayal arising from her brother's tacit censure of her as a lapsed Christian and as a woman who had deliberately elected to live 'in sin' with a married man. George Eliot could have presented Maggie Tulliver as a maligned innocent, as Charlotte Brontë had done with Jane Eyre; but this would not have been enough. Her life with George Henry Lewes was not a matter of speculation, as Charlotte Brontë's feelings for Heger became; it was a fact. What was needed, therefore, was something that would show that, far from being a 'scarlet woman', she endorsed utterly the general social consensus against the wrong-doer. The only difference lay in that, for her, 'sin' was not to be defined in terms of the mere breaking of certain social rules; it was, as Emily Brontë had shown in *Wuthering Heights*, the pursuit of egotistic needs and desires at the expense of the happiness and well-being of others. Thus, while for Charlotte Brontë the development of Jane Eyre from child to woman was an attempt to explain and justify an ideal that remained a dream, the life and death of the young Maggie Tulliver was for George Eliot a demonstration of the workings of a morality by which her own apparent culpability could be seen to be absolved.

Maggie Tulliver's failure to develop into maturity, her idealisations and vacillations, aspirations and fatal weakness, her ultimate emotional collapse in the face of a self-knowledge too painful to be borne, are all the results of those repressions that prevented her as a child from discovering her own natural, unenforced limits. In her attempts to break through the rigid barriers imposed upon her by others, she continually over-reaches herself; with every disillusionment, her sense of unworthiness increases, so that by the time her childhood is almost behind her, the downward pull is irreversible. Maggie, writes Bernard Paris,[120] 'has not the strength to become her own person'; she 'reverts to a childish dependence and returns to Tom for punishment and for protection from herself'.

The identification between author and heroine in *The Mill*, as in Charlotte Brontë's *Jane Eyre*, has been widely recognised, but the question that remains is whether George Eliot shared what Leavis has called Maggie Tulliver's 'large lack of self-knowledge'.[121] If she did not, then the degree of emotional seduction of the reader in the novel's *denouement* is unforgivable; if she did, however, the most that might be said is that the flood of sentiment in which Maggie and Tom disappear under the waters of the Ripple represents a gross over-statement on George Eliot's part of the washing away of Maggie's sins. If, too, the latter interpretation of authorial involvement is correct, then in this novel, perhaps more than anywhere else in George Eliot's work, we see that pattern of challenge followed by capitulation which is detectable in the lives and work of all four of these women writers facing alike the pressures and prejudices of a society so distrustful of their sex.

Silas Marner is the only other novel in which George Eliot focused specifically and centrally upon childhood. She herself described the work to her publisher, John Blackwood, as being about 'the remedial influences of pure, natural human relations'.[122] The impulse to write the novel, she told him, had come from a childhood memory of seeing 'a linen-weaver with a bag on his back'. But if we may thus interpret *Silas Marner* as 'the last of her novels inspired by her childhood',[123] we can also certainly define it as the first full-length work in which she leaves her own childhood firmly behind her and gives all her attention to the task of providing a body – both literally and figuratively – for an objective idea, the corruption of the spirit by the worship of matter. Eppie Cass, the *persona* of the Regenerative Child, is the instrument of that idea, and George Eliot defines her role at the outset with a three-line preface from Wordsworth's poem, 'Michael'.

> a child, more than all other gifts
> That earth can offer to declining man,
> Brings hope with it, and forward-looking thoughts.

In contrast with Eppie, we see in the figure of Silas a sad old man whose life 'had reduced itself to the functions of weaving and hoarding, without any contemplation of an end towards which the functions tended'.[124] His vision has been narrowed to all but the glint of gold, until the gleam of a child's fair head on his hearth awakens 'a hurrying influx of memories'.[125]

Significantly, however, the movement of growth in man and child has a reciprocal quality. 'As the child's mind was growing into knowledge, his mind was growing into memory'.[126] It is via this retrospection that Silas is enabled to come to terms with the present and the future.

> Silas now began to think of Raveloe life entirely in relation to Eppie . . . and he listened docilely, that he might come to understand better what this life was, from which, for fifteen years, he had stood aloof as from a strange thing . . . .[127]

Another aspect of this reciprocity of influence between the child and the man is seen as we recall that, initially, Eppie's own life had been saved by the light from Silas's door.

> That bright living thing must be caught; and in an instant the child had slipped on all fours, and held out one little hand to catch the gleam . . . . It came from a very bright place . . . .[128]

Silas's cottage was 'a very bright place' because 'the door was open',[129] releasing the light from within and enabling Eppie to enter. The door is open for the prosaic and practical reason that Silas is still vaguely looking for his lost gold; but at a deeper level the open door represents an element of incipient hope in the old man. As yet, he is blind to its meaning, as he is blind to the tiny shape of it as it crosses his threshold, but it foretells a receptivity within him that will work as much for Eppie's salvation as his own.

Robert Pattison has seen 'the *milieu* of *Silas Marner*'[130] to be 'the universe of Original Sin', but this is an argument that it is difficult to reconcile with George Eliot's philosophy. A more acceptable explanation of the novel's constitution and purpose would perhaps be that essentially it provides an allegorical representation of the successful application of the Religion of Humanity. Thus, the child's 'innocence' is shown as nurtured rather than corrupted by experience, resulting in an exchange of roles between child and man which brings maturity to the child and simplicity and peace of mind to the man. Thereby, the 'child is father', a notion which is at the heart of all that George Eliot held to be true about the interdependence of human life. The novel might therefore be said to contain the sum of her ideal view of the child's place and significance in human society. Variations on the contrast between maturity and immaturity appear throughout her work, until finally in *Daniel Deronda* we see the epitome of 'The Spoiled Child' in fruition in the characterisation of Gwendolen Harleth – the Maggie Tulliver that nearly was – the girl who 'will not rest without having the world at her feet'.[131] Overall, however, the 'message' of the Eliot child is essentially contained in the figure of Eppie Cass. In her decision to remain with Silas and to renounce the comfort and privilege of life as the squire's daughter, Eppie proclaims her loyalty to the simple world that, with Silas at its heart, has held her life in trust for her. It is a gesture that carries her from childhood into maturity in an unbroken flight, and provides George Eliot with her perfect demonstration of 'pure, natural human relations'.

It is clear that all four novelists were alive to the trends of contemporary thought on the subject of the child, tacitly acknowledging in their work the influence of such writers as Rousseau and Wordsworth; it is also clear that they held in common with each other and with other authors of fiction, notably Dickens, an awareness of the value of the child figure as a literary force. Through the child, the representative of the human being in embryo, could so well be shown the dangers of the world of experience. The warning directed to the adult world was thus twofold: first, of the vital need for understanding and moral guidance in the upbringing of the young; second, of the need for the reformation of adult beliefs and conduct in family life. In Emily Brontë we see a further dimension, inasmuch as she extended the little world of human childhood into concepts of maturity and immaturity of cosmic significance. We also see a somewhat surprising affinity of philosophical attitude between her and George Eliot – that is, in the form of their shared belief in the morally neutral processes of causality, depicted in similar terms in the progressions from sin to suffering in *Wuthering Heights*, *Adam Bede* and *The Mill on the Floss*. In all these novels, we are meant to see that their young offenders suffer, not because they are 'bad', but because they are foolish: not because they disobey some metaphysical imperative, but because, in their wilfulness and self-interest, they ignore the laws of cause and effect. Both novelists saw the notion of condemnation as pointless, although for different reasons. It was pointless to Emily Brontë because, for her, the soul in Reality is undefiled, but only briefly, in early childhood and in death, can this be realised. It was pointless to George Eliot because, sharing with Emily the belief that wrong-doing involves its own discipline, the price of failure to rectify one's life was the extension of anguish to the point where it becomes untenable.

Finally, there is the autobiographical element which we see connecting George Eliot and Charlotte Brontë in particular. Powerful threads of childhood pain and defiance link *Jane Eyre* and *The Mill on the Floss*. In both novels, the childhood sequences reflect their authors' attempts to dispossess themselves of the haunting shadows of the past. A note of challenge unites them: the echoes of Angrian heroes merge with the lonely voice of a St Teresa; but there is guilt, too, a guilt stemming from emotional needs that had been personal to both authors. Charlotte countered them with the story of a girl in whom virtue remained stronger than passion, and who was vindicated at the end, George Eliot with a girl for whom passion was stronger than prudence, and who accepted self-immolation as the due and proper price. The distinction is not too difficult to understand. George Eliot halted on the brink of a defiance that would have brought down upon her the outraged critical denunciations which the Brontës first received. They, in their mixture of honesty and naiveté, stepped out on to 'the other side of silence',[132] but we should perhaps bear in mind that in a not insignificant way they could afford to do so. The moral tone of their fiction might be seen to be dubious, but their life-style was not. George Eliot, on the other hand, was acutely conscious that her reputation was not such as to place her beyond reproach; it would be surprising if an instinct for self-preservation did not operate within her, albeit subconsciously, to keep the fictional moral tone high. Thus, perhaps, it is not merely adventitious that, while Jane Eyre marries her Rochester and Helen Graham her Markham, and Heathcliff dies in his bed, Maggie Tulliver is drowned, Janet Dempster is converted, Hetty Sorrel is transported and Molly Cass dies in the snow.

2

Matters of Belief: Religious and Ethical Attitudes

Today, in deference to the weight of time and tradition, we still apply the designation, 'period of change' to the Victorian era, despite the challenging events of more recent times: for this was the era that was to be recognised even by its participants as a kind of painful adolescence of the awakening Self, a time in which an ever-increasing number of human beings began, as Kant had exhorted, to have the courage to think for themselves, to 'dare to know'.[1] The results, not unexpectedly, were disturbing, and nowhere more so than in the area of religion, where a new 'disquietude and doubt'[2] began to undermine the foundations of long-established certainties.

Although the distinguishing aspects of nineteenth-century religious controversy began long before the purely nominal beginning of the Victorian period, it was from the late 1830s onwards that the most fundamental doubts began to be expressed. At that time, as the Brontë sisters and the young George Eliot grew from adolescence to maturity, the debate on religion broadened out; from being confined, as until then, simply to the nature of Catholicism, it now came to grips with the nature of religion itself and its validity in a new age of science. For most who thought at all it meant a re-examination of old beliefs: for many, a readjustment of attitudes. For some, it meant a total transformation, an almost wholesale abandonment of long-established alliances, and an often harrowing journey out into new, strange territories of the heart and mind. One such was George Eliot, whose life and thought suffered a dramatic and painful shift from the fervent certainties of Evangelical conversion to the anguished doubts of intellectual rationalism before reaching the somewhat uncertain haven of her own brand of the 'Religion of Humanity'. Others would make similar journeys, but few with the significance for literature and human thought in general as hers.

None of the Brontës was to make her position on religion quite as

37

clear as did George Eliot. Nor indeed can we assume that the views of one sister accorded altogether with those of the others. While all three shared the essential beliefs of their inherited Christian orthodoxy, their individual paths seem to have radiated out from this central point in different directions, and in one case – Emily's – the destination remains, in some aspects, extremely obscure. Certain basic similarities of experience and attitude, however, unite the sisters as a whole with George Eliot. In all four lives, for example, the earliest influences were of a 'Broad Church' environment, followed by exposure to powerful Evangelical pressures. The ensuing conflict resulted in a condition of adolescent religious 'crisis' which affected George Eliot and two of the Brontë sisters – Charlotte and Anne – in much the same way, with, in all four, the eventual rejection of religious hypocrisy and a passionate adherence to the belief that human understanding, sympathy and tolerance were more essentially Christian than ritual and dogma. For all of them, the writing of fiction was to become to a significant extent a means of expressing deeply felt ethical views.

The differences we find between the four in this area are of a kind that in the main relate to differences of background and upbringing. Firstly, with the possible exception of Charlotte, the Brontës do not appear to have taken anything like the same *objective* interest in religion as that shown by George Eliot. An obvious reason for this would seem to be afforded by the contrasts between lives constrained by Parsonage walls and that eventually brought into contact with a wide range of philosophical – including humanist – thought. Of the Brontës, it might be conjectured that familiarity with the subject of religion, if it did not necessarily breed contempt, might well perhaps have reduced curiosity towards it. Secondly, at no time do the Brontës appear to have been attracted to any kind of rational humanism as such. The absence of the cultural influences that might have encouraged this could be an explanation, but against that we have to place their apparently free access to a wide range of reading matter in the form of contemporary periodicals. Thirdly, for the Brontës, Evangelical ardour did not gush like a tidal bore into the quiet stream of Broad Church Anglicanism, as it did with the young George Eliot. The Reverend Patrick's sermons had never lacked Revivalist fire. As a boy in Ireland, he had been influenced at first hand by the vibrant spirit of early Wesleyanism, and the chord which it had struck in his Celtic nature was to reverberate there throughout the whole of his Anglican ministry. To his Haworth congregations, this did not go amiss, for a tradition of Methodism stretched back into the eighteenth century, when the famous William Grimshaw had thundered out his message to the ancestors of these very people.[3]

We have no record of what the Brontë children thought of their father's sermons. He was no Calvinist, hating what he called 'its appalling doctrines',[4] and adhering firmly to the hope of Universal Salvation and the *'good old plan'*[5] of the established Anglican Church, but he was not above using colourful 'hell-fire' analogies for the better guidance of his mostly simple, unlearned congregations, an approach which it seems more than likely that his children would have found much to their imaginative taste. On the other hand, it has been suggested[6] that the excessive fervour of their aunt, Elizabeth Branwell, proved repressive. A passionate Evangelical Methodist from Cornwall, one of the centres of religious Revivalism, Aunt Branwell was by all accounts a well-meaning but rather joyless woman who brought to the care of her dead sister's children a degree of puritan zeal that provoked mixed reactions. These seem to have ranged from a state of repressed catalytic anguish in Anne to near-open hostility and rebellion in the more inflammable Charlotte. Just how much the latter's attitude was owed to an objective difference of opinion on religion, however, and how much to the instinctive resentment of a growing young woman to the authority of another female not her natural mother it would be difficult to say; one might question whether the resentment did not significantly affect the difference of opinion. Charlotte's hatred of religious tyranny, rigidity and emotionalism was always itself conspicuously charged with some of the very intolerance it raged against, suggesting as much a personal as a philosophical source.

Nevertheless, Charlotte it was who, of the three sisters, showed the most direct interest in religion *per se*, both in her personal life and later in her fiction. According to Mrs Gaskell, Charlotte's friend Mary Taylor once reported: 'I have heard her condemn Socinianism, Calvinism, and many other "isms" consistent with Church of Englandism. I used to wonder at her acquaintance with such subjects'.[7] To Ellen Nussey in March 1846, Charlotte herself wrote:

I received the number of the 'Record' you sent . . . . I read D'aubigne's letter. It is clever, and in what he says about Catholicism very good. The Evangelical Alliance part is not very practicable, yet certainly it is more in accordance with the spirit of the Gospel to preach unity among Christians than to inculcate mutual intolerance and hatred.[8]

But it is in her fiction that we see Charlotte's views on religion and moral conduct to full effect. *Villette*, a work laden with anti-Catholic reference, brought from Matthew Arnold the shocked comment:

> Miss Brontë has written a hideous undelightful convulsed constricted novel . . . . Religion or devotion or whatever it is to be called may be impossible for such people now: but they have at any rate not found a substitute for it and it was better for the world when they comforted themselves with it.[9]

Charlotte's mind, he said, contained 'nothing but hunger, rebellion, and rage'.[10]

The implicit suggestion here that Charlotte was among those who sought a 'substitute' for religion was, however, incorrect, and this underlines an important contrast between her and George Eliot. Charlotte's retention of her orthodox faith argues for the presence of basic loyalties of a profound, if possibly critical, kind, and it is here claimed that the Brontë sisters did in the main sustain these loyalties to orthodox Christianity. Charlotte's treatment of religion in her fiction is explicit. It would be difficult to conceive of a more precise definition of her attitude towards the life-denying gloom and doom of the Calvinist mind than Jane Eyre's 'black marble clergyman', Mr Brocklehurst,[11] and the ice-cold, drearily sententious St John Rivers. On the other hand, in Jane herself, we have Charlotte's idea of true, unassuming Christian faith and virtue in action in an imperfect world. As already indicated however, it is in *Villette* that she shows most clearly both the intensity of her concern for religious truth and her contempt for the self-serving distortions of 'Churchianity' of all denominations. There can hardly be another novel whose central character is more powerfully antipathetic towards one religion in particular and to all religious excess in general. Identifying the views of an author with those of her characters is a doubtful procedure, but in Lucy Snowe we have what is palpably an authorial voice, speaking with impassioned directness of the Roman Catholic church as a prison of the mind, hiding its 'chains with flowers', its repressions with a 'large sensual indulgence' that permitted the victims of its 'slavery' to develop 'robust in body, feeble in soul, fat, ruddy, hale, joyous, ignorant, un-thinking, un-questioning'.[12]

Although she concedes that it is possible for a Romanist to hold to the 'purer elements of his creed',[13] in the deepest crisis of her life she rejects conversion (as had Charlotte in Brussels[14]) because she sees through the 'comfort' and the 'tenderness' to the ancient traditions of threat, coercion and persecution.[15] But it is not only Roman Catholicism that receives the scourge. In the verbal immoderations of Romanism, Lucy Snowe finds reminders of 'certain Wesleyan tracts I had once read [as had Charlotte] as a child; they were flavoured with about the same seasoning of excitation to fanaticism'.[16] Thus, the concern is revealed as a general one against all religious systems that resort to emotional seduction for effect. Nevertheless, through Lucy Snowe, Charlotte makes a statement of faith that has more than a ring of personal truth: 'I am not a heathen . . . . I am not unchristian . . . you believe in God and Christ and the Bible, and so do I'.[17] And, in Lucy's long speech to M. Paul, she goes on to define what we might see as the overall Brontë position:

> the more I saw of Popery the closer I clung to Protestantism; doubtless there were errors in every Church, but I now perceived by contrast how severely pure was my own, compared with her whose painted and meretricious face had been unveiled for my admiration. I told him how we kept fewer forms between us and God. . . . I told him I could not look on flowers and tinsel, on wax-lights and embroidery, at such times and under such circumstances as should be devoted to lifting the secret vision to Him whose home is Infinity, and his being – Eternity. That when I thought of sin and sorrow, of earthly corruption, mortal depravity, weighty temporal woe – I could not care for chanting priests or murmuring officials; that when the pains of existence and the terrors of dissolution pressed before me – when the mighty hope and measureless doubt of the future arose in view – *then*, even the scientific strain, or the prayer in a language learned and dead, harassed with hindrance a heart which only longed to cry – 'God be merciful to me, a sinner!'[18]

There can be little doubt that in this sustained and vehement protest, in the 'terrible, proud, earnest Protestantism'[19] of Lucy Snowe, we have the spiritual essence of her creator; and also that in the combination of open-mindedness and curiosity that led Lucy to attend three different Protestant chapels in Villette we have Charlotte Brontë's own odd mixture of tolerance and proscription. It is also surely clear that in Lucy's affirmation of allegiance to 'the Bible itself, rather than any sect, of whatever name or nation'[20] Charlotte was paraphrasing her own words, written to Ellen Nussey almost twenty years before; 'I know the treasures of the *Bible*; I love and adore them'.[21]

Brief mention was made, above, to Charlotte Brontë's rejection of conversion to the Roman faith whilst in Brussels. The word 'conversion' overstates the case: 'aberration' must have seemed a more appropriate one to Emily, to whom Charlotte wrote on 2 September 1843, describing her conduct. This strange circumstance merits close attention, as it casts an important light on certain aspects of Charlotte's nature that are central to our understanding of her. The background facts are that in 1843 Charlotte returned alone to the Pensionnat Heger in Brussels, having spent most of the previous year there with Emily as a fellow-pupil. After their aunt's death in October 1842, Emily had elected to remain at home as her father's housekeeper, while Charlotte, encouraged by both Madame and Monsieur Heger, decided to return to Brussels alone. It was an adventure to which she clearly looked forward keenly – and yet, at the same time with a strange sense of foreboding, expressed in the words written to Ellen Nussey three years later: 'I returned to Brussels after aunt's death against my conscience, prompted by what then seemed an irresistible impulse. I was punished for my selfish folly by a total withdrawal for more than two years of happiness and peace of mind . . . .'[22] The first shadow of things to come had already begun to form by March 1843, when her letters to Ellen Nussey hinted of loneliness and a certain disillusionment. 'As I told you before,' she wrote, 'M. and Madame Heger are the only two persons in the house for whom I really experience regard and esteem, and, of course, I cannot always be with them, nor even often . . . . Thus I am a good deal by myself'.[23] But she was now regularly giving English lessons to M. Heger himself and to his brother-in-law, M. Chapelle. At what point this intellectual stimulation turned, in Charlotte, to something more personal and more disturbing we cannot know, since she herself appears not to have recognised the true nature of her own feelings. We can only deduce from her conduct something of the growing ferment within her at this time, and the evidence here comes from the letter she wrote to Emily on 2 September 1843. In it, she speaks again of her increasing loneliness, of long, solitary walks through the streets of Brussels and the surrounding countryside. She then

writes of one evening in particular, when, finding herself unable to
return to the school with any sense of pleasure, she wandered into
the Cathedral of Ste Gudule. An 'odd whim', she told Emily, came
into her head.

> In a solitary part of the Cathedral six or seven people still
> remained kneeling by the confessionals . . . . I took a fancy to
> change myself into a Catholic and go and make a real confession
> to see what it was like. Knowing me as you do, you will think this
> odd, but when people are by themselves they have singular
> fancies . . . . After I had watched two or three penitents go and
> return I approached at last and knelt down in a niche which was
> just vacated . . . a little wooden door inside the grating opened,
> and I saw the priest leaning his ear towards me . . . . I actually did
> confess – a real confession . . . . Of course, however, the
> adventure stops there, and I hope I shall never see the priest
> again.[24]

To this extraordinary 'second confession' Charlotte added: 'I think
you had better not tell papa of this. He will not understand that it
was only a freak, and will perhaps think I am going to turn
Catholic'.

We may well wonder both at this strange event itself and at
Charlotte's revelation of it to Emily – almost as though, by thus
entrusting it to a safe ear she could rationalise it for herself. Her
attempt to explain it, however, in terms of the 'singular fancies' of
the solitary does not ring true. Only the year before, she had written
to Ellen Nussey:

> my advice to all protestants who are tempted to anything so
> besotted as turn Catholic – is to walk over the sea on to the
> continent – to attend mass regularly for a time to note well the
> mummeries thereof – also the idiotic, mercenary aspect of *all* the
> priests, and *then* if they are still disposed to consider Papistry in
> any other light than a most feeble childish piece of humbug let
> them turn papists at once that's all – I consider Methodism,
> Dissenterism, Quakerism, and the extremes of high and low
> Churchism foolish but Roman Catholicism beats them all.[25]

To this wholesale impeachment she added the rider that 'there are
some Catholics – who are as good as any Christians . . . and much

better than scores of Protestants'; but the fact remains that Charlotte clearly held throughout her life to the faith in which she had been born, and thus the Brussels 'confession' was, from a religious point of view, wholly spurious. A much more convincing explanation lies within the area of her emotional psychological condition at this time. From the evidence available to us, there can be little doubt that Charlotte developed an intense attachment to M. Heger, to which, eventually Madame Heger took exception,[26] and which led to Charlotte's leaving the Pensionnat on 1 January 1844, in circumstances in which much outward good-will was thrown over the very considerable tension that had preceded it. The emotional significance of the Heger relationship will be more fully dealt with in a later chapter, but it seems more than likely that the bizarre incident in the cathedral was the result of a culmination of guilt, apprehension and confusion from which Charlotte felt a desperate need to seek release. The letter to Emily fits into the same pattern.

To reach as nearly as we can to a final word on Charlotte's religious position, we must turn again to *Villette*, the novel of her full maturity, both as a novelist and as a human being. Despite its intimations of denominational bias, the novel portrays, in Lucy Snowe, a human soul in process of organic growth, moving towards an eclectic awareness of the good to be found in *all* religions, even in the hated Rome. Although there are times – especially in the struggles with Paul Emanuel – when the bias seems to have as much to do with the preservation of the personal identity of Lucy Snowe as with the Church of England or Rome, by the time the story ends the battle has been lifted out of the merely sexual and temporal into the dispassionate realms of the soul and spirit. With her hopes of happiness suddenly and tragically destroyed, Lucy Snowe faces the future with an un-selfpitying calm that seems to epitomise exactly Charlotte Brontë's own lifelong belief that 'there was some good reason, which we should know in time, why sorrow and disappointment seem to be the lot of some on earth', and that 'it was better to acknowledge this, and face out the truth in a religious faith'.[27]

It is from Mrs Gaskell that we first hear the classic story of Emily Brontë's Two Words on religion, quoted from an account by Charlotte's school-friend, Mary Taylor. 'I mentioned that some one had asked me what religion I was,' said Miss Taylor, '. . . and that I had said that that was between God and me. Emily (who was lying on the hearth-rug) exclaimed, "That's right." This was all I ever heard Emily say on religious subjects.'[28] We might wonder whether it was not from the extraordinary reticence of this one sister that the Brontë myth of religious silence first arose, and in some quarters still retains credence. Her disinclination to commit herself to any explicit statements of belief such as are seen in the work of both Charlotte and Anne has led to the kind of speculation of which an example is the linking of her name with that of F. D. Maurice,[29] of whom she was once reputed to have called herself a 'disciple', but most of whose writing was not done until after her death. In fact, there is nothing in her extant writings to indicate that she consciously acknowledged a debt to this or any other contemporary philosophical source. The influences that are most suggested by her work are much older ones. In her essay, 'The Butterfly', written, we must remember, when she was an adult, we can clearly trace not only her firm allegiance to the received faith of Christian orthodoxy, but also strong elements of Platonism. Although there is no evidence that Emily ever read a single word by or about Plato, or even for that matter studied any formal system of philosophy, nevertheless these Platonist elements, with their emphasis on life's dualities and contraries, and the division between the world of Illusion and the Eternal Reality, inform almost the whole of her creative expression. They are most noticeable in

(a) her stress upon the opposing influential forces in life – that is, the essential Spirit, immutable and free, represented by harmony and peace, versus the enslaved, earth-bound self, represented by violence, conflict, change and decay.[30]
(b) her belief in the necessary indestructability of the human soul.[31]
(c) her idea of death as the release of the soul.[32]
(d) her concern to probe the essence of being and to contrast it with the superficial and illusory.[33]

There is also a strong parallel to be seen at the end of *Wuthering Heights*, (with its suggestion of the survival and reunion of the spirits of Heathcliff and Cathy) with Plato's challenging argument on the immortality of the soul, that is, that the soul's own specific wickedness cannot destroy it. Whether Emily Brontë believed in a pre-birth existence of the individual soul, which, as Leslie Stevenson explains,[34] was a necessary part of Plato's statement on immortality, she did not reveal; although in her French essay on 'The Cat'[35] she showed that she adhered to the conventional belief in a Paradise that *preceded*, as well as follows, life on earth.

In the main, it would seem most likely that Emily arrived at her ontological insights by way of intuition rather than by study or instruction, and by the fits and starts of reason and reaction rather than via the consistency of philosophical dialectic. Nevertheless, from the early philosophy of 'The Butterfly', through such poems as 'I'll come when thou art saddest',[36] 'I'm happiest when most away',[37] 'The Philosopher's Conclusion'[38] and 'No coward soul is mine',[39] right through to the mature dissection of human emotion and its consequences in *Wuthering Heights*, a straight line is drawn. Following it, we can trace her reactions of shock, horror, rage and anguish to life's inherently tragic pattern, and witness the intermittent flashes of hope and mystic apprehension that continually recurred. Indeed, in the developing awareness of her own brief life, Emily Brontë herself presents a striking personal figuration of the soul's hard-won ascent from the Dark to the Light in the Platonic Theory of Knowledge. For her, the world was much as Plato had expressed it in his famous similes of the 'Sun', the 'Line' and the 'Cave'[40]: a world of images and illusions, motivated by 'a principle of destruction'.[41] Among contemporary English novelists, only Dickens is seen on occasion to have such a powerful sense of the corruptibility of human life. But, for Emily Brontë, there was another world, 'an eternal realm of happiness and glory',[42] or, as Plato had defined it, the 'Intelligible World',[43] the world of true knowledge, ruled by absolute goodness.

This leads us inevitably to the question often asked of Emily Brontë: *was* she, in the true sense of the word, a mystic? It is a question that bristles with difficulties, theological explanations being clearly inadequate to cover the preternatural experiences of a woman who was not by any strict definition a 'daughter of the church'. Yet possibly no aspect of her nature has attracted more interpretative comment, as Brontë scholars have sought to find in it the key to her religious attitudes, her views on life and the nature of her genius. In 1948, in what remains one of the most valuable discussions on the subject, Mildred A. Dobson distinguished between Emily Brontë's experience and that of the 'contemplative Christian in the highest stage of contemplative prayer'.[44] She nevertheless found the conditions necessary for the development of the 'intuitive faculty' of the mystic present in Emily's life: her habitual 'detachment from the world', and 'the attitude of mind whereby the transcience, the contingent nature, of all created being is apprehended by comparison with reality'.

> A thoughtful spirit taught me soon,
> That we must long till life be done;
> That every phase of earthly joy
> Must always fade, and always cloy . . .[45]

Even before she wrote this, Emily had turned her back on the 'common paths that others run' and expressed her true allegiance in the poem, 'Plead for me', written in October 1844:

> So with a ready heart I swore
> To seek their altar-stone no more,
> And gave my spirit to adore
> Thee, ever present, phantom thing –
> My slave, my comrade, and my king! . . .[46]

Here, we have the mysterious 'Visitant', before whom, says Mildred Dobson, 'she trembled, yet in whose presence she experienced pure joy'. This 'joy', a combination of ecstasy and agony, has distinguished mystical experience through the centuries, and it is incomparably expressed in the poem, 'Julian M. and A. G. Rochelle',[47] in the lines:

> But first a hush of peace, a soundless calm descends;
> The struggle of distress and fierce impatience ends;
> Mute music soothes my breast – unuttered harmony
> That I could never dream till earth was lost to me.
>
> Then dawns the Invisible, the Unseen its truth reveals;
> My outward sense is gone, my inward essence feels –
> Its wings are almost free, its home, its harbour found;
> Measuring the gulf it stoops and dares the final bound!
>
> Oh, dreadful is the check – intense the agony
> When the ear begins to hear and the eye begins to see;
> When the pulse begins to throb, the brain to think again,
> The soul to feel the flesh and the flesh to feel the chain! . . .

Allowing for the fact that this is a Gondal poem, and thus for its somewhat perorative style, it would hardly seem reasonable to deny that what is being described here is something both preternatural and intensely personal. And here, surely, is confirmation once and for all of the assessment of the entire body of Emily Brontë's poetry made by Kathleen Raine: that 'the same imagination speaks through all. The Gondal fantasy is only scaffolding'.[48]

As to the *nature* of Emily Brontë's mysticism, suggestions of 'Satanism', 'Daemonism' and 'Pantheism'[49] become patently absurd once the profundity of her thought is grasped. Nor can I agree with Mildred Dobson that Emily Brontë was 'predominantly pagan'. Despite what Charlotte called her sister's 'heretic spirit',[50] there seem to me to be the clearest possible indications in all her writings – and especially in the French essays – written, as already emphasised, when she was a mature twenty-four – that her essential fidelities were to Christian orthodoxy. For all that, there can be no doubt that Emily stood wholly apart from those 'chains' of religious conformity of which Charlotte had complained. She was, however, much less assured of her own innocence than was Charlotte, who, despite passionate outbursts of self-condemnation, could be deeply hurt by what she saw as others' misunderstanding of her motives. Emily, for example, in her poem beginning, 'I am the only being whose doom',[51] expresses the desolation of a self-knowledge that has revealed to her that not even the *victim* of corruption escapes its taint.

It is this aspect of Emily Brontë that separates her, too, from the youthful George Eliot in this context, for the latter, once the break with the old beliefs had been made, reacted initially with all the biting self-righteousness of the convert against certain suspect adherents of the abandoned faith. The censorious tone and content of the Eliot essay, 'Evangelical Teaching: Dr. Cumming',[52] would have been impossible to Emily Brontë. Perhaps because she was essentially a poet, Emily Brontë possessed, at twenty, the sympathetic insight into the universality of human folly that George Eliot, essentially a rationalist philosopher, gained only in her maturer years. In this respect, too, Emily differed from Charlotte, as was to be clearly seen in their respective final attitudes towards Branwell. For all her early adulation of him – possibly *because* of it – Charlotte at the end was to collapse into shocked disgust. No doubt hers was the greatest sense of personal let-down; possibly, too, her horror at how close she had herself come to falling into the same grievous error had made her harsh of judgement of one who had failed to find within himself the same resistance, not only to the wrong itself, but to the resulting pain and suffering. In contrast, we note the awareness shown by Emily and Anne of the *suffering* that lies at the heart of moral degradation; and here, again, it is possible to identify a link between the thought of Emily Brontë and that of Plato, of whom Stevenson writes:

> I doubt if one can attribute to him either of the simple views that individuals are to blame or that society is basically wrong. He would say, rather, that the two are interdependent. An imperfect society produces imperfect individuals, and imperfect individuals make for an imperfect society.[53]

Here we have the idea that forms the core of *Wuthering Heights* stemming from what John Hewish has called Emily Brontë's 'reaction to the absolutism, the "black and white" of Calvinist ideas'.[54] Writing of her resolution, via the 'healing' of Hareton and Cathy, of the novel's themes of vengeance and internecine conflict, Hewish observes:

> The point is, perhaps, that the object, the desired state of affairs, is not a matter of redemption or conversion of the religious sense, but a mutual one of fulfilment.

This is part of the rational element in Emily Brontë that tends to take us by surprise. The closer we come to her, the more we begin to realise that by far the deepest source of her understanding and compassion towards living things lay not in the impulses of the heart – powerful though these were – but in the realm of reason. It is, on the face of it, strange to reflect that, in Emily, M. Heger saw all the evidence of a profoundly analytical mind. He rated her genius even higher than Charlotte's and declared that she 'had a head for logic, and a capability of argument, unusual in a man, and rare indeed in a woman'.[55] 'She should have been a man – a great navigator,' he added, 'Her powerful reason would have deduced new spheres of discovery from the knowledge of the old; and her strong, imperious will would never have been daunted by opposition or difficulty; never have given way but with life'. It is perhaps remarkable that so percipient an observer should have failed to note the mystical element in Emily – unless, in the essay, 'The Butterfly', for instance, it was the *rational force* of the mystic vision that impressed him most of all. Here, Emily had envisaged, in the symbolism of the grub eating its way into the heart of a flower, the 'sad image of the earth and its inhabitants',[56] in which every creature lives only by the mutilation and destruction of another. It was a universe which at first appeared to her as 'a vast machine constructed only to bring forth evil: I almost doubted the goodness of God for not annihilating man on the day of his first sin'.[57] But after she has crushed the caterpillar with her foot, the sight of a butterfly recalls to her life's self-perpetuating laws, the laws of evolution and renewal, and she sees in this minute biological miracle the symbol of a vast and universal hope – the hope of mankind's liberation from sin and suffering into 'an eternal realm of happiness and glory'. For 'God is the God of Justice and mercy', and the transformation of grub into butterfly images 'the embryo of a new heaven and of a new earth whose meagrest beauty infinitely surpasses mortal imagination'. It is a restatement of the idea expressed in the poem, 'I am the only being whose doom', mentioned above; that is, that no earthly creature, be it beautiful or ugly, victim or tormentor, is free of the corruption of mortal existence; also of the idea expounded in 'The Cat' – that 'if hypocrisy, cruelty and ingratitude are the characteristics exclusively of mean people, this class includes everyone'.[58] But in 'The Butterfly' she penetrates beyond this to the ultimate law that governs all created life, and she finds it to be a law of restoration and renewal.

In this, yet again we see one of the foremost elements of mysticism: the ability to perceive the End in the Beginning, and *vice versa*. Instead of George Eliot's intermediate abandonment of faith, and Charlotte's and Anne's anguished conflicts, Emily appears to close the gap between doubt and the knowledge of ultimate good in one great leap of spiritual insight. Again, from her clear sense of the unity of all created things, of the All-in-Oneness of shared experience, stemmed her unfailing compassion, seen at its most definitive in the poem, 'Well, some may hate, and some may scorn',[59] which closes with the lines:

> Do I despise the timid deer
> Because his limbs are fleet with fear?
> Or would I mock the wolf's death-howl
> Because his form is gaunt and foul?
> Or hear with joy the leveret's cry
> Because it cannot bravely die?

No! Then above his memory
Let pity's heart as tender be:
Say, 'Earth lie lightly on that breast,
And, kind Heaven, grant that spirit rest!'

It was the compassion reflected in the nature of the finale of *Wuthering Heights*, when Heathcliff declares that 'there is a strange change approaching',[60] reveals that he no longer has the will for revenge, and finds his longed-for 'fulfilment'[61] in exultant death. Judgement is suspended, and in the ongoing relationship of Hareton and the second Catherine, Emily Brontë gives dynamic form to her 'Butterfly' thesis of life's capacity for healthful renewal. In the love that seems rather to give than to take, that is capable of self-knowledge and contrition is 'the embryo of a new heaven and of a new earth'.

Whatever view is held regarding the quality of Emily Brontë's vision, it would be difficult to deny that the pervading force of almost everything she wrote derived from an essentially *religious* sense of life, that is, the sense of the numinous, evoked by the mystery of an existence controlled by some transcendent yet immanent Power. Of itself, this need not be orthodox, nor even Christian, in origin, but although Emily Brontë makes no mention of the name of Christ, the nature of the morality that informs her work is unquestionably Christian. The culmination of the 'two children' theme in *Wuthering Heights*, for instance, is not the death of Heathcliff amid intimations of retribution, but lies in the reconciliation of the 'dark' and the 'fair' and the former's resulting transformation. The grub and the flower must die, but both have played their part in the birth of the butterfly:

> each suffering of our unhappy nature is only a seed for that divine harvest which will be gathered when sin having spent its last drop of poison, death having thrown its last dart, both will expire on the funeral pyre of a universe in flame, and will leave their former victims to an eternal realm of happiness and glory.[62]

The absence of 'Christ', taken with the frequent repetition of the name of 'God' and the theme of eternality is possibly significant. We might infer, perhaps, that Emily felt the individual personification to be too limited, too confined to the 'human' for her awful concept of the all-immanent 'God of justice' and of the presence that came to her on the wings of the wind and in the light of the stars.[63] Certainly, by the time she was adolescent Emily had moved as far from mere doctrinal religiosity as George Eliot was to do in her twenties; also, Emily, with her mystic 'God of Visions',[64] had found a 'substitute' for conventional worship which most people would have found more disturbing than atheism or agnosticism. It is little wonder that she felt that religion was a topic best kept between oneself and God. Nevertheless, and despite the dark, distorted creatures of her imagination, the doom of their lives and, as she saw it, of all life on earth, the intrinsic message of her creative labours was one of faith and of hope:

> I see Heaven's glories shine
> And Faith shines equal arming me from Fear[65]

and of ultimate, universal salvation:

> But God is not like human-kind;
> Man cannot read the Almighty mind;
> Vengeance will never torture thee,
> Nor hunt thy soul eternally.[66]

Finally, the same message appears in the concluding pages of *Wuthering Heights*. Life's impartial gift of resurgence is here seen both in the intimations of reunion between Heathcliff and Cathy and in the new, outgoing love of Hareton and Catherine. We may conclude that if Emily Brontë was not noticeably influenced by the great religious movements of the times, neither was she less moved by ideas of an essentially religious nature than her sisters and George Eliot, and although in her unique spiritual insights she possibly travelled beyond the ken of them all, she never relinquished her hold on the basic tenets of the Christian faith.

The general consensus of opinion on the youngest of the Brontës appears to be that she was the least gifted of the three, the most conventional in her religious views and the simplest in her approach to life. To this we must add that she was probably the bravest. Her steadfast endurance of nearly six years of governessing speaks for itself. Of those years, Anne spent four in one post, the longest period of any of her family. She worked mostly in circumstances of acute difficulty and loneliness, culminating in the final months of profound shock and disgrace, arising from Branwell's adventures at Thorp Green, where she also was employed. Added to this is the uncomplaining perseverance with which she faced her humdrum existence, surmounting illness, disappointment and a crisis of faith with a lack of the histrionic that seems positively heroic. 'She has so much to endure; far, far more than I have', Charlotte wrote to Ellen Nussey in 1841,[67] the year Anne took up her ill-fated position with the Robinson family at Thorp Green; 'when my thoughts turn to her they always see her as a patient, persecuted stranger'.

Anne's experiences at Thorp Green would have broken a lesser spirit. Emily had returned home, shattered in both mind and body, after only three months in the comparative harmony of Roe Head School, and had capitulated after what may have been a year, or possibly only six months, of her one attempt to earn her living as a full-time teacher. The deep waters of Anne's spirit astonished and intrigued George Barnett Smith in 1873 when he read *The Tenant of Wildfell Hall*. 'It is a curious question how this gentle woman, nevertheless, came to write such a narrative . . . which in some of its details is more offensive and repulsive than the great *pièce de résistance* of her next elder sister'.[68] A modern critic has extended the question to include all three sisters. Asking how 'three spinsters, brought up in an austere rectory in bleak Haworth', could have produced the work they did, Valentine Cunningham[69] finds a possible answer in the religious background. 'The Methodist matrix, while not perhaps *the* clue, is certainly one clue', he writes. Cunningham sees the sisters' novels as 'empty of real physicality', and claims that their 'dominant feeling'

is yearning for fulfilment, based on the authoresses' profound sexual innocence. But by appropriating the rhetoric of Methodism's love of God, exploiting the language of Divine love for earthly love, they deceived the world.

In furtherance of his point, Cunningham quotes G. E. Harrison, who, speaking of Emily, argues:

Knowing nothing of earthly passion, but being a connoisseur of the divine, she must needs use the thing she did know for the description of the love of which she was ignorant.[70]

We may wish to keep an open mind on the subject of precisely what Emily was ignorant of in this context, and what she was cognizant of, but the above statement, as well as the Methodist references, seems largely true of Anne, whose central theme in *The Tenant* is not human love, but the redemptive love of God for the sinner. Much Biblical quotation reinforces her narrative, together with religious metaphor, such as the likening of the suffering human being to a 'shipwrecked mariner'[71] and the penitent to 'a brand plucked from the burning',[72] that seem to stem direct from a Wesleyan source. Eventually, Anne came to adhere, like Emily, to the doctrine of universal salvation, and the belief that pain and suffering end with the experience of life on earth. Anne resembles Charlotte, however, in that she seems only to have attained religious peace out of intense spiritual conflict. In the poem, 'Vanitas Vanitatum, Omnia Vanitas',[73] she deplored, for example, all the evidence around her that 'Pleasure but doubles future pain/And joy brings sorrow in her train'. Her expression at this time owed much to the poet Cowper. In a poem dedicated to him she acknowledged this influence with the words:

> The language of my inmost heart,
> I traced in every line;
> *My* sins, *my* sorrows, hopes and fears,
> Were there – and only mine.[74]

It remains a mystery as to why, while she was still at Roe Head School, Anne turned for help in her doubts to a bishop of the Moravian church. Winifred Gérin suggests that Anne recognised that her 'need was beyond conventional remedy'.[75] The Moravians, Gérin explains, preached 'salvation by faith' as against the Wesleyan doctrine of 'salvation by works'. They admitted a dual nature in man which accepted the fact that even in the righteous man there still existed '. . . an "Old man" capable yet of sin and falling away'. But again we see how Brontë hope could not be extinguished. At the end of 'Vanitas Vanitatum', to the question 'What, then, remains for wretched man?' Anne gives the answer to 'Trust God and keep his statutes still/Upright and firm, through good and ill'.

Although, in the matter of her beliefs, as in most other things, Anne possibly shared more with Emily than with Charlotte, there were nevertheless differences which were rooted in their separate natures. While Emily's 'explorer's' instincts led her to seek her answers at the very heart of life's mysteries, Anne contemplated those mysteries from a distance, in bewilderment, but in patience and in a faith that ultimately proved equal to her bitterest trials. Spiritually, she could not go forth into the void, as physically she had so bravely done in her vocation as a governess, but neither would she give way. Anne Brontë's answer to her night of doubt was to cling with a fierce tenacity to the single, simple concept of a God of Love, and she allowed no evidence of personal pain, nor of the sin or weakness of others, to cause her to abandon it. It is possible that her achievement as an imaginative artist suffered as a result of this constant moral vigilance; perhaps her effort to be 'good' militated against that total commitment to a beckoning vision that is the hallmark of full genius. Anne could not kick against the pricks, like Charlotte; nor could she dare 'the final bound', like Emily.[76] Even when speaking out against injustice and oppression, there was at the root of her expression an unfailing sense of moderation, of *control*. But if her Christian obedience and restraint robbed her of the critical awe accorded her sisters, the verdict of George Moore on *Agnes Grey* – that is, that it was 'the most perfect prose narrative in English literature'[77] – remains to guard her position and to provoke closer and more percipient study of her contribution to nineteenth-century fiction.

In George Eliot's *Romola*, there comes a passage of dialogue in which, probably more than anywhere else in her work, she seems to put into the mouth of one of her protagonists something of her own innermost feelings about life and the world. The exchange comes towards the end of the novel, where Romola, angry and despairing at Savonarola's refusal to save her Medicean godfather from execution, practically accuses him of equating God's work with the furtherance of his own cause.

> 'And that is true!' said Savonarola, with flashing eyes . . . . The cause of my party *is* the cause of God's kingdom.'
> 'I do not believe it!' said Romola, her whole frame shaken with passionate repugnance. 'God's kingdom is something wider – else, let me stand outside it with the beings that I love.'[78]

In these words we have the essence of George Eliot's great

disenchantment with orthodox religion. Rational doubt about the existence of God and the hereafter may have been triggered by her acquaintance with such dissenting thinkers as Charles Bray and Charles Hennell, but a psychological reaction to her earlier love affair with Evangelicalism had already begun and only needed the meeting with these charismatic figures to give it point and purpose.[79]

The story of George Eliot's fluctuations of religious crisis are well-charted. Her commitment to Evangelicalism began under the influence of Miss Maria Lewis, the Principal Governess at Mrs Wallington's Boarding School at Nuneaton, which George Eliot attended from the age of nine until she was thirteen. She remained friends with Miss Lewis after transferring to Miss Franklin's School in Coventry, and, during a constant exchange of letters, was gradually but totally won over to the Evangelical position. Miss Lewis appears to have been the first of those many close human influences which George Eliot needed throughout her life to encourage and sustain her developing awareness of selfhood. The effects of her tutelage lasted until George Eliot was over twenty, taking the form in the latter of a 'gloomy Calvinism'.[80] This was the time of the daily Bible reading and the prayer meetings, and these rigid spiritual exercises were accompanied by a rejection of all forms of imagination and enthusiasm, an attitude such as had similarly affected Charlotte and Anne Brontë. A project which George Eliot began at this time – 'A Chart of Ecclesiastical History' – was a pointer to the formidable intellectual capacities of the future; its abandonment – when its author discovered that someone else had had the idea first – seems almost an ironic adumbration of the profound turnabout that was to affect her thinking by the time she reached her early twenties.

This second phase, again fully explored in Eliot biography, came about following George Eliot's meeting with Charles and Caroline Bray, whose Coventry home had become a centre of free-thinkers, among whom was Caroline's brother, Charles Hennell. Hennell's book, *An Inquiry Concerning the Origin of Christianity*, published in 1838, had initially been planned in response to his sister's need of confirmation of the legitimacy of her Christian beliefs. As much to Hennell's surprise as others', it had evolved, however, into a definition of the Christian story as myth;[81] from this conclusion, Hennell nevertheless attempted to extract certain essential and abiding moral truths that could be seen as forming a basis for a rationalistic interpretation. A Unitarian, as was his sister, Hennell was not disposed to deny the existence of a Creator, nor of an after-life. Like Strauss and Feuerbach after him, he was concerned primarily to identify and retain the spiritual and ontological essence of the Christian tradition within a rational framework.[82]

By this time, with her Evangelical fervour already beginning to cool, George Eliot was independently moving towards a radical shift of thought that was soon to take her further than Hennell, in his conservative position *vis-à-vis* God and Heaven, was prepared to go. There can be no doubt, however, that his book influenced her profoundly, producing in her what Basil Willey describes as a 'dreadful exhilaration':[83] exhilaration because 'here at last was the Truth which makes one free . . . but dread, because of the thought of one's father, one's home-circle, one's Church, and Miss Lewis'. Dread, too, possibly, because of the realisation of the price of such freedom in terms of individual discipline and responsibility. Young as she was, George Eliot no doubt realised that there is no true freedom without bondage.

At this stage, a paradox can be seen, for the element that remains stable throughout all George Eliot's oscillations towards intellectual and personal independence is her continuous need of the leadership and support of others. The nature of this need was psychological and emotional, its source very probably those deprivations of early childhood already mentioned. The result was a personality markedly divided between mind and heart, between phenomenal maturity of intellect and a recurrent susceptibility in the realm of feeling. These emotional disunities were foreshadowed by the phrenologist, George Combe, who declared that 'she was not fitted to stand alone',[84] an opinion later confirmed by her husband, John Cross, who said of her that throughout her life she had always needed 'some one person who should be all in all to her'.[85] Both had divined her most dangerous weakness, the tendency towards psychological collapse that was to recur at various crucial stages of her life. In the previous chapter, we saw something of its effects at work in her excessive emotional dependence on her brother, Isaac. In the present context, we note her wholesale submission to the persuasive proselytising of Miss Lewis, and in a future chapter mention will be made of her undue dependence on such individuals as Bray, John Chapman, Herbert Spencer and Dr Robert Brabant. Nevertheless, this basic frailty in George Eliot was, by another twist of paradox, the source of her greatest strength – the deep sympathy for human nature which was to be her substitute for a theistic religion. It is via the nature of this substitution that we see that her objection to Christian orthodoxy was not only the intellectual one – that is, that it rested on unprovable premises – but also that, in its rigid pursuit of the *letter* of the law, it let the spirit go by the board. 'It may enjoin charity, but it fosters all uncharitableness', she was to write in her famous essay, 'Evangelical Teaching: Dr. Cumming'.[86] The God of Calvinism – and of much of Wesleyanism and of the Evangelicals – a God 'who teaches love by fierce denunciations of wrath'[87] was a concept she could no longer tolerate. Adam Bede was essentially speaking for her when he said:

> I've seen pretty clear ever since I was a young 'un, as religion's something else besides doctrines and notions. I look at it as if the doctrines was like finding names for your feelings, so as you can talk of 'em when you've never known 'em, just as a man may talk o' tools when he knows their names, though he's never so much as seen 'em, still less handled 'em . . . .[88]

The influence of Feuerbach's *Essence of Christianity*, which George Eliot had translated in 1854, is clear. Feuerbach had described God as 'the commonplace book', wherein man 'registers his highest feelings and thoughts, the genealogical album in which he enters the names of the things most dear and sacred to him'.[89] And, for George Eliot, 'feelings' were of paramount importance. If religion was to have any meaning at all, this was where it must be found; and only in this most human connotation was the notion of 'God' a valid one.

> The idea of God is really moral in its influence – it really cherishes all that is best and loveliest in man – only when God is contemplated as sympathizing with the pure elements of human feeling, as possessing infinitely all those attributes which we recognize to be moral in humanity. In this light, the idea of God and the sense of His presence intensify all noble feeling, and encourage all noble effort . . . .[90]

But this view of God, she felt, was not the one which orthodox religion presented. Instead, the latter fostered the idea of God as a tyrant who scourged and punished, so that the Church's precept that we should love each other for God's sake came implicit with 'a strong principle of hatred'.[91] As we saw at the beginning of this section, her view was summarised with telling effect in the confrontation between Savonarola and Romola, between the full power and authority of the Church versus noble simplicity in the idealised figure of young patrician womanhood. Romola, the archetype of Purity betrayed, dons the garb of the Church in her suffering, but her motive, as Savonarola sternly reminds her, is not 'religious purpose' but 'disguise'.[92] Nevertheless, the need in her to do good, to find a 'religious purpose' for her life, remains, just as it did in George Eliot herself, when, throwing off the 'habit' of Evangelicalism, she sought her substitute. To Mrs Peter Alfred Taylor she wrote in July 1863:

> It seems to me that the soul of Christianity lies not at all in the facts of an individual life, but in the ideas of which that life was the meeting-point and the new starting-point. We can never have a satisfactory basis for the history of the man Jesus, but that negation does not affect the Idea of the Christ either in its historical influence or its great symbolic meanings.[93]

But if the Church had failed her, so, too, did some of the humanists. Translating *Das Leben Jesu* of David Friedrich Strauss between 1844 and 1846, she was sickened by its arid dissection of the Gospel story and by what she felt to be its reduction of a flesh-and-blood 'Jewish philosopher'[94] to a stylistic representation of myth. Something much more, she believed, was needed to explain the essential vitality and endurance of the Christian religion. It was in Ludwig Feuerbach, the German atheist philosopher, that she came as close as she ever would to finding it.

Feuerbach, whose psychological analysis of religion influenced Marx and to some extent such other seminal modern thinkers as Freud and Sartre,[95] thrilled her, when she came to translate his *Das Wesen des Christentums*, as Strauss never had.[96] Feuerbach's definition of the 'divine being' as 'nothing else than the human being, or rather, the human nature purified',[97] and, again, as 'pure, unlimited, free Feeling',[98] found her completely in accord. To Sara Hennell, she wrote, 'I everywhere agree'.[99] Feuerbach had written:

> it is our task to show that the antithesis of divine and human is altogether illusory, that it is nothing else than the antithesis between the human nature in general, and the human individual:

that, consequently, the object and contents of the Christian religion are altogether human.[100]

And to this end George Eliot applied her novelist's art with passion and fidelity. But if her work resonates with Feuerbachian 'feeling', with a palpable sympathy for the characters through whom she typifies erring, suffering humanity, there are times when the two religions of her life – that is, of Christianity and 'Humanity' – seem to become a little blurred, almost, indeed, to merge. In *Adam Bede*, for example, Dinah Morris, that shining angel of uncompromising Wesleyan Evangelicism, becomes increasingly humanistic in her dedicated caring for the doomed Hetty in her prison cell; and at the end Dinah is content to marry herself to Adam, a rustic-style imprint of Feuerbachian Man. We may wonder what George Eliot wants us to understand: whether these implications of reconciliation between orthodoxy and dissent indicate a serious proposition on her part of the need to effect some kind of unity – or whether they represent merely an instinctive reluctance to face the consequences of a complete and final severance from old ideas. It appears evident that the more 'humanistic' George Eliot's characters become, the less convincing they are.[101] Certainly, such over-idealised figures as Romola and Daniel Deronda do tend to suggest that she had difficulty in giving her humanist ideas a human form. Again, in *Middlemarch*, the insubstantial and insouciant Ladislaw has seemed to few readers to be the convincing match that George Eliot obviously intended him to be for the soaring heart of Dorothea Brooke. If we concede that Ladislaw brings Dorothea into touch with real life, it remains unfortunate that George Eliot did not perform the same service for him.

By contrast, all George Eliot's representatives of orthodoxy – her preachers, evangelists, ministers of religion of whatever colour – come across to us with all the vitality of their human strengths and weaknesses. *Scenes of Clerical Life*, for example, gives us three beautifully distinct delineations in the respective forms of Amos Barton, surrounded by his loving family, Edgar Tryan, Christ-like in his submission to poverty and suffering, and Maynard Gilfil, who like *Silas Marner's* Rufus Lyon, lives out a secret life of wasted passion. In *Middlemarch*, the contrasts are even more subtle. Here, we have not only those two so very different embodiments of comfortable clerical living, their Reverends Humphrey Cadwallader and Camden Farebrother, but, against them, hovering like some

uneasy spectre, the unforgettable Mr Casaubon himself, the sham
'modern Augustine', who, for Dorothea, 'united the glories of
doctor and saint'.[102] All these characterisations have a strong,
definitive quality, suggesting that, in forming them, George Eliot
was drawing upon the residual depths of personal knowledge,
observation and experience; if we apply the same criterion – that is,
of definition – to her humanist characters, we might conclude either
that she found some uncharacteristic difficulty in the presentation of
matters about which she felt deeply, or, more likely, that in this area
of her life there remained elements – albeit subconscious – of some
uncertainty. She herself provided some evidence of this in a letter
which she wrote to her friend, M. François d'Albert Durade, in 1859,
the year which saw the publication of *Adam Bede*:

> I have no longer any antagonism towards any faith in which
> human sorrow and human longing for purity have expressed
> themselves; on the contrary, I have a sympathy with it that
> predominates over all argumentative tendencies. I have not
> returned to dogmatic Christianity – to the acceptance of any set of
> doctrines as a creed, and a superhuman revelation of the unseen –
> but I see in it the highest expression of the religious sentiment that
> has yet found its place in the history of mankind, and I have the
> profoundest interest in the inward life of sincere Christians in all
> ages. Many things that I should have argued against ten years
> ago, I now feel myself too ignorant and too limited in moral
> sensibility to speak on with confident disapprobation: on many
> points where I used to delight in expressing intellectual
> difference, I now delight in feeling an emotional agreement.[103]

Just how far the pendulum had swung is shown in the words that
immediately followed:

> On that question of our future existence, to which you allude, I
> have undergone the sort of change I have just indicated, although
> my most rooted conviction is, that the immediate objects and the
> proper sphere of all our highest emotions are our struggling
> fellow-men and their earthly existence.

Despite the special pleading of this final sentence, this is conciliation
of a fairly high order, an attitude of compromise that she would
share with other liberal thinkers in the next two decades. U. C.

Knoepflmacher defines it as 'a conservative clinging' to orthodoxy's 'remains',[104] and cites both Matthew Arnold and George Eliot as examples: the former, for his ultimate concession to the influence of Hebraic conduct over 'three-fourths of human life',[105] the latter, for the apparent turnabout between her attack on the 'other-worldliness, of Dr Cumming and the poet Young,[106] and the portrayal, in *Daniel Deronda*, of an 'Old Testament righteousness based on the workings of an unknown and providential power'.[107]

Daniel Deronda surprises us in two ways: firstly, of course, for the Jewish element; secondly, for the uncompromising mysticism which pervades that part of the story; and in particular the empathy which is reflected in George Eliot's descriptions of it. Again, we might ask how this accords with her known rejection of the non-rational in religion. William Baker[108] reminds us that *Deronda* was not George Eliot's first reference to the mystical; in *Romola* also she had dealt with 'a similar area of experience'.[109] And he draws attention to the demonstrations of Knoepflmacher and Robert Preyer of the important role played by the 'non-real' parts of *Deronda* in George Eliot's philosophy;[110] such, for example, as Mordecai's 'waiting on the bridge for the fulfilment of his visions',[111] which belongs not to the realm of the impossible but to 'the force of imagination that pierces or exalts the solid fact'.[112] By this interpretation, the 'non-real' becomes a not unacceptable concept to the rationalistic mind. For all we may concede this argument, however, *Daniel Deronda* remains a book that comes strangely from an avowed agnostic, requiring of its author, apart from considerable research, a sympathetic understanding of the mind and feelings of a representative of proto-Christian orthodoxy concerning matters that can only be described as, at the very least, highly esoteric.

George Eliot's research for *Deronda*, according to her notebooks, drew mainly upon the work of the Anglo-Jewish scholar, Christian David Ginsburgh; in particular, his explanation of the theory of the soul's journey, via several reincarnations, back to its purified state within the Infinite Source from which it emanated.[113] (A coincidental link with Platonist elements in Emily Brontë's philosophy is here suggested.) Further, as Leon Gottfried observes:

> Daniel's story also borrows from that of Jesus, for Daniel's mentor is also a herald and a forerunner, a martyr and prophet who prepares the way by preaching the message of the coming of one

greater than himself and by initiating (baptizing) his successor when he appears . . . .[114]

The 'Christ-like Daniel,' adds Gottfried, 'is to be a saviour not only of the Jews, but, through them, of the Gentiles as well'. The powerful Messianism implicit in this doctrine seems at first sight a long way from an earthbound Religion of Humanity. One is left to conclude that, in *Deronda*, George Eliot was attempting to create a synthesis between explanations mystic and rationalistic of the soul's travail and destiny: in particular to show that if life did indeed have some eternal and cosmic Truth, then a necessary connection existed between this and ordinary human individual interrelationship. Thus, in the Jew's longing for fulfilment and his dread of exile, she crystallised once and for all everything she had ever written about human experience, its essential loneliness and uncertainty, its longing for something that 'should be all in all' to it, the shared human responsibility towards making all things new. We might well ask what separates this conception, with its mystic undertones, from that which forms the essence of orthodox Christianity. George Eliot did not live to tell us, but it is at least arguable on the evidence of her final book that a marked degree of reconciliation had taken place within her thinking *vis-à-vis* the old religion. Although the vision that marked *Deronda* was still primarily world-orientated, it was of a world that would be wholly new. At the novel's end, its individual lives stand on the brink of a great adventure that has both its physical and spiritual counterparts, as Mordecai prepares for his death, Daniel for his Mission and Gwendolen for her soul's journey of expiation. Here is confirmation that in this novel George Eliot drew together the two great strands of ethical thought that had influenced her life. The best of Christianity and the best of the Religion of Humanity meet in the characters of Mordecai (ironically, a Jew) and Daniel, a man of the world in the deepest sense; the spiritual transmigration to which Mordecai looked forward becomes a symbol of the fusion of Faith and Reason, Spirit and Flesh, God and Man. It was a tall order on George Eliot's part, which may well explain the difficulty she had in making either Mordecai or Deronda wholly convincing. Each is an idea first and a human being second, which is the wrong order of events for fictional characterisation. In leaving her story open, however, George Eliot was wise. As an expression of visionary belief in the possibilities of being, it could hardly be otherwise; but, as she had already said, in a letter written

just before the first part of *Deronda* was published, she saw her
writing as 'simply a set of experiments in life' –

an endeavour to see what our thoughts and emotions may be
capable of – what stores of motive, actual or hinted as possible,
give promise of a better after which we may strive – what gains
from past revelations and discipline we must strive to keep hold of
as something more sure than shifting theory.[115]

Of her own admission, then, George Eliot used her fiction to put to
the test her own phases of 'shifting theory', clothing abstract ideas
about life's meaning and purpose in a myriad human forms. In
characters such as Dinah Morris and Romola Bardi she attempted to
show the redemptive force of the highest kind of religion, that allied
with human love and caring; in Edward Casaubon she exposed the
sterility of the closed mind, and in a long line of 'egotists', from
Donnithorne to Tito Melema and Gwendolen Harleth she showed
the delusions of vanity and uncovered the corrosive acids of
self-seeking. It would almost seem true to say that George Eliot's
writing was her bible of the Religion of Humanity, and that it closed
with a book of 'Revelations'. The process throughout was
evolutionary, yet, at the same time, circular, both in the creative
and in the personal sense, as can clearly be seen if we parallel the
treatment of themes and characters in the novels with George Eliot's
own development from Evangelical to Agnostic, from ruthless
reaction to mellow, conciliatory enquiry.

We have seen that the reversion to a conservative 'middle-way'
was something which George Eliot experienced in common with
other intellectual figures of her time, just as she had earlier shared
with them the 'conversion' to rational dissent. She herself believed
that there was no private life that was not determined by a wider
public life, and her own continuous response to the fluctuations of
'shifting theory' would seem to have been of a piece with this
hypothesis.

Certain fairly close parallels of religious thought and experience
have been traced between all four novelists, especially as applicable
to the early years, when a mutual middle-of-the-road Anglicanism
was followed by the influence of Calvinistic ideas of a spiritually
narrow and life-denying kind. Periods of doubt and agonising

anxiety ensued, as answers were sought to life's cruel contradictions and to the conflict between the 'pure' religion as reflected in the life of Christ and its varied interpretations within the denominational churches. All four novelists rejected the latter's materialism and crude display, and all shared alike an abiding allegiance to that primal concept of spiritual love that, drawing the human heart to itself, forges common bonds of understanding, pity and service.

Essentially, in her Religion of Humanity, George Eliot was as much a Christian to the end of her life as was Anne Brontë, and all three Brontës, in their rejection of the spurious and despotic, as much rational dissenters as George Eliot. In this respect, it is interesting that once again we seem to see, as was noted in a previous chapter, that it is with Emily Brontë that George Eliot has most in common. The deepest implications of the 'two children' theme of *Wuthering Heights* strike a chord not dissimilar to that of the 'twin-self' concept of George Eliot's *Daniel Deronda*. In the latter's 'marriage' of souls, in which one self passes into its 'twin' at death and thus fulfils its spiritual being, we are not so very far removed from the concept of an ultimate unity of being which forms the intellectual core of *Wuthering Heights*. Furthermore, at the root of Emily Brontë's Platonist vision of the pre-natal and ultimate perfection of life lay an element of determinism very like George Eliot's own.[116] The law of life was good and was absolute; thus suffering was the result of, not the punishment for, disobedience. The logic, for Emily, seems to have extended to the conclusion that salvation was man's *necessary* destiny; in the strange story of Mordecai Cohen, George Eliot seems to be posing a somewhat similar idea. It is doubtful that we can infer from this that her own beliefs had changed so diametrically, but a degree of compromise seems palpably present in this as in some of her earlier work. What is certain is that a small part of her remained fascinated by religion's sanctified images of purified passion, represented, for example, by such figures as Thomas à Kempis and St Teresa.[117] Lives like these, of dedicated selflessness, remained for her a beacon; they shone, an uncertain but persistent light throughout all her work, assuming the forms of priest, monk and self-sacrificing womanhood, until they culminated in the Christ-like figure of Mordecai Cohen. Overall, the gap that remains between George Eliot's mature religious thought and that of the Brontë sisters is perhaps best summed up in Irving H. Buchen's valuable interpretation of Emily Brontë's metaphysical vision of life; this he concludes to be heaven-orientated, with earthly existence as a pale shadow of things to come. Buchen writes:

> if the childhood love of Heathcliff and Catherine serves as an
> image of heaven before birth, the love of Hareton and Cathy
> serves as a prefiguration of heaven after death. In short, to Brontë
> life is hemmed in at both ends by heaven.[118]

This, of course, could also be said of Anne Brontë, and to a large
extent of Charlotte. At first sight, it is the factor that finally, more
than any other, separates the sisters from George Eliot. The doubt
that nevertheless persists is whether the latter's agnosticism proved
inviolable to the end against the obvious need of her nature for some
basic personification of reassurance and support. The metaphysics
of *Daniel Deronda* might arguably suggest otherwise.

3

The Self and the World

One of those stories of the Brontë childhood that have proved irresistible to biographers is that of the 'mask' incident, disclosed by the Reverend Patrick in a letter to Mrs Gaskell dated 30 July 1855.[1] Suspecting, he said, that his children knew more than he had yet discovered, he decided to test them in a way that would encourage complete freedom of expression: 'happening,' he said, 'to have a mask in the house, I told them all to stand and speak boldly from under the cover of the mask.' In the event, the questions were banal, but the ploy was prophetic in a way and to an extent which the Reverend Patrick could hardly have foreseen. He could not have guessed that in the years ahead three of those children would adopt a series of metaphorical 'masks' and speak with a freedom of expression that would shock many of their contemporaries and ensure the three a major place in English literature into the incalculable future.

The primary purpose of the 'mask', of course, is to disguise, but it has a secondary function – as employed in the theatre – of providing for its wearer a complete change of identity. By their adoption of the male pseudonym, the Brontë sisters and George Eliot sought to make both functions work for them at one and the same time; anonymity went hand-in-hand with the most intrinsic change of *personae* possible. So drastic a change of the self could only be short-lived in effect, but it speaks much for the fears felt by the nineteenth-century women writers – that is, that recognition of their 'real' selves would attract a kind of criticism that had little or nothing to do with the quality of their literature and everything to do with their sex.

The effects of nineteenth-century sex-inequality on women generally, and on the Brontë sisters and George Eliot in particular, will be discussed in a subsequent chapter. Here, the concentration will be chiefly upon more general social pressures in an attempt to discover how much, if at all, such pressures affected the four and were reflected in their work.

Defining the two aspects of an age of revolutionary change as 'destruction' and 'reconstruction',[2] Houghton states that both these elements were apparent in the Britain of 1830, as the old order of administration faced the 'revolutionary legislation of 1828–1835 – the repeal of the Test and Corporation Acts, the Municipal Reform Act, and, above all, the Reform Bill'. In the first half of the nineteenth century, the population of England and Wales doubled.[3] The working classes, watching the steady advance of the machine, saw in it a desperate threat to their survival. At the same time, a new, wealthy and powerful middle class was arising, capable of imprinting its own ethos upon the age. Even those who were relatively unaffected by the actual physical events could not escape the sense of turmoil all around them, and it is this sense of general urgency and impending change that is, perhaps, the most important factor in relation to the four lives that concern us.

Innumerable references testify to the precocious interest in the political events of the day which the Brontës, encouraged by their father, maintained throughout childhood and early adolescence. We are told that Charlotte, whose paramount hero was the Duke of Wellington, sustained this interest to her early thirties, when she watched with anxiety the disturbances of the Europe of 1848.[4] Nor was the interest purely academic; the Reverend Patrick could tell of seeing the Luddites in action during his ministry at Hartshead,[5] and from Miss Wooler at Roe Head School Charlotte heard stories of similar local events of the recent past.[6] The Brontë girls were also to experience for themselves something of the Chartist agitation in the Haworth area.[7] Locally indeed, the changes had been considerable. 'The Township of Haworth'[8] grew in population between 1801 and 1851 from 3164 to 6848, it being estimated that in 1838 the local woollen industry was giving employment to twelve hundred handloom operators in Haworth alone. Later, with the migrations to the cities, the township's working population declined. Between 1801 and 1861 the population of Leeds increased from 53 000 to 172 000, and of Bradford from 13 000 to 104 000.[9] It was out of such conditions of undue growth and dispersal everywhere that were born both the opportunities of advancement for some and the bitter disillusionment of others that changed English life to its roots.

It is therefore perhaps surprising that the Brontë sisters' concern for the outside world seems to have been remarkably lacking in terms of practical *local* application. Mrs Gaskell tells us that Charlotte shared her father's diligence in 'visiting the sick' and 'in attendance at the schools',[10] adding that indeed all the Brontës were 'steady teachers at the Sunday school'. But nowhere do we find reports of them busying themselves with any regular and systematic parish visiting, such as we might perhaps have expected of the growing daughters of a parish priest. Yet conditions in the village must have created many social problems. There was 'not one water closet and no drainage system',[11] and by 1853 the number of children dying before the age of six had reached the appalling figure of 40 per cent. The impression given, however, is not that the Brontë girls did not care: rather, perhaps, that, 'cherishing and valuing privacy themselves, they were perhaps over-delicate in not intruding upon the privacy of others'.[12] This comment of Mrs Gaskell's seems to be contradicted to some extent by her later remark (reported above) concerning Charlotte's sick-visiting, but we might perhaps see it as a faithful reflection of the rather ambivalent nature of its subjects' attitudes to their relationship with society in general. The intensity of shyness and reserve which they exhibited in public apparently made the briefest social contact as painful to others as to themselves. Even on their walks, we learn, they 'seldom went downwards through the village. They were shy of meeting even familiar faces, and were scrupulous about entering the house of the very poorest uninvited.'[13] Their natural inclination was to seek the 'solitude and freedom of the moors'. In the light of these facts, the matter of the Brontës' relationship with the outside world becomes an increasingly uncertain one, especially when they grew older. We might perhaps conclude that, in the light of the emphasis they came to place upon the delineation of individual human personality, their interest in political and historical events considerably abated with the years.[14]

Looking first at Charlotte, the work that springs immediately to mind is *Shirley*, the only one of her four completed novels in which social and economic problems constitute a central part of her theme. It has been pertinently asked, however, why Charlotte chose to go back almost forty years to the activities of the Luddites, when the Chartist agitations were currently on her doorstep. One answer to this has been that 'Charlotte wanted to use the Chartist Movement as her background, but was told that the events of that agitation were too near and burning to be fit for treatment'.[15] The point is reasonably made that for the 'daughter of the minister of a disturbed parish'[16] to exploit what was, for many, a situation of tragic consequence for the purposes of a novel – especially a novel in which her own Tory alignment would be obvious – would be likely to seem insensitive and could possibly even be 'dangerous'. Then of course there is the possibility that Charlotte may have been influenced, even if subconsciously, by what had been in the 1840s almost a literary cult of the past. Kathleen Tillotson writes that during this time 'many writers were coming to prefer a setting which was neither historical nor contemporary, but which lay in a period from twenty to sixty years earlier'.[17] She notes a 'variety' of motives:

> the wish to avoid the specific associations of strictly contemporary novels . . . the desire to escape from the moral constrictions of the present, the wish to record change . . . the feeling that the writer's imagination is most readily and valuably stimulated by early memories.

Then, she says, 'There are the special cases of the "autobiographical" novel and others . . . these "go back" in order to have room to come forward, but nevertheless usually stop well short of the present'. In *Jane Eyre*, says Tillotson, Charlotte was 'disguising or dissociating herself' from her own remembered experience '(so that Jane is at Lowood a quarter-century before Charlotte was at Cowan Bridge).' In *Shirley*, Charlotte's motive was possibly very similar, although it is interesting that she herself was later to observe that she could not 'write books handling the topics of the day'.[18] Nor, she added, 'can I write a book for its moral . . . . To manage these matters rightly they must be long and practically studied, their bearings known intimately, their evils felt genuinely'. It is my own view that the closest approach to an understanding of Charlotte's choice of theme in *Shirley* is obtained in examination of her reactions to the critical reception of *Jane Eyre*. This was almost unanimously favourable, but in his review in *Fraser's Magazine*, G. H. Lewes, after praising the book's artistry, sounded the following note of caution to its author:

> Keep reality distinctly before you, and paint it as accurately as you can: invention will never equal the effect of truth.[19]

During the course of the personal correspondence that ensued between them, Lewes expanded on the theme, eventually provoking Charlotte to reply:

> When I first began to write, so impressed was I with the truth of
> the principles you advocate, that I determined to take Nature and
> Truth as my sole guides . . . .
>
> My work . . . being completed, I offered it to a publisher I
> tried six publishers in succession; they all told me it was deficient
> in 'startling incident' and 'thrilling excitement'. . . .[20]

For all that, the correspondence with Lewes had its effect. Charlotte,
said Mrs Gaskell,[21] 'carefully studied the different reviews and
criticisms that had appeared on "Jane Eyre", in hopes of extracting
precepts and advice from which to profit'. Lewes's views in
particular, writes Franklin Gary,[22] explicitly influenced Charlotte in
'matters of artistic aim and method of presentation'. This would
seem strongly to suggest that Charlotte's *primary* consideration in
her choice of theme in *Shirley* was artistic rather than social, and that
she looked about her for an appropriate vein in which to discharge
the kind of ideas which she had been persuaded would counteract
any over-indulgence of the emotional and imaginative in *Jane Eyre*.
Her own comments on *Shirley* seem, albeit guardedly, to confirm
this. To Lewes, on 12 January 1848, she wrote

> I mean to observe your warning about being careful how I
> undertake new works . . . .
> If I ever *do* write another book, I think I will have nothing of
> what you call 'melodrama'; I *think* so, but I am not sure. . . .[23]

And in her opening chapter to the novel itself she warned:

> If you think, from this prelude, that anything like a romance is
> preparing for you, reader, you never were more mistaken . . . .
> Do you expect passion, and stimulus, and melodrama? Calm your
> expectations . . . . Something real, cool, and solid, lies before you;
> something unromantic as Monday morning . . . .[24]

If, however, Charlotte's use of social themes in *Shirley* was in the
main an artistic expedient, the issues dealt with were of a kind in
which deep human feeling was involved, and the exploration and
celebration of human feeling were at the very core of her entire
creative expression. It is all the more to her credit that, having
decided to focus upon a social problem, she disciplined herself to
approach the task with appropriate sociological objectivity and

thoroughness. She consulted the files of the *Leeds Mercury* for the years from 1812 to 1814 for accounts of the Luddite disturbances,[25] and from these she drew her descriptions of the woollen industry in the West Riding in 1811–12, of the dire effects upon it of the Continental blockade and of the ultimate suspension of the Orders in Council. In all these general matters her fidelity to the facts was meticulous. Her only evasions were in connection with particular incidents involving individuals. It has been pointed out, for example,[26] that in adapting the events at Cartwright's Mill at Rawfolds to her own 'Hollow's mill', she omitted to mention the fact that one of the soldiers was subsequently court-martialled and flogged 'for cowardice or reluctance'. Similarly, her reference to four ring-leaders being 'safely shipped prior to transportation' was a watering-down of the historical truth, which was that seventeen men were executed and six transported for seven years. However, the suggestion that Charlotte was not influenced here wholly by her Tory sympathies, but partly by a wish to avoid her hero, Robert Moore, appearing as a 'vindictive butcher' seems reasonable.

Asa Briggs, on the other hand, claims that Charlotte 'deliberately set out to make *Shirley* like a piece of actual life'.[27] Although, he says, 'she lacked George Eliot's power of historical and sociological synthesis', she understood and could faithfully describe her own northern society. The result, he affirms, is that *Shirley* 'is an important contribution to the literature of regional interpretation'. This, however, as Briggs goes on to show, is not all that *Shirley* is, and it is in the novel's two other related themes – the governess theme and the feminist theme – that Charlotte's essential self converges with her assumed 'social' self in a consistent attack upon a single target close to her heart. The issue which came to be known as the 'Woman Question' is examined in the chapter of that name; it is pertinent at this point to note its prominence in *Shirley*, the only quasi-'social' novel which Charlotte ever wrote. Its treatment here, however, is a curious mixture of attack and retreat, most of the attack being conveyed in bursts of feminist dialogue from the mouth of the spirited Shirley Keeldar, none of which, however, really amounts to anything in any practical sense. What is significant, in the light of subsequent criticism of the novel, is that the feminist cause is absorbed into the general theme of social inequality, thus forming a single voice of protest. This gives to the novel a unity of structure which largely refutes such charges as that of G. H. Lewes,[28] who called the work 'a portfolio of sketches', claiming that whole chapters could be omitted without destroying the story. Counter to this is the argument for 'design' which comes from Jacob Korg,[29] who states that *Shirley* is a 'philosophical novel' (as distinct from social), in which 'action is meaningful only when it springs from sincere individual desire'.

Intentional or otherwise, *Shirley's* blending of the social and personal strata is understandable when we realise that this novel was coming to birth at the very time that Charlotte's two sisters were dying. It is clear that her reflections upon the tragic disappointments and frustrations that had haunted her sisters' short lives were inevitably primary influences upon the slowly forming work. Thus, via the individual and social elements in this novel we see something that would later form the paramount focus of the work of George Eliot – an awareness of the tragic universality of human frailty trapped by an implacable fate. *Shirley* was Charlotte's translation of subjective experience into terms that were not merely social but formed a synoptic view of the human struggle for unity and fulfilment. If the *approach* was new for Charlotte, the *ideas* it served were not. The long and painful journey towards self-realisation and wholeness had been given powerful expression in *Jane Eyre*, and we see the same pattern given deeper complexities in what Nina Auerbach has called the 'divided self'[30] of Lucy Snowe in *Villette*. In this novel, she writes, is located 'Charlotte Brontë's key "myth", the perpetual war between fire and ice, within the isolated and estranged self, reaching towards a reality that can coalesce into nothing beyond projection.'

This self-division in Charlotte accounts for the recurrence in all her novels of their characteristic elements of disorientation. Jane Eyre, tearing herself away from Rochester, cries, 'Where to go?'[31]; Caroline Helstone, separated against her will from Robert Moore, asks, 'What was I created for . . .? Where is my place in the world?';[32] while Lucy Snowe, seeming never quite able to find her way round Villette, exists for much of her time in a dream-like state of suspended reality, induced by a combination of prolonged solitude, drug-torpor and nervous exhaustion. She is, as Philip Momberger puts it, tortured by a 'sense of spiritual exile',[33] in which even 'Nature seems not only inscrutably alien, but actively hostile'. Momberger sees this alienation, together with a sense of guilt, as common to the search for the self of the Brontë hero, and certainly where Charlotte is concerned it would seem to have been a part of her own rather uncertain approach to the initial stages of authorship. Between the private impulse towards concealment, the professional need to satisfy her critics and the personal urge to speak of what she truly felt, we can see her being pulled in different directions after the rejection of *The Professor*. The passionate psychological conflicts of *Jane Eyre* were followed by *Shirley*'s brave attempt at objectivity and then by the profound heart-searchings of *Villette*. As Tony Tanner explains,[34] commencing with the 'partial' (and 'male') version of her experiences in *The Professor*, Charlotte alternated the 'female subjectivity' of *Jane Eyre* with the 'objective account' of *Shirley*, until, in *Villette*, she 'found the most appropriate female narrator to explore in a sufficiently complex way the tensions and alternations in her own inner and outer experience'.

Perhaps, finally, we must return to *Shirley* for the most reliable clue of all to Charlotte Brontë's idea of the true function of the self *vis-à-vis* the creative artist and the world. In Chapter 26, Shirley Keeldar's lame young cousin, Henry Sympson, tells her that he will write a book so that he can dedicate it to her. She replies: 'You will write it, that you may give your soul its natural release.'[35] This may leave a great deal about the creative process unsaid, but it possibly tells us as much as we can ever know about Charlotte Brontë's own personal priorities in the complex relationship between the creative self and the social *milieu*.

Among the first reviewers of *Wuthering Heights*, the writer in *Douglas Jerrold's Weekly Newspaper* foreshadowed much subsequent opinion by calling it a book 'baffling all regular criticism',[36] and the difficulty has since been reflected in the number of contrasting views that have been expressed. Much of the opposition has centred on the novel's 'mystic' versus 'realistic' nature, with the conclusions being more or less equally divided between the two camps. These polarities would seem to stem from the modern tendency towards literary categorisation, in which the danger exists that in the attempt to affix neat 'labels' to a work we shall ignore its only valid perspective – the author's own creative vision. In Emily Brontë's case, the vision behind *Wuthering Heights* was intrinsic to her view of life itself. This view – of life's essential meaning and purpose – was explored in the previous chapter; its significance in the present context lies in its emphasis upon life's contrasting dualities, and upon an interpretation of Reality as transcendent and absolute, all of which concepts are given symbolic form in the novel. It is a token of

Emily Brontë's genius that, despite this preoccupation with essential and cosmic meanings, she achieved in *Wuthering Heights* one of the most authentic portrayals of mundane realism in all literature. The very narrative itself, with its alternations between storm and calm, reflect on the most fundamental level the changing elements of the natural world. The rough dialect evokes a crude country scene; the characters – wild, passionate, often cruelly individualistic – are living symbols of the stark magnificence of the moors themselves in all their changing moods.

It was once, perhaps truly, said that *'Wuthering Heights* ignores society',[37] although, as has recently been pointed out, Emily Brontë was fully aware of the social significance of the position of women at that time. Merryn Williams, observing that Emily had 'a sound knowledge of the laws affecting women around 1800', writes:

> Heathcliff can make Isabella a prisoner and after she leaves him . . . he can force her to come back . . . and he can at any time claim their child . . . .
>
> *Wuthering Heights* shows the enormous powers of the head of the household, and how they can be used against the weaker members of the family . . . .[38]

Whether this awareness was due to research on Emily's part, or merely a result of her wide reading of current newspapers and journals, we do not know. Perhaps, however, it is not so very surprising that a woman whose central focus on life was metaphysical rather than material, cosmic rather than local, should take more note of issues *outside* her own limited area than of those within it. Charlotte, holding to the view that her sister had little awareness of 'what is called "the world"',[39] stated that Emily had hardly more 'practical knowledge' of the community immediately around her 'than a nun has of the country people who sometimes pass her convent gates'. And yet, Charlotte added, 'she knew them'. And it is this knowledge, of a society that Emily Brontë 'knew' at the most profound level, that we sense in *Wuthering Heights*. The story, for all its inherent metaphysical purpose and structure, yet remains one of the most powerful projections by any author of a world intimately known, and both loved and despaired of. With 'Thackeray, Trollope, Mrs. Gaskell, and the rest of the great novelists,' writes Geoffrey Tillotson,[40] Emily provided '"Thackerayan Truth"'.

The relationship of the Self to the Other lies at the very heart of *Wuthering Heights*. Again, however, the sheer simplicity of Brontëan 'truth' has created difficulties for modern critics writing for a world in which the haste to establish a freedom between the sexes that can be *seen* to exist has resulted in the burial of human spiritual qualities beneath a towering façade of sensuality. It has thus become harder by the minute for us to accept that a normal girl – that is, neither a lunatic nor a nun – could seriously and honestly devote a whole book to the analysis of human love in terms that at times seem uncomfortably other than human, and end it with the simple suggestion that love only 'works' when the surrender of self-will is made the primary ingredient. As W. H. Marshall, writing of *Wuthering Heights*, points out:[41] 'realization of the Self is to be achieved only by moving beyond the immediate limits of the Self'.

in order to achieve self-realization, man must commit himself to the universe and to society, but in so doing he destroys the equilibrium in which, presumably deluded, he has maintained his own existence. In this sense commitment means sacrificing the demands of the physical and emotional aspects of the Self; the realization of the larger Self that supposedly follows must then be seen in terms of the spirit, specifically of the individual soul of the Christian tradition.[42]

This may seem a long way from the love of Heathcliff and Cathy, but it is the explanation of why their self-centred love is doomed, and of the introduction of the 'alternative' love of Hareton and the younger Catherine. In this alternative version, we see that apparent incompatibility yields to rapport only when Catherine, hitherto by far the more aggressive of the two, surrenders her will to humility and compassion. This completes the dual love pattern between self-will and self-surrender in *Wuthering Heights*, concerning which Mary M. Visick has offered an illuminating comparison with the sense of Blake's poem, 'The Clod and the Pebble'.[43] Unlike Blake, Emily chose to give the last word to the *unselfed* soul, no doubt because in her Platonist view of life she saw it as the logically necessary conclusion to any account of being in absolute terms; and, for her, the conflicts of *Wuthering Heights* like all the conflicts of self in the world, were conflicts of essences and absolutes in individual human guise. It is because of this that *Wuthering Heights* is sensed by most to be such a disturbing book; but it is also a hopeful one. If

Heathcliff and Cathy are symbols of what life can become when self-interest is unrestrained, it is nevertheless clearly pointed out that they are powerless to stem life's innate capacity for restoration. It is left open to conjecture as to what their individual destinies might be, but we have glimpsed enough of Emily Brontë's thought to know that judgement was not a concept she found acceptable; if suffering was one way in which the flawed soul might find salvation, it was enough that it was so. But there was another and a better way, whose prerequisite was self-forgetfulness. Therefore, 'Earth lie lightly on that breast/And kind Heaven, grant that spirit rest!'[44]

Even less than her elder sister was Emily concerned with social matters of the day. Life itself – not simply society – was her passionate preoccupation. It has indeed been claimed of her that even in the close relationship of love she showed 'no sense of the otherness of the other person';[45] that 'ultimate passion' was for her a 'kind of recognition of . . . one's true and absolute self . . . .' Yet it surely remains that, in the intense, individualistic expression of *Wuthering Heights*, everything that makes – and breaks – the relationship of human beings with one another in an ordinary, everyday world is defined. Here, the worst of human folly and the best of human potential, both individual and, in the widest sense, social, is delineated with a clarity that it is difficult to imagine can ever be surpassed.

Ever since 1924, when George Moore[46] sent a minor shock through the world of literary criticism by declaring Anne Brontë's genius to be even greater than that of either of her sisters, the chorus of faint praise directed towards the youngest of the Brontës has been steadily deepening in tone. Writing of *Agnes Grey* that it was as 'simple and beautiful as a muslin dress', Moore put its 'fifty-odd' year neglect down to critical 'blindness' and claimed for it the distinction of being 'the one story in English literature in which style, characters and subject are in perfect keeping'. He went so far as to argue that 'if Anne had lived ten years longer she would have taken a place beside Jane Austen, perhaps even a higher place'. In 1949, Phyllis Bentley proclaimed Anne to be 'in her own right a minor classic',[47] and was followed, ten years later, by Ada Harrison and Derek Stanford, who decried the tendency for Anne to be regarded as 'a sort of humble footnote to her sisters' pages'.[48] More recently, Inga-Stina Ewbank has praised, among other qualities, Anne's 'realism',[49] and Winifred Gérin has stated that *The Tenant of Wildfell Hall* could well be called 'the first manifesto for Women's Lib'.[50] All these assessments point to an author fully awake to the world around her and concerned to declare her interest on some of the important questions of the day. In particular, as will be shown later, Anne showed herself to be keenly alive to what was to become known as the Woman Question.

The difference between Anne's two novels is itself of some significance, but there is a sense in which this difference is less marked than might at first seem. On the face of it, *Agnes Grey* is essentially an 'autobiographical' work, whereas *The Tenant* concerns itself with certain questions of great social importance, particularly in connection with the status of women and the upbringing of children. Paradoxically, however, the latter work was directly motivated by certain personally experienced events – those connected with the tragic moral breakdown of Branwell Brontë following his dismissal from Thorp Green – while *Agnes Grey*, on the other hand, provides as part of its inherent organism a close exploration of the typical characteristics of a particular kind of contemporary society, and its attitudes to those seen as its dependent 'inferiors'. In its own way, this novel ranks perhaps on an equal footing with *Shirley* as a protest against social inequality, especially in matters of class and sex. Although there can be no doubt that Anne drew upon incidents and characters known personally in her five years as a governess, it is clear, as the book's opening line reveals, that she had a wider aim in view than that of mere reminiscence. 'All true histories contain instruction,'[51] she wrote, and, a few chapters on, declared that her aim was 'not to amuse, but to benefit those whom it might concern'.[52] In the event, this proves to be a fairly wide canvas, for the book explores a variety of human relationships, and views the function of governesses objectively, yet with a probing intimacy. There is a refreshing lack of emotionalism. Sentimentality, notes Ewbank, 'is completely absent from *Agnes Grey*. There are fewer tears in this novel than in any other mid-nineteenth-century novel that I have read.'[53] It is an impressive achievement bearing in mind that the quality of *Agnes Grey* that most compels attention is that which springs directly from the involvement of Anne's deepest self in the miseries stemming from injustice. Moore described that quality as 'heat',[54] a burning of the heart, which he distinguished from 'violence, rhetoric or vehemence' and defined by reference to St Teresa, Heloise's letters to Abelard and the style of Jane Austen in *Sense and Sensibility*.

Anne's anger at social injustice may have had a personal base, but it did not remain there. She could relate the anguish of her own family to other fathers and sons, to other sisters. Returning from Thorp Green, with the shadow of Branwell's disgrace upon her, Anne had written in her diary: 'I have had some very unpleasant and undreamt-of experience of human nature',[55] and pencilled in the back of her prayer book was found the line: 'Sick of mankind and their disgusting ways'.[56] This was all Anne revealed of whatever had taken place at the Robinsons, but from someone as controlled, as compassionate, as she it tells us much. But it was characteristic of this most dauntless and most realistic of all the Brontës that she did not yield to the sickness within her, but, instead, faced and outstared her monster, and then quietly sat down and wrote *The Tenant of Wildfell Hall*. As in Charlotte's case, much of Anne's social concern lay directly in the context of the position of women, as will be shown in Chapter 5; however, at the core of *The Tenant of Wildfell Hall* was something that went deeper than concern for any one life, or for any particular group of people at any given historical time. Anne's sense of social significance, like Emily's, was subsumed under a wider, more general attitude to morality. To her deeply religious nature, injustice of any kind held implications that dangerously threatened spiritual well-being. Thus it is that the great culminating drama of *The Tenant of Wildfell Hall* is not in the triumph of Helen Huntingdon's bid for independence against all the laws and conventions of her time; it is in the death struggle of Arthur Huntingdon as Helen sits beside him and fights desperately to save his soul. Like Emily, Anne conceived of the human self, or soul, as an entity in the making; thus commitment to other human beings was both a Christian duty and a necessary part of self (soul)-creation. In a letter to Ellen Nussey, written little more than a month before her death, she said:

> I long to do some good in the world before I leave it. I have many schemes in my head for future practise [sic] – humble and limited indeed – but still I should not like to see them come to nothing, and myself to have lived to so little purpose.[57]

As it was, *The Tenant of Wildfell Hall* was to be Anne's last challenge to a world which she, more than either of her sisters, had come to know at its worst. It was a challenge which she directed with a courage and honesty rare among women writers of her time. Few would wish to dispute that courage. All that perhaps we might question is whether Anne – or, for that matter, either of her sisters – fully realised the differences that lay between themselves, their lives and their views and those of the vast majority of the society of which they were part. With their penetrating logic, their uncompromising rejection of ambivalent standards of morality and their insistence on the human right to *feel*, they shocked the world; it is possibly equally true that in its reaction to their work the world shocked *them*.

George Eliot once said that her writings belonged to 'successive mental phases',[58] and nowhere is this more clearly seen than in the gradual shift of emphasis in her novels from a reliance on personal recollection of people, places and events to a more objective awareness of society as a whole. After *The Mill on the Floss*, she noticeably ceased to hug the shore-line of personal observation and, except for occasional resort to the 'spare-parts' bank of real-life personalities, began increasingly to base her characters upon a synthesis of intellectual ideas and psychological insight and intuition. It was when she failed to get the balance right, when the idea took over from the human being, that the result would be one of those failures of characterisation that would seem all the more unhappy for having been preceded or followed by a masterpiece. Examples are the curiously flat personality of Daniel Deronda, and the text-book historicity of much of *Romola*, which, even to contemporary eyes, contained 'somewhat too much of the dry bones of archaeological research'.[59]

We do not have to look far into George Eliot's work for evidence that her vision of life was pre-eminently social – to the extent, that is, that 'society' meant not merely a cohesion of individual lives, but individual lives joined at each 'equivalent centre of self'.[60] Long before the publication of *Middlemarch*, which established her as a novelist of major social sensibilities, her preoccupation with this inter-relationship was manifest. Similarly, her ethical philosophy had long been centred not on some speculative and future ideal, but on a universal, here-and-now meliorist belief in the power of the human will.

Like Ruskin, whom she revered, George Eliot was passionately convinced of the need for some breakthrough into a larger, more comprehensive way of living. Again, like Ruskin, she felt that a merely individual salvation was not enough: the expansion of being itself ought to be general and social.[61]

It is in *Middlemarch* that we see her applying this ideal with the greatest concentration, at the same time showing, in numerous individual lives, how success or failure depended on internal factors within those lives more than on their extraneous circumstances. The theme of self-frustration forms a major focus in a novel in which the individual and the social continuously interrelate. The two most notable exponents are Dorothea Brooke, 'whose mind was theoretic, and yearned by its nature after some lofty conception of the world',[62] and Tertius Lydgate, who 'had come to Middlemarch bent on doing many things that were not directly fitted to make his fortune or even secure him a good income'.[63] The problem which George Eliot exposes is crystallised in her use of the word 'theoretic'; for both Dorothea and Lydgate fail to assess their own and others' lives realistically. Each makes the same kind of drastic misjudgements that inevitably effect the failure of their dreams. Life, instead of being a noble self-fulfilment and a sharing of exalted aspirations, becomes a lonely and painful process of self-education. For Dorothea, the result is happiness in a humbler but truer destiny than that which she had fondly imagined for herself; Lydgate, on the other hand, is aware to the end that 'he had not done what he once meant to do'.[64]

It is in *Middlemarch* that we see most clearly George Eliot's concept of the relationship of self to the world. In its delineation of the deadly egotism of Casaubon and Rosamond, the deceiving and self-deceiving Bulstrode, even the likeable but feckless Fred Vincy, she points the moral that illumines all her work – that, as Redinger describes it, 'salvation can come only through the achievement of selflessness and awareness of other-than-self'.[65] By selecting as her background a social setting of infinite variety, she was able to explore an almost unlimited number of human possibilities as characters continuously touch and change each other's lives. It is a situation very much to the taste of a novelist dedicated to the art of experiment. The reader, however, faced with the 'distancing' quality of that ubiquitous, yet detached, authorial voice may occasionally wonder how 'theoretic' were some of her own social and intellectual attitudes. The question is particularly pertinent in the present context, for selfhood was a subject that had given her much personal difficulty from girlhood.

From that early Puritan 'fear of self'[66] there had developed in her what Gerald Bullett calls her 'pathological self-dislike',[67] which, he argues, led to her 'deification of duty' and her constant habit of 'pointing the moral'. Another explanation of her 'passionate devotion' to the idea of the 'renunciation of self' and the 'pursuit of social duty'[68] has been given by reference to the combination in her of Evangelicalism and 'Romantic ardour'. We might also wonder, perhaps, whether a combination of feminine self-idealisation and the onus of an increasingly sibylline reputation did not urge her towards expressions of this sort. One of the clearest examples occurs in *Daniel Deronda*, where Mordecai tells Mirah that 'women are specially framed for the love which feels possession in renouncing. . . . This is the surpassing love, that loses self in the object of love'.[69]

In her own life, the 'renunciation of self' was the one basic ideal to which George Eliot held throughout the great intellectual *voltes face* that shaped her as a human being and as a novelist. As faith yielded to reason, the numinous to the scientific, the infinite to the finite, the ideal of renunciation remained to light her vision of a world in which could be realised the perfection of the human nature. Creatively, however, feeling – which, in theory, was as important to her as to the Brontës – seems often to give way to analysis, and to a didacticism which George Eliot took pains to deny[70] and yet at the same time declared (rather ponderously) to be an inevitable part of authorship.[71] We might conclude, perhaps, that, ironically, the preoccupation with what she saw to be the real problem of the self – its egotism – tended towards a self-*consciousness* in her that was part and parcel of the very quality she abjured. It is further possible that an effort to counter this resulted in the erection of barriers between herself and those of her characters which were drawn from deep springs of feeling within her: thus the creation of those idealised characters which have provoked critical judgements such as that of Gerald Bullett concerning Romola – that, 'if she walks like a procession, she talks like a proclamation'.[72] To the end, a small part of George Eliot remained true to religion's sanctified images of purified passion, represented by such figures as Thomas à Kempis and St Teresa. These lives of dedicated selflessness remained for her a beacon; they shone, an uncertain but persistent light throughout all her work, assuming the forms of priest, monk and self-sacrificing womanhood, until they culminated in the Christ-figure of Mordecai Cohen.

The picture of George Eliot that emerges, therefore, is of an artist in whom the self was divided into a number of conflicting aspects, which might be delineated thus:

Self-Renunciation	*v.*	Self-Commitment
Self-Dislike	*v.*	Self-Idealisation
Self as Self	*v.*	Self as Teacher
(i.e., spontaneous feeling)		(i.e., didactic objectivity)

Given these self-orientated tensions in her work, we might question whether any of George Eliot's novels can properly be called 'social' *per se*, whether they are not, rather, configurations of her theories about the individual self in its relationship with other individual selves. At the same time, as we have already seen, where these theories were expressed in terms of major idealised characters, such as Romola and Deronda, the effect was at times to objectify to the point at which reader-credibility was seriously strained. Secondary characters, on the other hand, almost unfailingly redeemed the situation. Barbara Hardy, remarking on the 'deadness' of *Romola*, makes an exception – as had Margaret Oliphant before her – in relation to the incidents involving Tito.[73] From this, it seems true to say that George Eliot draws closest to her characters when her essential self is furthest from them, when, in other words, she is free from that self-consciousness that stemmed from ideological pressures within her. If *Felix Holt*, her 'political novel', truly deserves Mrs Oliphant's strictures upon it – that it left an impression on the mind 'as of "Hamlet" played by six sets of grave-diggers'[74] – it is surely for the reason that the human drama of the Transomes, especially as focused on the person of Mrs Transome herself, is insufficiently integrated with the political events to give to these events – and to Felix Holt himself – a palpable sense of reality. If we compare this novel with, say, *The Mill on the Floss*, or *Middlemarch*, we can immediately see the force obliquely applied to social or political themes, however tenuous, by the involvement of well-defined secondary characters. In *The Mill*, for example, the moral deadness of 'respectability' is beautifully caught in the Dodson family, who, we are told, see their brother-in-law's economic downfall as a 'judgement'[75] which 'it would be an impiety to counteract by too much kindness'. Again and again in the Eliot novel, the struggle is of individuals, seen as affected by, and affecting, other lives conjoint with theirs within the group. With William Marshall, we might conclude that, 'for George Eliot, the individual being, the Self, determines the moral nature of the world',[76] and this, of course, was all of a piece with 'her belief in an inflexible law of moral consequences'.

It emerges that the differences in this context between George Eliot and the Brontës, which at first sight may have appeared obvious and considerable, are in fact more a matter of emphasis. There is the Brontës' overtly 'individualistic' approach compared with George Eliot's overtly 'social' one. But, as we have seen, the latter's socially-orientated ethical philosophy was invariably directed towards the working out of *individual* problems within the group – just as the Brontës, in their concentration upon individual destinies, cast considerable light upon the society to which these individuals belonged. Again, as might be expected with women writers of the period, the creative process in all four authors showed similar impulses towards escape and expansion. There was, first, the desire for freedom from limiting aspects of the external world – as, for instance, Charlotte Brontë's resentment of the intrusion on her creative needs of her governess duties[77] – and, secondly, freedom from interior restraints upon full self-realisation – as, for example, George Eliot's rejection of conventional religion. All expressed in their work the craving of individuals, especially women, for a wider experience of life, a fuller sense of self-identity.

In the Brontës, the themes of imprisonment and isolation – and their contrasting correlations, freedom and unity – are so dominant as to require no stressing. In one form or another, they are central to the work of all three sisters. It is not difficult to appreciate why the Brontës should have been so obsessed with the horror of imprisonment, and its symbolic connections with death. Their isolated lives were hemmed in by a graveyard, which was linked in both a practical and imaginative sense with repeated experience of family tragedy. The connection between this ever-present reminder of negation and the sense of spiritual and intellectual limitation which each sister suffered is plain. That Charlotte longed to spread her wings is seen in her many letters to her friends;[78] that Emily asked only of life that her *soul* might be free – but asked repeatedly – is clear in the great bulk of her poems; and that Anne regretted to the day she died that she had not had opportunity to make more of her life in the world is the concluding message of the last letter she wrote (quoted on p. 79). We might summarise these aims, perhaps, by saying that Charlotte wanted to *do*, Anne to *be* and Emily to *know*. The early realisation that frustration was inevitable led, especially in Charlotte and Emily, to a Quixotic longing for things to be *more* than they are in the ordinary run of a lifetime, and Emily, in particular, painted the definitive picture of the connection between a combination of repression and injustice and the creation of monsters.

In George Eliot's 'day-dream'[79] selves, we can see at work similar efforts – although more complex – to resolve the same kind of problems. Her aim, directed not only on her own behalf, but, as she saw it, for all humanity, was to widen the vision of the human being, to 'let in a little conscience and refinement'.[80] In her delighted reception (mentioned earlier) of Feuerbach's identification of 'divine being' with 'human nature glorified' and with 'pure, unlimited, free Feeling', links can be seen with Charlotte Brontë's explicit expression of the need for feeling in human affairs. Andrew and Judith Hook show how, in *Shirley*, Charlotte pinpointed the roots of division between people in terms of what is described as 'the denial of the world of feeling built into the existing social order'.[81] Similarly, in this part-'political' novel, written in the revolutionary year of 1848, Charlotte shows as little sympathy for out-and-out political radicalism as George Eliot was to do in *Felix Holt*. In the latter, written between the Spring of 1865 and May 1866, Peter Coveney traces a 'refining'[82] process in George Eliot's political attitudes from her revolutionary phase of almost twenty years before. The work of 'an inherently radical and committed mind', the novel, Coveney claims, sets out to explain:

> why, in face of that 'groaning, travailing creation' it descried in its youth . . . it found itself within the conservative political tradition of Burke, Coleridge, Scott and Wordsworth, rather than with the Radical mainstream of Benthamite reform.

In sum, then, we find that in all four novelists the trend towards objectivity was, paradoxically, to a considerable extent subjective. Their paramount motivation, subconscious or otherwise, was towards a self-expression that would be personally satisfying and enlarging. As Marshall observes:[83] 'More than any other literary type, the novel offered indefinite [sic] opportunity for the embodiment of individual experiences through which the Self and a new basis for certitude were to be discovered'. The methods which all four authors adopted had certain essentials in common, differing in the main in terms of focus and interpretation. For George Eliot the concept of selflessness took on almost the dimension of a religion, yet in their creative expression the Brontës were the more truly selfless, the reason stemming from their simpler, more honest acceptance of reality. In them, we see the perfect expression of that 'enthusiasm' which Coleridge[84] defined as the 'oblivion and swallowing-up of self in an object dearer than self, or in an idea more vivid'. In contrast, we have seen that in George Eliot the *fear* of self distanced her from her characters, as did her didacticism, the latter being possibly a defence against the demands of complete self-commitment; in other words, as Henry James[85] was to put it, 'instead of feeling life itself, it is "views" on life that she tries to feel'. In fairness to her, we should nevertheless remind ourselves how panoramic those 'views' were.

4
Love and Sexuality

Few areas of discussion on the world of the Victorians present us with greater difficulty than that which pertains to their attitudes to love and sexuality. So great have been the changes between those attitudes and our own that before we can assess the former with any confidence it is necessary for us to make considerable adjustments to our own prevailing assumptions.

The problem derives not merely from the fact of today's greater candour in confronting the issues related to love between the sexes, but also from fundamental differences in our interpretation even of the language which we use to describe them. When currently we speak of 'lovers', for example, and of 'making love', the received connotations are explicit. But no such unequivocal clarity pertained to the use of these words in the English romantic novel of the period under review. For the most part, social convention rather than physical intimacy was the defining element. Thus, for example, in George Eliot's *Felix Holt*, Esther Lyon, at a time when she barely knows Felix and is only superficially attracted to him, can speculate upon his one day being 'a regular lover',[1] by which she merely means that he will formally present himself as a suitor within the accepted guidelines of nineteenth-century courtship. By the same token, Charlotte Brontë's Caroline Helstone in *Shirley* muses upon Robert Moore's 'love-making'[2] at a point when his awareness of her is still merely that of an affectionate cousin.

Sometimes, too, our modern perceptions of human emotions transpire to be not so much 'progressive' as reactionary. An illustration is today's generally adopted attitude towards emotional friendships between people of the same sex. It is difficult, in our post-Freudian world, to realise that to Victorian sensibilities such overtly innocent attachments were only very seldom held to be abnormal or offensive. Rather, for the most part they were seen as rather beautiful and inspiring. This is important to our understanding of the Victorian approach to sexuality in general, for such attitudes were not so much due to any classical realism in that approach as to a conception of love that was determinedly idealistic;

something Houghton has described as 'a curious blending of Protestant earnestness and Romantic enthusiasm, with a strong assist from chivalric literature'.[3] Particularly relevant to two of our novelists was the way in which friendships between women were viewed. George Eliot's many neophyte 'daughters' afford interesting examples, as will be seen later in this chapter; we recall, too, Charlotte Brontë's reference to her own 'hot, tenacious heart',[4] whose 'warmest affections' were 'lavished' upon her lifelong friend, Ellen Nussey.

The universal acceptance of the innocence of such female affections, though probably justified in most cases, was nevertheless owed in the main to a myth which was fostered by almost as many women as men – that is, that the nature of the female was such as to be 'above' sensuality of a sexual kind – the effect of which tended to cast women in rigid moulds of 'good' or 'bad', and to see them, where the sex relation generally was concerned, as virtually either cataleptic or wanton. By the same token, parenthood and the family were exalted by the presence of the 'good' wife and mother into symbols incarnate of their heavenly 'antitypes',[5] while the 'bad' mother – usually by interpretation the woman for whom home affairs were not totally satisfying – would generally be held to be the agent primarily responsible for the corruption of family life.

A further, and paradoxical, element in the general social situation is of special interest since it bears particularly upon the fictional attitudes noticeable in our four authors. Part of the 'emphasis on romantic and wedded love', Houghton points out,[6] was in fact 'a protest against marriage'. It was 'a revolt of the heart against a system which denied its impulses, and which, in the absence of love, was a source of personal distress and social evil'. By 'system', was meant, of course, the prevailing tendency for marriage to be used as an instrument for the promotion of interests other than romantic. Houghton writes:

> in the best fiction – notably in Thackeray, George Eliot, Trollope and Charlotte Brontë – it was not a daydream people found but a passionate insistence that those feelings [of love] should be a reality, and a bitter arraignment of the system that ignored them.[7]

For all, however, that this was undoubtedly true, there were problems for authors writing in an age culturally so insulated from reality; an age in which 'Thackeray might satirize prudery', but 'was ready enough to praise *Punch* because it contained nothing unfit for little boys to read, or for women to enjoy without blushing'.[8] And an age in which, as Eva Figes has pointed out, women authors had 'other restraints imposed on them' besides the general social ones; there were 'the restraints of a commercial publishing system which would reject reflections on and of the world too far from the general consensus'.[9]

The above comment is perhaps particularly illuminating in connection with the two elder Brontës, whose intentions in the treatment of the love theme have attracted an almost bewildering array of contrasting critical opinions. Overall, the effect has been a polarisation between two opposing schools of thought: on the one hand, that which sees Brontë love themes as whiter than white – that is, wholly 'spiritual' – and, on the other, that favouring the deep-dyed purples of Freudian sexual connotation. For the former school, such statements as Ernest Raymond's, that 'spiritual, disembodied love is a characteristic of all three Brontë sisters',[10] leaves one deeply uneasy, for while it is certainly true that there is a marked lack of what Raymond calls 'animal sex' in their work, the same might be said of almost all English romantic novels of the period. We recall some of the sickly heroines of Dickens – for example, Dora Copperfield and Little Dorrit – and Thackeray's tendency to sentimentalise his virtuous women and to overstate his 'bad' ones to the point almost of unreality. On the other hand, Margaret Lane has surely done Brontë criticism a service with her use of the phrase, 'ingenious absurdities'[11] to describe some of the more bizarrely speculative theories about Brontë sexual psychology which have emerged in recent years. With particular reference to *Wuthering Heights*, she expresses surprise that so far no-one has 'written a thesis to prove that . . . Cathy's preference for lying in a cradle of branches on a windy day is an anagram of sexual symbolism'.[12] In fairness to both schools of thought, the Brontës' treatment of love in their fiction does leave considerable room for speculation, and the one direct statement we have on the subject – Charlotte's reply to Harriet Martineau's criticism of her 'incessant' preoccupation with 'the need of being loved'[13] – is somewhat circular. 'I know what *love* is as I understand it',[14] Charlotte wrote, adding, without altogether clarifying:

and if man or woman should be ashamed of feeling such love, then there is nothing right, noble, faithful, truthful, unselfish in this earth, as I comprehend rectitude, nobleness, fidelity, truth, and disinterestedness.

Charlotte Brontë's treatment of love is especially interesting, since, so far as can reasonably be adduced, she alone of the sisters did, as she put it, 'know' what that emotion was. Unfortunately, just what the knowledge was is not easy to arrive at, for, as most of her modern biographers and critics would seem to agree, Charlotte's own personal response to sexual emotion was deeply complex. Statements to the effect that she was 'always in battle between her strong morality and her equally strong sexual intimations',[15] and that she 'knew a great deal about sex, but would have loathed the idea that she did',[16] seem accurately to reflect the continuing pattern of that response. Throughout her fairly short life, Charlotte had no less than four offers of marriage, but seemed to have set herself impossibly high criteria by which to assess all would-be suitors who came her way. In 1839, for example, while her instincts in all probability served her well in prompting her to reject the extremely pragmatic advances of her best friend's brother, the Reverend Henry Nussey, her explanation for doing so held more than a touch of the unreal:

> I had not, and could not have, that intense attachment which would make me willing to die for him; and if ever I marry, it must be in that light of adoration that I will regard my husband.[17]

Five months later, the visit to the Parsonage of a young Irish curate named Bryce clearly at first delighted her; 'I . . . laughed at his jests',[18] she reported to Ellen Nussey; but when the young man, encouraged by her response, began to show a more personal interest, she reacted with a primness more reminiscent of a passage from Jane Austen than from one of her own ardent stories. 'I cooled a little', she told Ellen, '. . . because he began to season his conversation with something of Hibernian flattery, which I did not quite relish.'

The advice she gave to others was even more surprising; 'respect',[19] she told Ellen, was much more to be desired in a relationship than passion: '. . . if you can respect a person before marriage, moderate love at least will come after; and as to intense *passion*, I am convinced that that is no desirable feeling'. And 'respect' – or, rather, the lack of it – was to be her excuse nine years later for rejecting her publisher's managing clerk, James Taylor. However, her description of the curiously disturbing effect he had on her is interesting:

> each moment he came near me –and that I could see his eyes fastened on me – my veins ran ice. . . . I grow rigid – stiffening with a strange mixture of apprehension and anger . . . .[20]

And Taylor's departure, after a visit to Haworth, produced a surprising reaction:

> his absence and the exclusion of his idea from my mind leave me certainly with less support and in deeper solitude than before . . . something in my heart aches and gnaws drearily . . . .[21]

From these responses, it seems reasonable to suspect that Charlotte's enthusiasm for the sexual relationship increased with distance. So many gaps still exist in our knowledge of the Brontë lives that we can only speculate as to causes, but it is at least evident that motherlessness and the tragic loss of her two elder sisters, Maria and Elizabeth, left her with an exaggerated *need* of love, which, in a perfectly natural way, she translated into romantic, and often quite erotic, forms at an early age – that is, in the prolific Juvenilia. But inexperience of the social world held her love hunger imprisoned in a prolonged immaturity, and it is in the light of this explanation that we must surely see the supreme emotional experience that eventually released the novelist in her and both cauterised and completed her as a woman.

It has been justly observed that the 'Heger affair has preoccupied both Brontë and Gaskell scholars beyond the point of saturation'.[22] Nevertheless, it is only here, in Charlotte's response to her Belgian teacher, Constantin Heger, that we find the key to the intense love relationships of the novels. Everything that disturbed her contemporary readers – the wild impatience with the world as it was, the passion that seemed to have no bounds – all were rooted in the personal defiance with which she emerged, chastened but unrepentant, from this salutary experience. The conflicts of Jane Eyre, of Caroline Helstone, of Lucy Snowe, were all variant symbols of that great conflict within herself between emotional need and an impossible idealism that derived partly from residual puritanism and partly from a profound sexual innocence and social naiveté.

Charlotte's attachment to Heger clearly began as a mixture of hero-worship and simple heart-hunger. It is at least arguable that there it would have remained but for the response of the Hegers themselves, which apparently changed, due to Madame's growing suspicions, from warm friendliness to an understandable coolness. The unfortunate outcome of this was that Charlotte felt compelled to resign her teaching position at the Pensionnat and return home. There, driven to desperation by a lack of communication with her beloved 'Master', she wrote him a series of letters that, even by today's standards, it is difficult to see as other than love-letters.[23]

> Once more goodbye, Monsieur; it hurts to say goodbye even in a letter. Oh, it is certain that I shall see you again one day – it must be so –   (24 July 1844).

> Day and night I find neither rest nor peace . . . . Forgive me then, Monsieur, if I adopt the course of writing to you again. How can I endure life if I make no effort to cease its sufferings?   (8 January 1845).

> I have tried meanwhile to forget you . . . . To forbid me to write to you, to refuse to answer me would be to tear from me my only joy on earth . . . when day by day disappointment comes . . . I lose appetite and sleep – I pine away.   (18 November/? 1845/).

Those commentators who have seen Charlotte's behaviour in the Heger affair as evincing the presence of an intense passion and a preparedness to commit adultery[24] have much circumstantial evidence on their side. Nevertheless, it is my own view that assumptions of this sort risk being over-simplistic; at the very least, they must answer to the powerful evidence – reflected in the novels – of Charlotte's essential, scrupulously moral, nature. More persuasive, to my mind, is the view that, 'had Charlotte been allowed to continue to enjoy the frank friendship of her master, an altogether saner attitude of mind might have been preserved'.[25] As it was, Heger's few letters to Charlotte (which have not survived) would seem to have been astringent almost to the point of heartlessness if her own letter of 18 November (above) is to be taken as evidence. It is surely significant that on the edge of this particularly anguished letter the professor noted the name and address of a local shoemaker.

Perhaps the truth of the Heger affair is too simple, too prosaic, to be of great interest to us. As already suggested, Charlotte had shown a repeated tendency to withdraw from relationships that brought her down to earth. It is thus conceivable, perhaps, that, by what might be called a reverse process, the Hegers unwittingly intensified to a perilous and almost uncontrollable extent what would otherwise have passed as no more and no less than a belated manifestation of schoolgirl infatuation. Possibly the explanation offered by Kathleen Tillotson errs on the side of a too unadulterated objectivity, but in the absence of conclusive proof in either one direction or the other, it must at least be accepted as tenable:

> M. Heger's marriage was a datum, in no sense a frustration, but rather an encouragement; he was married, therefore he could, she thought, accept the ardent feeling she offered him, as belonging to a quite other kind of relation. The moment that he hinted that misunderstanding was possible, she ceased writing. The relation has been much misunderstood.[26]

Whether Charlotte ceased writing because she realised – or cared – that 'misunderstanding was possible', or because, in the face of impenetrable silence, she simply despaired, we shall never know. Meanwhile, the words of the final letter of 18 November must leave us always in doubt:

> To forbid me to write to you . . . would be to . . . deprive me of my last privilege – a privilege I never shall consent willingly to surrender.[27]

Despite this uncertainty, any minimisation of the connection between the Heger experience and Charlotte's delineation of love themes in her novels is as serious a threat to our understanding of her as is over-expansive speculation. The connection in the novels is continuous, and accounts entirely for the peculiarly evocative sexual force that we find there. Mrs Oliphant described the latter as 'the desire of a lonely creature longing for its mate',[28] and Thackeray wrote to a friend in February 1852 that Charlotte had 'had a story and a great grief that has gone badly with her'.[29] The ways in which that story and that grief entered the novels can be seen to form a basic pattern, of which the following were the dominant features:

The Master/Pupil relationship – connected with the schoolroom

in all the novels except *Jane Eyre*, but represented here also by
what Charlotte called the 'hierophant' figure.[30]

The 'rejection' experience – common to all the heroines except
Shirley Keeldar.

The 'inequality' syndrome – represented by the constraints
imposed upon women's freedom of expression in relations
between the sexes: voiced, for example, by Jane Eyre and by
Caroline Helstone in *Shirley*.[31]

Voyeurism – an emphasis seen particularly in *The Professor* and
Villette in the characterisations of Mlle Reuter and Mme Beck,
symbols of Charlotte's awareness of Mme Heger's jealous
watchfulness.

Of all these elements, the Master/Pupil relationship is, of course,
the most consistent. It is also the most significant. This is not simply
because it relates directly to her deep personal attachment to M.
Heger, but because it also affords us an important clue to Charlotte's
psychosexual development. This unvarying compulsion to place
her heroines in some kind of willing subjection to a dominant male
suggests that within Charlotte herself there might well have been a
subconscious reluctance to assume the responsibility of an adult and
equal male/female relationship. That Charlotte, who so feared
death,[32] should also to some extent fear life is not so very surprising
given the tragic synonymity of those terms in Brontë experience. In
the escapist and dream-fulfilling sagas of the Juvenilia, all the
material and emotional insecurity of a painful reality could be
forgotten. In her fiction, as Robert Keefe has suggested, 'she could
become the master of fate'.[33] But it is hardly to be expected that such
autonomy should not carry a price: that Charlotte, hovering
between the real and the ideal, should not at times feel like a lost
soul, fearful of what either state might bring to her, wandering
amidst her isolating fears like Lucy Snowe through the alien
boulevards of Villette. The connection in that novel between author
and heroine becomes even clearer when Lucy's 'forbidden' garden
is 'vulgarized'[34] for her by love-letters tossed from a window of the
nearby boys' school; her thoughts then seek shelter in her
'childhood', into which 'the rude Real burst coarsely in – all evil,
grovelling, and repellent as she too often is'.[35] Like Lucy, Charlotte,
too, had kept the 'rude Real' at bay, but her fiction afforded her the
chance to confront it with the same thrilling sense of impunity in the
face of danger that comes with throwing tit-bits to tigers behind

bars. This is why, perhaps, in the novels we observe such a marked and consistent gap between *language* and *action*. While Charlotte seems always careful to keep her heroines' feet firmly in the paths of rectitude, she allows herself considerable play with words. This applies especially to the thoughts and dialogue of her male characters, which quite often come close to what, by the standards of her time, could be called eroticism. An instance is the courtship play of words that precedes the parting of Jane Eyre and Rochester, when Rochester protests:

> you please me, and you master me – you seem to submit, and I like the sense of pliancy you impart; and while I am twining the soft, silken skein round my finger, it sends a thrill up my arm to my heart. I am influenced – conquered . . . .[36]

It is as if, within the safety of the unreal, via the language of poetry and of passion, Charlotte sought and found release from the emotional restrictions which for so long had been a constant part of her life. Not long after the completion of *Shirley*, she herself put something of this into words in a letter to her publisher's reader, W. S. Williams:

> The loss of what we possess nearest and dearest to us in this world produces an effect upon the character: we search out what we have yet left that can support, and, when found, we cling to it with a hold of new-strung tenacity. The faculty of imagination lifted me when I was sinking, three months ago; its active exercise has kept my head above water since . . . .[37]

An even more interesting example of Charlotte's use of the language of passion is seen in *The Professor*, because here the autobiographical role of narrator is transferred from female to male, with the result that we have what has intriguingly been described[38] as an author 'making love to herself'. Unremarkable as this adoption by a woman author of a wholly masculine view might seem to us today, in its own time it was revolutionary, since what was involved in this particular novel was the sustained portrayal of a young man's feelings about women in general and in particular, and his awakening impulses to sexual love. Jane Austen, it will be recalled, always took special care to avoid this problem, and neither Dickens nor Thackeray were invariably convincing in their portrayal of the opposite sex, the latter having been described as 'completely inhibited'[39] in the handling of sex and the female. Charlotte's inability, therefore, to achieve a consistent credibility in this area in *The Professor* is less remarkable than are those moments when her hero, Crimsworth, displays a palpable sense of masculinity: as, for example, where he discovers that even when love is dead, sensuality retains an independent power over him, leaving

> an irritating sense of degradation in the very experience of the pleasure. When she stole about me with the soft step of a slave, I felt at once barbarous and sensual as a pasha.[40]

Such passages might incline us to agree with the statement that 'Charlotte had strong masculine components to her personality'.[41] This aspect of her nature was indeed sensed by her chief contemporary critic, George Henry Lewes, who, in an article in the *Edinburgh Review* in January 1850, remarked on the 'over-masculine vigour'[42] of *Jane Eyre* and *Shirley*. The same observation could be made of Emily, of course, even of Anne in certain passages of *The Tenant of Wildfell Hall*, and could well be applied to much of the sinewy intellectualism of George Eliot. This is a characteristic of all four authors which will be explored in the following chapter on The Woman Question, where the validity of the tendency to attribute certain qualities – such, as in this case, creative *energy* – exclusively to the male sex will be challenged. We do not need Charlotte's own statement to the effect that it was 'natural' to her 'to submit, and very unnatural to command'[43] to appreciate that her deepest instincts were predominantly female. These instincts are patently evidenced in the feminine bias of the great love stories that formed her novels, and no less so in a personal life throughout which she showed so clearly her need, as Thackeray discerned, for a 'Tomkins . . . to love her'.[44] But, as will be argued in the following chapter, a certain apparent conflict between the male and female sides of her nature did account for considerable equivocation in her treatment of the sex relation in her work.

Both as a woman, however, and as a novelist, Charlotte's maturity became fully apparent with the publication of *Villette*, her last completed novel, which followed upon her own harrowing experiences of both love and grief. In Lucy Snowe we see for the first time in Charlotte's fiction a heroine capable of distancing herself sufficiently from her own problems to show concern for another being for whom she has no special emotional attachment – in this case the anxious little Paulina Home. There is an astringency in her concern as was the case, with very few exceptions, in Charlotte's real-life attitude to children, but its objectivity strikes a new note in her approach to the major characters of her fiction. Only in *Villette*, too, do we see the Master/Pupil relationship divested at last of those strong elements of adolescent idealism and hero-worship to develop slowly and painfully into a clear-sighted acceptance of life as it is. For the first time, a Charlotte Brontë heroine does not have unreservedly to *admire* before she can love. M. Paul does not have to be apotheosised in verse, as was Crimsworth in *The Professor*, nor 'emasculated' as was Rochester, in *Jane Eyre*, nor 'educated' as was Robert Moore in *Shirley*. He remains consistently egotistical, explosive, opinionated, an infuriating mixture of dominance and tenderness, to the end. Charlotte's challenge to the world, seen in her repeated concepts of Ideal Love, dissolves in *Villette* into a quiet capitulation to reality, just as it was eventually to do in her own life when she accepted her father's curate, Arthur Bell Nicholls, in marriage.

This was the man of whom, five years before, Charlotte had told Ellen Nussey, 'I cannot for my life see those interesting germs of goodness in him you discovered; his narrowness of mind always strikes me chiefly'.[45] But if Nicholls was no Zamorna, the virile Gothic hero of all those wild, passionate stories of her Juvenilia, his dogged persistence and courage in the face of Charlotte's resistance and the Reverend Patrick's almost pathological opposition were amazing. And if Charlotte was not swept off her feet, she was at the last carried a considerable way towards that deep respect and affection which she had long since declared was more important than passion. When the engagement was announced, she told Ellen Nussey:

> I am still very calm. . . . What I taste of happiness is of the soberest order. I trust to love my husband. . . . I believe him to be an affectionate, a conscientious, a high-principled man; and if, with all this, I should yield to regrets, that fine talents, congenial tastes and thoughts are not added, it seems to me I should be most presumptuous and thankless.[46]

As pre-nuptial letters go, it must stand as one of the staidest on record. But, on reflection, it is not difficult to see *why* Charlotte accepted Arthur Nicholls. Alone now in that bleak parsonage, with only an old and infirm father for company and with middle age advancing resolutely upon her, the future must have seemed to her like some grim abyss. Here, at least, was a helpmate. Moreover, he was one who would stand by her in the trust she saw as sacred upon her above all others – the care and support of her father to the end of his days. 'I stipulated that I would not leave Papa',[47] she told Ellen Nussey, and to her old school teacher, Margaret Wooler, she wrote:

> Mr. Nicholls seems deeply to feel the wish to comfort and sustain his declining years. I think – from Mr. N's character – I may depend on this not being a mere transitory, impulsive feeling, but rather that it will be accepted steadily as a duty – and discharged tenderly as an office of affection.[48]

In the event, through the nine months of life that remained to her after her marriage, Charlotte's decision to accept Nicholls was more than vindicated. A month before she died, she wrote again to Ellen Nussey:[49]

> No kinder, better husband than mine, it seems to me, can there be in the world . . . . [15 February 1855]

> . . . I find my husband the tenderest nurse, the kindest support – the best earthly comfort that ever woman had . . . . [21 February 1855]

He was, she said at the end, 'my dear, patient, constant Arthur'.

It was a story more moving, perhaps, than anything she had ever written, for it told of the depths of feeling of which people are capable who, like Nicholls, are no Rochesters or Paul Emanuels, but instead appear, on the surface at least, to be quite ordinary people; it told, too, of the slowly maturing awareness of a woman who at the end became possessed of more, much more, than the 'moderate love' she had been prepared to settle for.

Leslie Stevenson, describing *Wuthering Heights* as a 'terrible and beautiful'[50] story based on an over-mastering love, claimed nevertheless that that love was 'devoid of sexual passion'. It is a view that has been echoed in many quarters – and strenuously countered in as many others. Two opposing schools of thought as to the novel's essential nature emerge; I propose to call them 'the Spiritual' and 'the Sexual'.

It is clear from the outset that any attempt to find possible sources of the fiction in fact, as was possible with Charlotte, will here be of no avail. So far as is known – and there is no internal or external evidence to suggest otherwise – Emily formed no closer human attachments during her brief life than those she felt towards the members of her own family circle. As was indicated in the discussion on her religious attitudes, the impulses of her heart turned inward, and then, increasingly, towards an invisible, spiritually apprehended goal. But it is part of the puzzle that we perceive concerning her that this girl, who seemed to seek no comfort on earth, no husband, no lover, no close companionship, could yet write of these things in her poetry and her novel with such fierce integrity and conviction. Whether this was due to some hidden emotional experience, whether to an equally carefully concealed yearning for such (as in Charlotte), or whether it was all what Leavis has rather unpersuasively described as 'a kind of sport',[51] are questions that will probably never be satisfactorily answered. Indeed, the answer that eludes us could well be formed of an admixture of several, or all, of these factors. Failing answers, all we can do is to try to determine what were the effects that Emily Brontë wished to produce, and from these deduce her motivations as nearly as we can. In this section, *Wuthering Heights* only will be dealt with, because it is felt that it is here, in the human representations lacking in the poetry, that Emily's attitudes to the connection between the emotions and human life are seen at their most true and revealing.

Immediately, we are forced back into the thicket of conflicting opinion, the crux of which, as was outlined above, shifts continually around the question of the novel's spiritual versus sensual intent. One commentator,[52] referring to the 'curiously chaste relations between Cathy and Heathcliff' has written:

unlike most young lovers, they do not kiss and hold hands . . . Emily Brontë does not even hint at such a thing; one feels she would have rejected the idea with disgust. The closest they come to normal sexual contact is when Heathcliff holds her in his arms as she lies dying in bed. The novel is permeated with sexual passion. It crackles in the air like electricity. Yet the thunderstorm never breaks.

The first reaction to this is to wonder whether we have all been reading the same book; for, while the last three sentences are surely true, it is not correct that Heathcliff holds Cathy 'as she lies dying in bed'; throughout the afternoon and early evening that precedes her death in childbirth, Cathy is sitting up in her room in a chair, and remains so during the interlude with Heathcliff.[53] It is also not correct that 'they do not kiss and hold hands'. We are told that 'she put up her hand to clasp his neck and bring her cheek to his, as he held her: while he, in return, covering her with frantic caresses . . . .'[54] Later, he implores, 'Kiss me again . . . .'[55] The further statement – that 'Emily cannot even imagine a sexual relationship between Heathcliff and Isabella without a shudder of disgust; it has to be transformed into bitterness and sadism'[56] – is even stranger. Apart from the fact that it is difficult to see a valid logical connection between an author's omitting to portray an event in fiction and his ability, or otherwise, to imagine such an event, there is the matter of appropriate form. This is dictated by a novel's plot and characterisation, which, in the case of *Wuthering Heights*, and the relationship between Heathcliff and Isabella, clearly requires those very factors to which objection is taken. At this point in the novel, Heathcliff is in full pursuit of the revenge for which he has waited so long. We recall the fifteen-year-old boy, sitting on a stool by the kitchen fire at the Heights, musing with dispassionate concentration upon this very problem. 'I don't care how long I wait',[57] he tells Nelly, 'if I can only do it, at last'. On that occasion, it was Hindley who was the enemy, but, with time, Heathcliff's malice, and his power, extend over both the Earnshaw and Linton families; Isabella Linton falls within its focus, and Heathcliff, in his marriage to her, tastes a satisfaction that is far beyond the power of mere sensuality to afford him. Emily therefore is not here concerned with sensuality; she is concerned with an even more basic element – revenge.

Many commentators, however, failing to find more or less explicit sexual reference in the book have interpreted this as indicating that the main love relationship is therefore meant to be seen as an exercise in spiritual symbolism. One describes it as 'Emily Brontë's way of giving expression to some all-devouring spiritual experience',[58] while another explains the novel's alleged absence of sex to be due to its presumed focus on a non-temporal, non-secular concept of 'paradise lost and paradise regained'.[59] The love between Heathcliff and Cathy, it is argued, is 'never corporeal, just as it is never temporal'. This kind of love, it is claimed, 'precludes sexuality and thereby procreation'.[60] The argument becomes even more muddled by the intervention of what we might call the 'incest lobby' – those who believe that there is sufficient internal evidence in the novel for the theory that Heathcliff was in fact old Earnshaw's natural son.[61] Some who hold this theory see it as an explanation for the *absence* of sexual desire in the two protagonists, while others have concluded it to be the basis of the particularly intense love relation between them; incorporated in the incest argument is also the not wholly unreasonable suggestion that Heathcliff could have consummated his love for his 'sister', and thus become the second Cathy's father.

If anything, the speculations of those who see the novel in terms of a powerful sensuality are even more inventive than those of the 'Spiritual School'. An example is the description of the book as 'a passionate paen to Eros',[62] and others include the presentation of such incidents as Heathcliff's numerous victories in disputes over the entry of various doors and windows as symbols of 'sexual conquest', and the breaking of Hareton's pipe as a deprivation of his 'male sexual force'.

Since Emily Brontë does not make any of these intriguing possibilities manifest beyond a shadow of doubt, the problem remains. The explanation – offered in connection with the incest theme[63] – that she retreated through 'natural shyness', or in the face of contemporary moral taboos, seems barely credible when we recall what she actually did write; this included a passionate five-page love scene between a wife and her long-lost lover (spiritual or otherwise) in her bedroom, with her husband practically at the door.[64] More importantly, one questions the basic validity of arguments that have a dichotomous effect upon the interpretation of a unified work of art. Their implication here is that the love content of *Wuthering Heights* is an either/or situation – that is, either 'sexual' or 'spiritual' – thus excluding the possibility that it could reasonably, and by intent, be both. As indicated in a previous chapter, it is my own view that Emily Brontë was *primarily* concerned to delineate in dramatic form her philosophy concerning the corruption of purity and the conflict between good and evil to which she had given a first tentative expression in her essay, 'The Butterfly'. This is why, in *Wuthering Heights*, the crucial 'sin' is Cathy's, when she returns from the material comforts of Thrushcross Grange and for the first time sees Heathcliff as 'dirty'.[65]

This is the first and major turning-point in the book, a moment of false vision that can never, by either of the pair, be redeemed; it permanently distorts their lives. The second, climactic, turning-point comes at the story's end when the younger Catherine, recognising that the hostility between herself and Hareton arises from her own resistant self-will, openly acknowledges her fault, asks for forgiveness and seals their friendship with a kiss.[66] The Platonist imagery, together with the sense of something supra-human in the mortal conflict of souls between Heathcliff and Cathy, are the elements that give to the book its unmistakable 'spiritual' significance. But Emily was dealing with human beings and with very human emotions, and it should not disappoint the 'spiritual school', even if it does not surprise the 'sexual' school, that, while remaining faithful to her main intent, she renders to the physical body the things that belong to it. It is my own contention that if we look carefully at the factual evidence in the novel, we find that this is precisely what she did.

Taking the three main works of the Brontës and comparing them with the two full-length novels of George Eliot that stand nearest to them in time – that is, *Adam Bede* and *The Mill on the Floss* – a breakdown of the references to physical sexual contact yields the following interesting results: *Wuthering Heights* – 9 references (excluding two incidents of childhood and adolescence);[67] *Jane Eyre* – 11 references;[68] *The Tenant of Wildfell Hall* – 11 references;[69] *Adam Bede* – 4 references;[70] *The Mill on the Floss* – 5 references.[71]

From this, it is clear that not only did Emily Brontë equal both her sisters in the presentation of physical demonstrations of love between the sexes, but also that she and they individually considerably exceeded the performance of George Eliot, writing more than a decade later. Furthermore, the extended love scene between Heathcliff and Cathy is considerably more explicit than any of the references in the other books, many of which amount to no more than hand-touching or hair-stroking, or the heroine sitting on her lover's knee.

So why, we may well ask, have so many critics felt the relationship between Heathcliff and Catherine Earnshaw to be categorically 'non-sexual'? What does it lack – or what does it possess – that leads to so strong a conviction? It cannot be denied that the *essence* of this relationship, as conceived within Emily herself, is metaphysical: that she is concerned paramountly with an exploration of the universal significance of love and hate, of the effects of 'giving' and 'taking' on human destinies. Equally, however, it is surely an ineluctable fact that running alongside this metaphysical view is a continuous thread of raw, dynamic *force*, or *energy*, that is extremely physical and that at times speaks with as true a voice of physical, sensual passion as it was possible for any English novel to portray in the mid-nineteenth century. Beside it, even the electricity that flows between Rochester and Jane Eyre seems static, and the deliberately controlled langour of the crisis of the Maggie Tulliver/Stephen Guest relationship in George Eliot's *The Mill on the Floss* becomes almost soporific. From Heathcliff and Cathy emanates a sensual vitality so palpable that it creates in us a continual expectancy of climax. But the only climax, if we can call it that, is of the violent physical frustration of Heathcliff at Cathy's grave, and it is to be another eighteen years before the culmination is reached. Then, as Heathcliff nears his own death, something begins to happen which we do not understand. Heathcliff changes. After nights spent out on the moors alone, he tells Nelly Dean of strange experiences, of a growing belief that he is no longer alone, of the approach of an indescribable joy.[72] All his protracted bitterness is forgotten; a mysterious excitement takes possession of him; it is as though he knows something that we do not know. And Emily Brontë does not tell us what this is precisely. To the end of the book, the meaning of these events remains obscure. All we know is that Heathcliff dies exultant, and that afterwards there are mysterious stories of a ghostly couple seen together on the moor.

Thus, what we are left with is a sense of two separate and valid impressions in unresolved isolation – on the one hand, the novel's intrinsic sexual force, and, on the other, its persistent metaphysical tone, which seems finally to emerge as the dominant factor. It is, I believe, this deliberate separation on Emily Brontë's part of the story's natural and supernatural elements that provokes the division of critical opinion on the book's treatment of love. Arguably, it might be concluded that neither view is wholly right nor wholly wrong, but that each is limited by its exclusive focus. Perhaps we can reasonably and satisfactorily infer that, via the inherent conflict between body and soul, matter and spirit, with which she had long been preoccupied, Emily Brontë was here giving expression to her deepest apprehensions of the human experience, as well as to her Platonist philosophy about life's cosmic significance overall.

Apropos of these various speculations, we are reminded of the truth of Charlotte's famous words about her sister: 'an interpreter ought always to have stood between her and the world'.[73] It is an unfortunate aspect of interpretation that, given enough time, it can become an imaginative literature all its own.

Happily, in the case of Anne Brontë no such interpretation is required: or, rather, those interpretations of her impulses and motivations that we have serve us nothing like as well as the explanation provided by Anne herself.

Of the three sisters, Anne was the least concerned to write a 'love story' as such. Her essential concern, in fact, was not love, but 'truth'.[74] In her Preface to the second edition of *The Tenant of Wildfell Hall* she declared her motives with engaging unequivocation; they were not, she said, to 'amuse the Reader', nor to 'gratify' her 'own taste', nor yet to 'ingratiate' herself with the Press and Public, but were 'to tell the truth'. The book, we are further told, was written not to entertain but to warn, not to edify, but to expose the true nature of 'vice and vicious characters', drawn from a direct and personal experience of the fact that 'such characters do exist'. It is therefore clearly reasonable to deduce that the dissolute lives that occupy a large portion of the novel derive from true-life models encountered by Anne during her duties as a governess, as well, of course, as from the unique knowledge that was hers of her own brother's behaviour at Thorp Green Hall in the summer of 1845. This it was, we recall, that had prompted the reference in her Diary to some 'unpleasant and undreamt-of experience',[75] and bearing these words in mind the message of the 1848 Preface to *The Tenant* takes on a special significance. The basic cause of so much 'sin and misery',[76] she declared, was society's propensity towards 'delicate concealment of facts', and for 'whispering "Peace, peace", where there is no peace', leaving the young to acquire their 'bitter knowledge' of the 'snares and pitfalls' of life 'from experience'. Similar overtones of personal knowledge are heard in Helen Huntingdon's impassioned speech on the need for wider and more equal teaching of the young of both sexes:

> I would not send a poor girl into the world unarmed against her foes, and ignorant of the snares that beset her path; nor would I watch and guard her, till, deprived of self-respect and self-reliance, she lost the power or the will, to watch and guard

herself; – and as for my son – if I thought he would grow up to be what you call a man of the world – one that has '*seen life*', and glories in his experience, even though he should so far profit by it, as to sober down, at length, into a useful and respected member of society – I would rather that he died tomorrow! – rather a thousand times!'[77]

Anne's own emotional life is, like Emily's, a matter on which we can only speculate. Her relations with her father's personable young curate, William Weightman, who arrived in Haworth in August 1839, is a Brontë riddle almost as much disputed as that of Charlotte's feelings for M. Heger. Weightman has been variously and confidently described as 'the man she loved'[78] and the 'Mr. Weston in *Agnes Grey*'.[79] According to Charlotte, 'Celia Amelia', as she dubbed Weightman, was also attracted to Anne. To Ellen Nussey, she reported:

He sits opposite to Anne at church sighing softly and looking out of the corners of his eyes to win her attention – and Anne is so quiet, her look so downcast – they are a picture.[80]

What we do *not* have – apart from some undesignated love poems – is any material evidence that establishes beyond a doubt that Anne's affections for him went significantly deeper than did those of the other members of the Brontë family. Winifred Gérin appears to have relied entirely for her interpretation of the affair upon the almost literal correlation of fact and feeling which she believes exists between the novel, *Agnes Grey*, and its author. That the novel *was* autobiographical is plainly evident, both from the nature of its inception as *Passages in the Life of an Individual*[81] and from the relation of events to those in Anne's own life. But authors of fiction do not write on oath; no threat of contempt of court waits upon every comma. However sincere the expressed intent to tell the truth and nothing but the truth, the creative writer will for the most part as instinctively and tenaciously evade total self-exposure as the individual in the dock. Anne could say with all honesty of *The Tenant of Wildfell Hall* that she had told only of those things which she had seen *for* herself, but this affords us no guarantee that either in that novel or in *Agnes Grey* she had told us what was true *of* herself. If Mr Weston was indeed modelled on Willie Weightman, then *Agnes Grey*'s happy ending has a tragic irony, for Weightman never declared himself to Anne, and in 1842, at the age of twenty-eight, and while she was away at Thorp Green, he contracted cholera and died. He was deeply mourned by all the Brontës, especially the Reverend Patrick, who had looked on him almost as a son, and by Branwell, whom he had befriended and helped possibly more than had any other human being outside the immediate family. Afterwards, Anne wrote several mournful poems of love, including the following, dated two years after Willie Weightman's death:

> Yes, thou art gone! and never more
> Thy sunny smile shall gladden me;
> But I may pass the old church door
> And pace the floor that covers thee.
>
> May stand upon the cold, damp stone
> And think that, frozen, lies below
> The lightest heart that I have known,
> The kindest I shall ever know.[82]

The words and sentiments are suggestive, but, as has been pointed out, even more love poems were written by Emily, 'for whom attempts to find a lover have been singularly unsuccessful'.[83] Despite this, *Agnes Grey* provides us with Anne Brontë's first clear early warning of an attitude to love and marriage that was to be far from conventionally romantic. Here, in a novel of deceptive gentleness, was foreshadowed the unequivocal condemnation of the marriage of social convenience that was to appear, a year later, in *The Tenant of Wildfell Hall*.

With *The Tenant*, Anne stepped entirely outside the area of personal involvement into a realm known to her only by bitter and anguished observation. As well as being a cry of protest against the social conventions of the time which allowed young people to grow up in ignorance of the dangers into which a false step could lead them, it was also about inequalities between the sexes, in education and in marriage, and about a whole spectrum of false standards passed down by one generation to the next. Most shocking of all to certain of its contemporary readers was the book's views on marriage. At a time when husbands quite literally – and legally – had complete control over the affairs of the home, including their wives and children, here was a novel in which a wife not only bars her bedroom door against her husband but also finally, after fighting him over the upbringing of her child, walks out on him, taking the child with her in defiance of the very laws of the land.[84] Moreover, this astonishingly modern heroine then proceeds to earn her living not as a governess, or a housekeeper, but as an *artist*.

Paramountly, however, Helen Huntingdon is not a feminist figure. This aspect is only a secondary feature of her battle with her husband; primarily, her struggle is a moral one. She opposes Huntingdon not because his masculine standards inhibit or frustrate her, but because his immorality threatens her and threatens the future of her child. And in opposing him she challenges the whole society of which he is a part, a society in which marriages are contracted for gain and in which amusement is a euphemism for dissipation of all kinds. It was a society of which Anne Brontë had seen much during her long, lonely years away from home.

One of the greatest achievements of *The Tenant of Wildfell Hall* is the complete credibility of the evolutionary process which we observe in Helen Huntingdon's emotional experience. We see her change from a normal, high-spirited girl in love with her husband, through all the stages of sickening disillusionment, to the final acceptance of reality and the knowledge that her love has turned to hate. The contrast between this unflinching acceptance of the truth and the conventional feminine attitude, as represented by Helen's friend, Milicent Hargrave, is portrayed with beautiful irony in the letter which the latter sends to Helen:

> I hardly know what to say . . . or what to think . . . . . If I *am* to be Mr Hattersley's wife, I must try to love him; and I do try with all my might; but I have made very little progress yet . . . . . 'Then why have you accepted him?' you will ask; and I didn't know I had accepted him; but mamma tells me I have, and he seems to think so too. . . . mamma is so delighted with the idea of the match; she thinks she has managed so well for me; and I cannot bear to disappoint her. . . . Mr Hattersley, you know, is the son of a rich banker . . . . he is so diametrically opposite to what I imagined my husband should be.[85]

Utterly ruthless, too, is the book's portrayal of sexual double standards. Faced with Helen's knowledge of his infidelity, Huntingdon attempts to establish a special case for the male versus the female:

It is a woman's nature to be constant – to love one and one only, blindly, tenderly, and for ever . . . but you must have some commiseration for us, Helen; you must give us a little more licence . . . .[86]

She does – until, driven to the point at which self-respect rebels, she becomes the first heroine in an English novel to set, by implication, a whole new ethic of equality in sexual behaviour.

Perhaps only now, after nearly half a century's revolution of attitudes towards sexual relationships, is it possible for us to see Anne Brontë's work in true focus. A. Craig Bell,[87] in the spirit of George Moore, has described *The Tenant of Wildfell Hall* as a 'masterpiece', compared with which, he writes, 'the novels of George Eliot, Dickens, Thackeray, Trollope and the rest of their contemporaries, are sexless and wooden'. We may find so summary a dismissal impossible to accept, but the tribute to Anne Brontë's boldness remains a valid one. Over fifty years before Hardy, and nearly eighty years before Lawrence, she offers us a picture of a woman as a complete and independent entity, and she takes the tradition of the Byronic Hero and turns it on its head.

There is an interesting contrast between George Eliot's own emotional life and her treatment of personal relations in her novels. We do not link George Eliot with the great Love Story, as we do Charlotte Brontë, or even Emily. In a George Eliot novel, the love relationship is only a part of a whole which reflects aspects of human interrelation in essentially social terms. Thus, in *Adam Bede*, we have the love of Adam for Hetty and that of Hetty for Donnithorne, and of Seth for Dinah Morris, all forming segments of a community in organic interaction. In their different ways, the same is true of *Middlemarch, Felix Holt, Romola* and *Daniel Deronda*. The nearest we come to a truly dominant love theme is in *The Mill on the Floss*, and here it is problematic whether the central love is not that of a sister for a brother. But if George Eliot's primary interest as a novelist was in the group rather than the pair-bond, we find, by contrast, that in her own life she showed a marked tendency to form close and extremely dependent relationships, often of an unfortunate kind. All these attachments have already been mentioned. The earliest, to her strict Evangelical school-teacher, Maria Lewis, is perhaps the most readily understood, because, like Charlotte Brontë's to M.

Heger, it falls into the time-honoured Master/Pupil tradition; also, it occurred when George Eliot was at an age when the impulse to find some religious or political crusade to which to nail one's colours is an almost mandatory part of the growing-up process. The subsequent attachments – to Bray, Spencer, Brabant, Chapman, even Lewes himself – might similarly be seen as logical and appropriate stages along her intellectual journey from conformity through rebellion to full intellectual and spiritual emancipation. The factor that makes them somewhat singular is their intensity, which in some cases seems to have been almost pathological. Long before we meet George Henry Lewes, we arrive at the conclusion that for George Eliot to meet and work with a man of any intellectual capacity approaching her own was for her to become emotionally involved. The entire pre-Lewes course of her life seems to have been a continuous search for that 'some one person', described by Cross, 'who should be all in all to her'. Having at last found him in Lewes, it is as though she came temporarily to rest, and was thus able to turn out from herself and, for the first time, see the wider world as something with a validity of its own, and not merely as an extension of her own troubled psyche. The word 'temporarily' may seem an inappropriate description of a period of emotional and intellectual union that lasted a quarter of a century. But the collapse into emotional insecurity that immediately followed upon Lewes's death seems powerfully familiar. This collapse, resulting in the marriage of a sixty-year-old woman to a man of forty, would seem to justify the suspicion that there remained unresolved problems within George Eliot's psychological constitution that possibly no one human being could ever cure. Redinger has described the Eliot/Lewes union as a true 'marriage', though without, she says, 'great passion. Each had given that to someone else; their basic relationship was comradely, a sharing of interests, joys and tribulations'.[88] Presumably, the 'someone else', in George Eliot's case was meant to be John Chapman, almost certainly the closest of her early relationships, though just how close this was is uncertain. All that we can assume with absolute confidence is that, within the restrictions of their circumstances, George Henry Lewes was, in her own words, 'the Husband whose perfect Love has been the best source of her insight & strength . . . .'[89] The suggestion has been made that, after he died, Lewes was discovered by George Eliot to have been unfaithful to her,[90] and that this accounted for her 'astonishingly quick' decision to marry Cross, but again a dearth of conclusive evidence argues for caution. Remarkable as this marriage was, we have to place it into the perspective of a life which from the very beginning is seen to have been dominated by feelings of psychological inadequacy. As an act of self-protection, therefore, it is all of a piece with an already familiar pattern. We might surmise that the self-imposed estrangement from her early, deeply-held religious faith – and thus from her family – had something to do with this, causing the long succession of dependencies upon 'lover-substitute' figures, all of whom, in one way or another, failed her. In dying, Lewes failed her, too, and after he had gone it seems that the darkness of isolation returned and could not be borne. Only one 'lover-substitute' now remained: John Cross, the friend whom she and Lewes had called their 'nephew'.[91] In the letter she wrote to him five months after Lewes's death the note of panic is unmistakable:

Dearest N.

I am in dreadful need of your counsel. Pray come to me when you can – morning, afternoon, or evening. I shall dismiss anyone else.

You will probably not get this till the Greek Kalends, for I never know where you are. If I address you at Cornhill, you will be at the club, if I address you at the club, you will be at Weybridge, and if I address you there you will be gone on a distant visit.

Your much worried
Aunt.[92]

Implied here is the suggestion that Cross was avoiding a commitment which he sensed to be closing in upon him. But Cross, too, had recently suffered a deep personal loss – his mother had died ten days after Lewes; it is therefore perhaps not so surprising that, less than sixteen months after this double tragedy, he and George Eliot were married. No satisfactory explanation has ever been offered as to why, during the honeymoon in Venice, Cross apparently attempted suicide by jumping into the Grand Canal.[93] Did this man, whose most intimate contacts with the female sex appear up until then to have been those of a son and a brother, find marriage to a woman as intense as George Eliot too disturbing? Her emotional needs had always been greater than those of many women; probably at no time had they been greater than at this particular moment.

This brings us to another aspect of George Eliot's nature that has to be looked at in this context, although I would not wish to overstate it. More than one critic has remarked on a certain sexual ambivalence to be noted in her personality. Ruby Redinger,[94] for example, writes: 'Where [she may have felt] in the great family of man–woman did she belong?', emphasising that it was not until 1920 that Virginia Woolf could write of the dilemma experienced by everyone at some time or other of the awareness of the other sex within them. George Eliot, claims Redinger, although undoubtedly essentially feminine, was also powerfully man-like, which, she argues, accounted for the tendency shown in Cross and others to over-emphasise her femininity. It would perhaps also account for her own nervous insistence (to her passionate friend, Edith Simcox) that she had 'never in her life cared very much for women'.[95] Miss Simcox's embarrassing attentions rendered the untruth forgivable, but untruth it was, for in 1843 George Eliot was addressing her friend, Sara Hennell as 'Beloved Spouse'[96] and writing to her in 1849 in the following terms:

> Dear love
>
> I have given you a sad excuse for flirtation but I have not been beyond seas long enough to make it lawful for you to take a new husband – therefore I come back to you with all a husband's privileges and command you to love me . . . . I sometimes talk to you in my soul as lovingly as Solomon's Song.[97]

The fact is that, whether she wished it or not, a powerfully magnetic attraction existed between George Eliot and members of her own sex. In addition to the deep, long-standing friendships with such as the Hennell sisters, Barbara Leigh Smith (Mme Bodichon) and Bessie Rayner Smith (Mme Belloc), fame brought her a wide circle of doting 'daughters', who turned to her for varying degrees of affection and inspiration. Among the more importunate ones were those who suffered from what Marghanita Laski has described as 'a lack of normal emotional satisfaction',[98] of whom Elma Steuart and Edith Simcox led the field. From the security of her union with Lewes, George Eliot returned these compliments with a carefully measured graciousness; and in *Felix Holt* we find her defending such attachments: 'Surely every young woman has something of a daughter's feelings towards an older one who has been kind to her'.[99] Only in the case of the extraordinarily gifted Edith Simcox did she appear to show any resistance, but this was understandable perhaps in the light of Miss Simcox's frequent and embarrassing indulgence in foot-kissing. For the reasons already mentioned, it is difficult for us today to form an unbiased judgement of the situation described here. As Haight warns:

> In reading Edith Simcox's record of her wild passion for George Eliot, we must guard against interpretations that could never have entered the writer's mind . . . . she lived sixty-seven years full of active, useful work without violating the social mores. In reading her private account of George Eliot we should, as Geoffrey Tillotson suggests, allow for the intermingling of fantasy with fact.[100]

As for George Eliot herself, her twenty-five years of apparently ideal union with Lewes speaks for itself; whatever brief trails of emotional commitment may have preceded this, there can be no doubt that this relationship touched the deepest sources of her being and released those creative powers which she subsequently brought to their full potential. As Anna Theresa Kitchell writes:

> of the men who influenced her early years – Charles Bray, Charles Hennell and Herbert Spencer – no one had the special sympathies and special interests which were necessary to start her on her way. George Eliot needed exactly the kind of companionship Lewes offered her.[101]

The implications here are of special interest when we consider the most notable difference between the work of George Eliot and that of the Brontë sisters – that is, the former's presumed greater objectivity in the treatment of human relationships. She is as committed as Charlotte and Anne Brontë to the themes of female independence (as reflected in Dinah Morris, Maggie Tulliver and Dorothea Brooke); and of false standards in marriage (as in the unions of the Casaubons, the Lydgates and the Grandcourts) but her view is detached, because – we might conjecture – no urgent personal need directs it. It has been argued that the ambiguity of her social status inhibited her creative expression.[102] Against this, however, it might equally be argued that if the relationship with Lewes was indeed contributory, as suggested, the conclusion we might draw is that this union, which she herself described as a 'perfect love',[103] lulled into relative quiescence those emotional urgencies which, by contrast, gave to Charlotte Brontë's art its peculiar force. For, often, in her handling of the sexual relationship, George Eliot adopted a procedure which was the reverse of that seen in Charlotte Brontë, whose language, as noted above, often carried a boldness not reflected in actual events. For whatever reason – perhaps more personal than objective – George Eliot tended to use language that was implicative and analogous rather than clear and direct. Barbara Hardy has argued, for example, that in *The Mill on the Floss* 'the sexual implications of Maggie's relationship with Philip Wakem would have been more moving and incisive if they had gone beyond hints and implications'.[104] In *Adam Bede*, where Hardy finds 'the sexual *lacunae*' even more noticeable, she suggests that the odd lack of sexual detail between the two otherwise excellently drawn characters of Hetty and Donnithorne 'seems to be the product of omission rather than of reticence'; and it will not do, she adds, 'to excuse the omissions on the ground that they are conventional or historically necessary. Hetty and Arthur are not a shadowy idyllic couple . . . . And Arthur is by no means a hero without sexuality.'

On the other hand, it must be conceded that, in George Eliot's hands, hints and implications are often extremely effective. The sequences in the wood between Donnithorne and Hetty powerfully convey the couple's physical attraction to each other,[105] while Donnithorne's essential sexuality is graphically emphasised in the sensual imagery connecting him with his favourite mare, Meg.[106] 'Horse imagery' appears to even more compelling effect in *Deronda*, this time to transmit two very different kinds of sexual significance. First, in the courtship of Gwendolen Harleth by her cousin, Rex Gascoigne, the young man's inadequacies as a lover are unmistakably adumbrated in the challenging ride that ends in his fall from his horse.[107] Second, in the Gwendolen/Grandcourt courtship sequences, the horse becomes the symbol of a relationship in which hints of sexual command and mastery alternate between the pair; here, too, is a repetition of that powerfully sensual combination of tension and langour that so markedly stamped the Maggie Tulliver/Stephen Guest climactic river journey in *The Mill on the Floss*.

By contrast, the reticence with which George Eliot deals with the Casaubon marriage in *Middlemarch* is the more striking. It has been pointed out that this reticence 'is compatible with a truthful and complete account of what it was like for Dorothea to be married to Casaubon, and what it was like for Casaubon to be married to

Dorothea';[108] at the same time, 'if we compare it with contemporary novels in France and Russia, it leaves out a lot'. Among these omissions, of course, is the possibility of Casaubon's impotence, but in this the novel is hardly different from any other English novel of its time. On the other hand, *Middlemarch* appeared more than twenty years after the main Brontë novels; therefore, we might perhaps have expected comparisons between the sisters and George Eliot in this respect to yield a greater degree of development in the treatment of sexual themes than is in fact the case. For a possible explanation, we again have to return to the peculiar circumstances of George Eliot's private life. The pressures upon her to counter the social stigma of her liaison with Lewes cannot be overlooked when we examine her methods of dealing with matters so intimately connected with her own life. By the nature of that life, she was, as an author, infinitely more vulnerable *vis-à-vis* her readers than were the Brontës with theirs. We should not forget either that, to the extent that she does deal with the objective facts of sexuality, she does so without the special pleading that we see, for example, in Charlotte Brontë's *Jane Eyre*, where Rochester's *roué* life is partly mitigated because his wife is not only insane but *immoral*. For George Eliot, the task was to confront the realities of seduction, adultery, pregnancy – even, in certain cases, murder – with compassion, but without excuse or dissimulation. At a deeper level, of course, this too might be interpreted as a very subtle form of special pleading – that is, that we should be tolerant and understanding of imperfect lives. The fact is that the more we look at an author's methods simultaneously with a study of his or her life, the more difficult it becomes to distinguish in any precise way between the objective and the personal.

One of the facts to emerge most clearly from an examination of the attitudes of all four novelists in this area is that of the dangers inherent in any attempt to 'periodise' literature for the sake of categorisation. The notion, for example, of the Brontës as belonging, as a 'family', to the Romantic Tradition, and of George Eliot as representing a new standard of 'maturity' in Victorian fiction, are both concepts that have been given an airing,[109] but can be seen to be as slippery as the implication upon which they are based, that there exists some evolutionary type of movement between them. Nor is it only *Emily* Brontë who upsets the convenient evolutionary picture. Anne Brontë's readiness to grapple with awkward social realities reveals her as defying not only the literary and social conventions of her time but also any efforts of posterity to detect an 'upward' movement in literary realism between these two so very different creative forms. While it is true to say that George Eliot exceeded Anne Brontë in the variety of subjects dealt with, it is equally obvious that this is a distinction that we can never be sure that Anne would not have disposed of given the greater generosity of time.

On the whole, more than any marked movement between the four, the most notable and significant factor is seen to be something which they share – that is, a passionate personal conviction of the importance of the *quality* of human relationships. In the realms of the emotions, especially those connected with love and sexuality – in courtship, marriage, child rearing, the family – it is feeling, rather than form, that dictates both the movement of events and the method of presentation. As I shall later pinpoint more closely, the traditions of both Romanticism *and* Realism uniquely merge in this particular group of writers.

5

The Woman Question

'Life has taken on a new unloveliness', wrote Mrs Roy Devereux in 1895, 'and the least beautiful thing therein is the New Woman'.[1] She was talking in, and about, an age in which 'the Girton Girl and the Lady Doctor became recognized sub-groups'[2] of a new feminine species, among whom matters such as 'venereal disease, contraception, divorce and adultery were made the common talking points'.[3] The enormity of the change, and of the shock it produced is best appreciated when we recall that little more than thirty years had elapsed since John Stuart Mill had published his pungent criticism of a society that not only tolerated but even insisted upon such invidious distinctions between the sexes that turned women into virtual slaves. The female sex, said Mill, was brought up to believe that its 'ideal of character'[4] was the very opposite to that of men's, 'not self-will, and government by self-control, but submission, and yielding to the control of others. All the moralities tell them that it is the duty of women, and all the current sentimentalities that it is their nature, to live for others; to make complete abnegation of themselves, and to have no life but in their affections'.[5]

Given, then, that those thirty years clearly constituted something of a watershed for the 'women's movement', it might seem remarkable that such advances as had been made had taken so long, even among women themselves, to be accepted. Reasons for this, however, are not hard to find. The years that followed the publication of Mary Wollstonecraft's historic treatise, *A Vindication of the Rights of Woman* (1792), were years of general revolution, of a great and widespread social movement. It is hardly to be wondered at that in this wholesale revolutionary struggle, succeeded by the Napoleonic wars, the specific complaints of women were lost in the general birth throes of the Common Man. Nearer home, at the very moment that the Brontë sisters and George Eliot were growing from childhood into adolescence, much of English society was experiencing both the vast repercussions of industrial change and a widespread political and social reaction to the horrors of revolutionary fanaticism. It was a time for cohesion, not division, for national and general causes, not individual and specific ones.

Apart, however, from these practical reasons for the diffidence of women towards the projection of their own social needs, there were the natural fears of a weak minority in the face of a brutally strong majority and the mesmeric influence of long years of social conditioning. So set was the social ethos that even those changes that did take place tended to reinforce discriminatory attitudes. As Françoise Basch explains,[6] the abandonment towards the end of the nineteenth century of the old Pauline conception of the tempting and sinful woman was followed by the notion of women's 'natural' inferiority – that is, their inherent incapacity for intellectual exercise. This in turn led to the idea of what Tennyson was to term 'distinctive womanhood',[7] a notion of woman as having a distinct nature and function, usually of an unnaturally elevated kind, so that from being some sort of moral 'will-o'-the-wisp' she now became a kind of female 'light of the world'. When all is said and done, the fact is that during the period in which the Brontë sisters and George Eliot were growing up, and on to the end of the century, the life of woman, be she Saint or Sinner, Vegetable or Virgin Mary, had possibly never before been more codified and restricted in Western culture.

It cannot thus be surprising that even the best of our women novelists were less vocal on the subject of the Woman Question than might have been expected. In recent times, there has been a tendency for both Charlotte Brontë and George Eliot to be taken to task for failing to confront the problem more explicitly,[8] but such criticism takes little account of the enormous psychological pressures on those women for whom the vocation of authorship meant a more than usual exposure to social scrutiny. The use which the Brontë sisters and George Eliot in particular made of the male pseudonym is evidence in itself of the need felt for protection from the invidious effects of such exposure. For the Brontë sisters, Charlotte explained the position thus:

Averse to personal publicity, we veiled our own names under those of Currer, Ellis and Acton Bell; the ambiguous choice being dictated by a sort of conscientious scruple at assuming Christian names, positively masculine, while we did not like to declare ourselves women, because – without at that time suspecting that our mode of writing and thinking was not what is called 'feminine' – we had a vague impression that authoresses are liable to be looked on with prejudice. . . .[9]

The decision was not without a certain ambivalence in effect. Introducing herself to Harriet Martineau in November 1849, Charlotte wrote: 'Currer Bell offers a copy of "Shirley" to Miss Martineau's acceptance, in acknowledgement of the pleasure and profit ~~she~~ [sic] he has derived from her works . . . .'[10] By leaving visible the deleted word 'she', Charlotte drew Miss Martineau's attention to the truth about her, possibly in the hope that Harriet Martineau, as a fellow female, would accord her the sympathetic response denied to her by Southey in 1837.[11] Miss Martineau was intrigued. 'I now addressed my reply,' she records, 'externally to "Currer Bell Esq." and began it "Madam"'.[12]

To G. H. Lewes, Charlotte was more emphatic: 'I wish all reviewers believed "Currer Bell" to be a man', she wrote: 'they would be more just to him. You will, I know, keep measuring me by some standards of what you deem becoming to my sex; where I am not what you consider graceful, you will condemn me'.[13] And when Lewes's review of *Shirley* in the January 1850 issue of the *Edinburgh Review* proved her correct, she told him: 'I can be on guard against my enemies, but God deliver me from my friends!'[14]

For George Eliot, concealment was doubly important. Writing to Charles Bray in 1853,[15] she asked him not to reveal that she was the author of an article on 'Evangelical Teaching' in the *Westminster Review*, because, she wrote, 'the article appears to have produced a strong impression, and that impression would be a little counteracted if the author were known to be a *woman*'. In addition to the fear of sex-discrimination, there was also the urgent need to protect herself against society in her relationship with Lewes. 'Whatever may be the success of my stories', she wrote, 'I shall be resolute in preserving my incognito, having observed that a *nom de plume* secures all the advantages without the disagreeables of reputation'.[16]

Such ploys, however, reveal how weak was nineteenth-century feminism, even among the most aware and articulate of women. As Basch points out,[17] such open and acknowledged feminists as Harriet Martineau, Anna Jameson, Barbara Bodichon and Mrs Hugo Reid 'only very rarely and incompletely called the old idea into question'. She adds: 'The political and sexual dimension of female emancipation could only be asserted as a consequence of a general liberalisation which had hardly started before 1870'. Indeed, brilliant and vital as much of the nineteenth century now seems to us, it will not go down in history as one of generosity to women.

To what extent feminine frustration accounted for the proliferation of women authors at this time is an interesting question. 'Innumerable Victorian women,' writes J. A. Sutherland,[18] 'hoped to emulate Charlotte Brontë and write themselves out of the restrictions which the age imposed on their sex.' Starting with the eldest of the Brontës, then, how much was Charlotte's own career as a novelist due to this same psychological compulsion? We know that she longed for what she called 'a stake in life',[19] for some call to action and a sense of purpose to her being. 'Haworth seems such a lonely, quiet spot, buried away from the world', she wrote to Ellen Nussey in January 1844, adding:

> something in me, which used to be enthusiasm, is tamed down and broken. . . . I shall soon be twenty-eight; and it seems as if I ought to be working and braving the rough realities of the world, as other people do. It is, however, my duty to restrain this feeling at present, and I will endeavour to do so.

Her 'duty' at this time, as she saw it, was to remain with her father, then losing his sight from cataract, and bereft of both Branwell and Anne, away at Thorp Green. It was a situation typical of the pattern of life for the Brontë sisters once the close companionship of childhood was behind them. Loneliness, family anguish – caused by Branwell's disgrace – finally, the successive tragedies of illness and death. But as early as 1836 there is evidence that Charlotte's frustrations stemmed in the first place more from a repressive *ennui* than actual adversity. On 29 December she wrote to Southey,[20] enclosing some of her poems, clearly hoping for some encouragement, but all she got – three months later – was his famous rebuke that 'literature cannot be the business of a woman's life, and it ought not to be'. Her reply was eloquent of that agonising conflict of woman between submission and rebellion which was to be the burden of Charlotte's life and work until she died:

> I never trouble anyone else with my thoughts. I carefully avoid any appearance of preoccupation and eccentricity, which might lead those I live amongst to suspect the nature of my pursuits . . . . I have endeavoured not only attentively to observe

all the duties a woman ought to fulfil, but to feel deeply interested in them . . . sometimes when I'm teaching or sewing I would rather be reading or writing; but I try to deny myself; and my father's approbation amply rewarded me for the privation.[21]

But Charlotte was tougher than such propitiation suggested, and her concern was not only for herself but also for her sisters. 'I want us *all* to go on', she wrote in 1841[22] to Aunt Branwell from Upperwood House, Rawdon, where she was governess to the White children. 'I know we have talents, and I want them to be turned to account.' The work of governessing was something she had told Ellen Nussey 'I *hate* and *abhor'.*[23] But in the event, the promise of the Brussels adventure, when it came the following year, brought only sadness and disillusionment, and now the 'duty' to her ailing father over-rode all personal considerations. Mary Taylor recorded her impressions of that time:

When I last saw Charlotte [February 1845] she told me she had quite decided to stay at home. She owned she did not like it . . . she thought that there must be some possibilty for some people of having a life of more variety and more communion with human kind, but she saw none for her. . . . Such a dark shadow came over her face when I said, 'Think of what you'll be five years hence!' that I stopped, and said, 'Don't cry, Charlotte!' She did not cry, but went on walking up and down the room, and said in a little while, 'But I intend to stay, Polly.'[24]

Just what her decision cost her is revealed in the very first letter she wrote to Mary after that meeting:

I can hardly tell you how time gets on here at Haworth . . . one day resembles another – and all have heavy, lifeless physiognomies – Sunday – baking day and Saturday are the only ones that bear the slightest distinctive mark . . . . I shall soon be 30 – and I have done nothing yet . . . . There was a time when Haworth was a very pleasant place to me, it is not so now . . . .[25]

If, then, Charlotte Brontë 'failed' her sex, it must be said in her defence that what she most lacked was not the courage to *do* something but an apprehension of what, if anything, it was *possible* to do. She agreed with the more liberal-minded among men who argued that the condition of women depended upon themselves, but she felt that there were 'evils – deep-rooted in the foundations of the social system – which no efforts of ours can touch . . . .'[26] Of these, she wrote to Mrs Gaskell, 'it is advisable not too often to think'.

It was a perplexity that, unknowingly, she shared with George Eliot, as also she did her fear of the 'hardening' effect on women that the more overt kind of feminist challenge might have. Writing again to Mrs Gaskell in September 1851, she referred to an article in the *Westminster Review* which she mistakenly attributed to J. S. Mill:

> When I first read the paper, I thought it was the work of a powerful, clear-headed woman, who had a hard, jealous heart, and nerves of bend leather; of a woman who longed for power, and had never felt affection . . . . I believe J. S. Mill would make a hard, dry, dismal world of it; and yet he speaks admirable sense . . . especially when he says that if there be a natural unfitness in women for men's employment there is no need to make laws on the subject; leave all careers open; let them try; those who ought to succeed will succeed, or, at least, will have a fair chance; the incapable will fall back into their rightful place . . . .[27]

From this, it seems clear that Charlotte had no argument with the principles of feminism. Her doubts concerned its practice. The emphasis on 'affection' also raises the question as to whether her own lifelong sense of futility might have been considerably appeased if what Mrs Gaskell had called 'woman's principal work'[28] had meant for her what it had meant for Elizabeth Gaskell – marriage and the bringing up of four energetic little daughters. To W. S. Williams, Charlotte wrote:

> When a woman has a little family to rear and educate and a household to conduct, her hands are full, her vocation is evident; when her destiny isolates her, I suppose she must do what she can, live as she can, complain as little, bear as much, work as well as possible.[29]

The echoes of the age-old female response are very clear, as is the life-denying sense of limitation that lay at its root. The times were still too young for women properly to judge how they might most effectively make the compromise between the conflicting worlds of

'affection' and achievement, self-denial and self-expression; and
Charlotte Brontë was a woman of her times. As things were, her
'destiny' isolated her without her 'vocation' being at all evident.
And yet, unfortunate as this was in the personal sense, there were
for the Brontës, as Lord David Cecil has pointed out, important
literary compensations.

> Their feminine limitations kept their eyes close to first-hand
> experience, which means close to life. Their area of vision may be
> narrower than that of a man but it is more certainly the area of
> reality.[30]

These limitations, too, engendered in all the Brontës, but most
articulately in Charlotte, a view of art as asexual, or androgynous,
and the role of the author as rather like that of the Renaissance
painter – that is, as truth-tellers with special, enhancing powers. In
defence of the right this gave her to be judged without reference to
her sex Charlotte could be fiercely outspoken. Writing to W. S.
Williams about the reception by various critics of *Jane Eyre*, she
stated: 'To such critics I would say, "To you I am neither man nor
woman – I come before you as an author only. It is the sole standard
by which you have a right to judge me – the sole ground on which I
accept your judgment.'[31] Even in private and personal life, she
believed that there should be a sexual 'no-man's land', where male
and female could interrelate free of sexual connotation, and she
resented deeply the constraints which social convention placed
upon women in this respect. In a letter to Ellen Nussey in 1845 her
words held a bitter edge:

> If women wish to escape the stigma of husband-seeking they
> must act and look like marble or clay – cold – expressionless,
> bloodless – for every appearance of feeling, of joy – sorrow –
> friendliness, antipathy, admiration – disgust are alike construed
> by the world into an attempt to hook a husband . . . .

It was part of the passionate plea for the freer expression of human
feeling that was to become the dominating continuum of her work.
The bitterness increased as she adjured Ellen to be true to her own
nature:

> do not too harshly repress sentiments and feelings excellent in

themselves because you fear that some puppy may fancy that you are letting them come out to fascinate him – do not condemn yourself to live only by halves because if you showed too much animation some pragmatical thing in breeches . . . might take it into its pate to imagine that you designed to dedicate your precious life to its inanity . . . .[32]

If the sexual hostility here surprises us, we do not have far to seek for the explanation, nor do we have to be trained psychologists to understand it. The date of the letter gives us the clue. This was the beginning of the second year of Charlotte's return from Brussels, and the beginning of her slow, agonising realisation that the friendship with M. Heger, in which she had felt so secure, was in fact a delusion. Whatever the truth of the matter, the only explanation of her own naiveté that she was prepared to accept was that she had been betrayed by the conventions of a society that forced people to accept crude standards of thought and action; such conduct, she believed, misinterpreted, and thus inhibited, natural feeling and drove people apart. It is tempting to see *all* Charlotte's sexual equivocation as stemming from this source: from the mixture of adoration and resentment that had slowly and bitterly consumed her during these two years. But this sexual dichotomy had been present in Charlotte long before she met Heger. The pattern of alternating domination and submission had been a significant feature of the erotic adventures of the Juvenilia. It was indeed a basic component of her personality. The womanly, managing, love-hungry little busybody that was Charlotte Brontë had also a tough, 'masculine', surviving streak in her – very similar to that detected by Kathleen Tillotson in the characterisation of Jane Eyre –[33] that not all her protestations of feminine submissiveness could hide. We are accustomed to see Charlotte as the 'womanly' sister, Emily as the 'manly' one and Anne as the 'little girl': but we would be gravely mistaken on all counts to take these analogies too far.

In the previous chapter it was argued that the identification of creative vigour in art with what we commonly call 'masculinity' was not necessarily a valid one, and that Charlotte's essential instincts were 'predominantly feminine'. While holding to this basic viewpoint, I would nevertheless affirm that the masculine side of her nature should be taken into account when we seek to explain her attitudes towards the Woman Question. From childhood, she had shown a marked bias in favour of male heroes, both in real life and in her early writings, which bristled with accounts of wars, soldiers and epic adventures in foreign lands. But these were no mere reflections of doting femininity. Charlotte followed the exploits of her 'men of action' with an aggressively participative spirit that, even today, might seem more appropriate to a boy than a girl. Her well-known worship of the Duke of Wellington – who was translated in the Juvenilia into that magnificent Byronic anti-hero, Arthur Augustus Adrian Wellesley, Duke of Zamorna – exceeded anything of the kind indulged in by either Emily or Anne. The influence of Branwell seems indisputable. This was the influence which Winifred Gérin has claimed shaped 'consciously or unconsciously, the second self to which [Charlotte] gave a masculine name'[34] – that is, 'Charles Thunder' or 'Charles Townsend' – in her early authorship, and there can be little doubt that Charlotte revelled in the masculine freedom of that *alter ego*.

It can thus be seen that Charlotte's attitudes towards the problems of her own sex oscillated between extremes. On the one hand, there was resentment and rebellion, on the other a residual conservatism; a sense of duty, combined with a desire for female propriety, was in conflict with an aching yearning for liberty; finally, sharply defined male and female attributes within her were not only in conflict with one another, but also with a strong artistic impulse towards androgyny. The divisions in her mind reflected the deep divisions of her nature. The woman in her saw the justice of the female argument and felt keenly for the *in*justice of a male-biased society; but the male in her was subconsciously resistant, resulting in a withholding of full support. That these psychological disunities should frequently invade her work is hardly surprising. The male *persona* of *The Professor*, for example, is more than a convenient authorial disguise in a book that was essentially autobiographical; it afforded Charlotte the opportunity to gratify her frustrated emotional needs by adopting the male role. In this alone it was remarkable, for although writing *about* men was something women learned to do, writing *as* them was a bold leap into the dark which separated Charlotte even from her own innovative sisters. Moreover, *The Professor* supplies the first example of that uneasy sexual dichotomy that was to form a continuous thread throughout her novels. Here we have, on the one hand, the extraordinary spectacle in Victorian eyes of an almost wholly 'liberated' young woman, who finds nothing untoward in entertaining a young man *tête-à-tête* in her lodgings, who also takes the initiative in contacting him after they have lost touch, and who further insists, after they are married, on being a joint bread-winner – yet, on the other hand, who continues to call him 'Monsieur' – 'actually as if you were something superior', marvels Crimsworth's friend, Hunsden.[35] It is the first of the 'Master/Pupil' relationships, in which Charlotte's heroines are consistently seen to hover between challenge and capitulation. By an interesting reversal, Crimsworth, the 'dominant male', is shown as apparently yielding to his bride's brave new dreams for the future with a splendid show of sweet reason. In Charlotte's extended exposition of his thoughts can we doubt that we have the very epitome of her notion of what, in the best of all possible worlds, should be man's response to his existential partnership with woman?

> I put no obstacle in her way; raised no objection; I knew she was not one who could live quiescent and inactive, or even comparatively inactive. Duties she must have to fulfil, and important duties; work to do – and exciting, absorbing, profitable work; strong faculties stirred in her frame, and they demanded full nourishment, free exercise: mine was not the hand ever to starve or cramp them; no, I delighted in offering them sustenance, and in clearing them wider space for action.[36]

Splendid words. But it is all too good to be true, and Charlotte – via Crimsworth – spoils it in the very next sentence.

> 'You have conceived a plan, Frances,' said I, 'and a good plan; execute it; you have my free consent, and wherever and whenever my assistance is wanted, ask and you shall have.'

It is the voice of the 'Master' still, kindly but patronising; and, for all her aspirations, Charlotte clearly does not know it.

In *Jane Eyre*, however, the aspirations are noticeably stronger. A fiercer rebel yet than Frances Henri, Jane takes her stand against the traditional male stance of 'provider', wiping what she takes to be a 'sultan'-like smile off Rochester's face with the words, 'I'll not stand you an inch in the stead of a seraglio . . . if you have a fancy for anything in that line, away with you, sir, to the bazars [sic] of Stamboul . . . .'[37]

However, Jane's need to look up to the man she marries results in something even less edifying than the usual submission. In the inelegant reversal of the material roles of dominance and dependency in Rochester, we see a blatant capitulation of Charlotte's own function as an artist, for her solution is worked out not on a moral and intellectual level, but in the crude physical terms of blindness and maiming. In other words, by making Rochester less than a man, by reducing him to the physical dependence of a child – the traditional recipient of female care and support – she endeavours to suspend any doubts which she or her readers may have as to his suitability as a husband for a heroine of such rectitude. But, as Geoffrey Wagner observes, 'to "extinguish" the male universe . . . is hardly the answer'.[38]

The pattern of male domination and female resistance and escape is repeated in the interlude with St John Rivers, and Jane is allowed to come disturbingly close to a paralytic submission to this ruthless young pedagogue. In his own cerebral way, Rivers is even more the Byronic tyrant than Rochester, and Jane, no less than her creator, seems to find the type almost irresistible. But Rivers lacks the one quality that for Charlotte is indispensable; he is a man of 'marble', a man without the capacity of ordinary human feeling. And so he is ultimately disposed of in a fair fight; he lives to pit his implacable moral will against innocents abroad.

It has been argued that by the time she came to write *Shirley*, Charlotte had matured psychologically, artistically and intellectually and was ready to see the problem of female inequality in the wider context of other inequalities.[39] That *Shirley* was intended to be a story about power, and its direct relation to human fulfilment on all levels, seems very likely. Possibly it was conceived of as a dispassionate, largely optimistic portrayal of how the relation worked in individual lives, particularly those of women, whom Charlotte would naturally see as being among the main victims of deprivation. The light-hearted opening certainly suggests this conception of the story, as does the obvious contrast in the delineation of the two heroines: both young, both without immediate family, but one wealthy, free and independent, the other confined within the well-intentioned but misogynistic guardianship of a clerical uncle.

At heart, he could not abide sense in women: he liked to see them as silly, as light-headed, as vain, as open to ridicule as possible; because they were then in reality what he held them to be, and wished them to be, –inferior: toys to play with, to amuse a vacant hour and to be thrown away.[40]

When Caroline suggests she should work, her uncle is angry.

'Don't mention it again . . . put all crotchets out of your head, and run away and amuse yourself.'[41]

'What with? My doll?' asks Caroline of herself.

Only Shirley is free, because, in Shirley, power is equated with money; and it is to Shirley, self-confident and secure, that Charlotte gives some of her most overtly feminist speeches.

If men could see us as we really are, they would be a little amazed; but the cleverest, the acutest men are often under an illusion about women: they . . . misapprehend them, both for good and evil: their good woman is a queer thing, half doll, half angel; their bad woman almost always a fiend.[42]

As Keefe reminds us, her 'androgynous nature begins with her name',[43] (a reference to the fact that nineteenth-century usage of the name 'Shirley' was almost exclusively male). She moreover makes a number of fine, sabre-rattling speeches of a feminist kind, but as ever, there comes at the end the inevitable capitulation. In Shirley Keeldar, this is preceded by a conflict of needs, described by Frederick R. Karl[44] as being between the feminine search for a 'unique self' and 'the urgency of fulfilment by a male'. Thus, Shirley is tamed. The 'pantheress! beautiful forest-born!'[45] ends by declaring that she will accept 'no hand which cannot hold me in check',[46] and then unites herself with a man who seems never to amount to more than a mere shadow on a page. Possibly we are meant to be reassured by Shirley's own last words on the subject: 'Louis would never have learned to rule, if she had not ceased to govern: the incapacity of the sovereign had developed the powers of the premier'.[47] The submission, then, is in itself a kind of control: a tacit gesture of courtesy to male pride; but submission still, by the very fact of its recognition of the conventions that evoke and support that pride.

Written at the time it was, with such an accumulation of personal tragedy so recently behind its author, *Shirley* inevitably reflects an almost inextricable tangle of both personal and social concern.

Beneath its light banter, its dry irony and flashes of slapstick humour, there is in *Shirley* a sense of deep bitterness, of profound despair. On the fate of many of the local single girls, for example, Caroline muses:

> [They] should have more to do – better chances of interesting and profitable occupation . . . . The brothers of these girls are every one in business or the professions . . . their sisters have no earthly employment, but household work and sewing . . . . They expect them to do this, and this only . . . all their lives long, as if they had no germs of faculties for anything else . . . .[48]

She ends with an impassioned plea in which we can surely hear echoes of the long years of frustration at the Haworth Parsonage:

> Fathers! cannot you alter these things? . . . Keep your girls' minds narrow and fettered – and they will still be a plague and a care, sometimes a disgrace to you: cultivate them – give them scope and work – they will be your gayest companions in health; your tenderest nurses in sickness; your most faithful prop in age.[49]

It is, however, in speeches such as this that we can identify the problem which feminists from her own day on have seen in Charlotte's witness to the female cause, for the underlying tone here is wistfully idealistic.

It was not until she wrote *Villette* that Charlotte finally came to terms with disillusionment. Her sisters were gone, her own future seemed set in loneliness and resignation, the world would not change, no matter what she felt or wrote; there was a limit, even in art, to the amount of control it was possible to impose on events and remain true to life as it was. In *Villette*, Charlotte at last accepted this, and it is thus her most realistic book. Paradoxically, however, although in this novel she returns to a narrower concentration on the problems of the individual love relation, there is a much greater sense than in *Shirley* of concern for the general nature of human experience. The battle for 'uniqueness', although still confronted with occasional feminist connotations, is here lifted out of this more limited area to become a battle for the establishment of a wholly personal 'self', an independent, and largely androgynous, identity. Lucy Snowe, in her foreign – that is, alien – settings, is only secondarily a woman in search of love; principally, she is a human soul, ageless and sexless, in search of itself. The loneliness that is so hateful to her is nevertheless a sort of necessity, for while it drives her in on herself, it also ultimately separates her from illusion, both of a general and personal kind. Philosophically, for example, she learns to discriminate between a hated faith and its individual adherents. 'Whatever Romanism may be, there are good Romanists,'[50] she tells herself. Emotionally, she learns that the 'love' she had felt for one man (Dr John) is infatuation, and the game of mutual antagonism which she had played with another (Paul Emanuel) is love.

In *Villette*, the feminist elements are the more convincing for being absorbed into the overall development of character than, as in *Shirley*, being offered in set 'chunks' of dialogue or narrative. We see, for example, how Paul Emanuel taunts Lucy with the traditional notion of women as superior ministrants to the human race after she has complained of her ordeal of close and lonely confinement wth the 'cretin', Marie Broc. Later, 'the mocking spirit'[51] of the little professor delivers a frontal attack on what he calls 'women of intellect', a species which he sees as:

a sort of 'lusus naturae', a luckless accident, a thing for which there was neither place nor use in creation, wanted neither as wife nor worker . . . . He believed in his soul that lovely, placid, and passive feminine mediocrity was the only pillow on which manly thought and sense could find rest . . . and as to work, male mind alone could work to any good practical result.[52]

Lucy Snowe, however, is given more real independence than any other of Charlotte Brontë's heroines. Although she calls Paul her 'king'[53] and says that 'to offer homage was both a joy and a duty', yet the process of alternating resistance and submission is mutual; the relationship throughout is such as might almost be described as one of equitable inequality. Charlotte has not entirely lost her attachment to the notion of the dominant male – indeed, in Paul and John Graham, we have here *two* Byronic heroes; but it is significant that *Villette* is the only novel of Charlotte Brontë's that does not end in marriage. M. Paul is 'lost' to Lucy, just as in real life Charlotte's own beloved professor had been lost to her, in a way that, for her, was equally unexplained and uncomprehended. The result in both cases was a coming to grips with the self and reality.

If this can be translated into terms applicable to the Woman Question, perhaps it might be said that at the end Charlotte appeared to have come to believe that the most important problem for women was not the simple one of transformation of their lives; prior to that was the need for a new and more honest identification of themselves, both as women and as human beings.

> Woman is a female to the extent that she feels herself as such . . . . The fact is that she would be quite embarrassed to decide *what* she *is*; but this is not because the hidden truth is too vague to be discerned: it is because in this domain there is no truth.[54]

Emily Brontë was not a woman to repeat herself, but if she could have read this statement of Simone de Beauvoir's, she must surely have uttered yet again those two small words which were her sole contribution to the debate upon religion: 'That's right'. This is because, to Emily Brontë, alone among our four authors, and indeed among most of the women of her day, the Woman Question, like the Religious Question, was largely a *non sequitur*. This is not to say that she would not have been aware of the injustices that prevailed against women; it is inconceivable that anyone living under the same roof as Charlotte could have been. It is certainly not to say that she did not herself suffer on account of her sex. Indeed, it seems highly probable that, of the four novelists here under review, she suffered the most; it is the *nature* of her suffering that, in relation to other women, we cannot simply take for granted.

It has been said, by those who knew her and since, that she was like a man. She should have been one, said M. Heger[55] after observing her intellectual capacities and experiencing the occasional disputatious nature of her will. Since intellectual capacity, however, was generally as a matter of course equated solely with human masculinity, this perhaps tells us more about the conformity of individual male opinion to the mass than it does about Emily Brontë. In our own time, C. Day Lewis has aligned her 'proud recalcitrance, her preoccupation with themes of captivity, exile and freedom'[56] with 'the limitation of not being a man'. The argument is persuasive, but an important element is missing. In almost all those women we can call to mind who have battled against a specific sense of sexual repression – from Mary Wollstonecraft to Harriet Martineau, and the Misses Davies and Clough on into our own time – there always appears to be present a specifically sex-based assertiveness, an attitude of confrontation that leaves no doubt as to the nature of the argument and the allegiance of the protagonist. In Emily Brontë, there is no sign of this at all. There is not one word, not a single protest, claim or pronouncement of hers that we know of that compares even with the statements of Charlotte in *Shirley*, for example, or of Anne in *The Tenant of Wildfell Hall*. *Wuthering Heights* offers no particular feminist focus, unless we count the equality of suffering, nor does Emily Brontë's own life, unless we accept with Winifred Gérin that Emily's note in her diary paper of Victoria's accession to the throne indicated that the event was 'artistically satisfying'[57] to her because it meant that 'a woman . . . almost her own age' had achieved 'this unique position in the land'.

We come closest to understanding Emily Brontë when we realise that the freedom she sought right from the beginning, and that she tried to define in her poetry and in her fiction, was not categorically sexual, or social, but *existential*. She did not want the freedom of maleness; she wanted freedom from the restraints and the inherent self-alienation and *division* of sexuality itself; and in *Wuthering Heights* she wrote what has surely been most accurately called 'an investigation into being, probably the only ontological novel of consequence in the English language',[58] a book that is 'not so much asexual as pre-sexual', because it is about 'that existence itself which is the locus of our freedoms'. Accepting this, we might conclude that, for Emily, being a woman merely aggravated a sense of exile and dichotomy whose source was not in some supposed superiority of one sex over the other, but rather in the fatal flaws of human-kind in its relation to true being.

The problem raised by this kind of interpretation is that it suggests something almost supra-human, which I would maintain Emily Brontë neither was nor wished to be. She has been seen by some as a woman 'indifferent'[59] to the 'need for love and companionship', and as neutral to the 'social norms of her time'.[60] Yet this was a girl who almost pined to death when away from home,[61] and used such phrases in her diary paper as 'merrily',[62] 'contented' and 'undesponding' when safely settled back at Haworth, with all her restless, worrisome, difficult family around her. In common with all human beings, Emily Brontë experienced life on more than one level. The difference we find in her is that she seemed to respond fully only to that inner centre of being which draws the faculties to deeper echoes than our mundane senses can readily comprehend and comfortably bear. For such individuals, human problems are seen within a universal and cosmic context. We look in vain to them for simple answers to simple questions. Thus, in *Wuthering Heights*, Emily Brontë provides no categorical statement on the Woman Question because, for her, the question is subsumed under the larger ones of justice and freedom as universally applicable. These are primarily posed in the novel by the origins and sufferings of Heathcliff, his mutually annihilating motivations towards self-fulfilment and revenge and the various kinds of love which form the movement of the story. A notable difference in the male versus female theme between this book and those of Emily's sisters is that, here, the 'victim' of society is the male, Heathcliff, who is abused materially by Hindley and emotionally by Cathy. It might, in fact, be said that Emily Brontë had no need to postulate sex-equality; by this unusual transfer of powerlessness from the female to the male she created a situation in which sex-equality tacitly exists. Another deeply significant element here is that the true source of Heathcliff's suffering is not, as he himself believes, in the gulf that develops between him and the beloved, but in their mutual struggles to realise themselves *within each other*, rather than as united, sharing but independent entities. Looked at in this way, *Wuthering Heights* can be seen as a reflection of the dangers hinted at by Mary Wollstonecraft in her expression of the sexual ideal: 'men and women were made for each other, though not to become one being.'[63] And it is in this that we see Emily Brontë to have been, as a female writer, unique in her time – possibly, for that matter, *any* time: that is, in her challenge to the man/woman 'one-flesh' notion of time-honoured sexual tradition. Through the most powerful kind of love imaginable she reveals how tragically illusory is the desire for absolute union in human terms, showing it to be incapable of providing that perfect harmonisation of needs and desires that such absolutism requires, and to lead, instead, to a mutually-imposed tyranny of separate wills. By contrast, in the love bond of the second generation of the novel, she shows something of that shared exploration of the 'equal but different' which, if pressed, she would possibly have cited as offering the greatest hope of human happiness.

Thus, by a characteristic paradox, Emily Brontë becomes the only one of our four novelists to say virtually nothing about sex-equality, and yet to say, perhaps, everything on the subject that matters most.

It is ironic, on the other hand, that the Brontë sister whom tradition has dubbed 'The Gentle Anne'[64] should have been the one whose ringing challenge to contemporary sexual assumptions seems to have shocked her Victorian world almost more than did the work of her sisters. Tom Winnifrith suggests[65] that part of the reason for this could have been the accumulative effect of 'suspicions' concerning the morality of *Jane Eyre* and *Wuthering Heights*, suspicions which *The Tenant of Wildfell Hall* 'confirmed'. One of the reviews quoted by Winnifrith also underlines the kind of prudery focused on women to which the Brontë sisters were especially averse:

> So revolting are many of the scenes, so coarse and disgusting the language put into the mouths of some of the characters . . . that our object in the present paper is to warn our readers, and more especially our lady-readers, against being induced to peruse it . . . .

It is not, the reviewer continues, a fit novel 'to be obtruded by every circulating library-keeper upon the notice of our sisters, wives and daughters'; in other words,

> unfit for perusal of the very class of persons to whom it would be most useful (namely imaginative girls likely to risk their happiness on the forlorn hope of marrying and reforming a captive rake).

Anne, however, was not simply unrepentant; she was defiant. She had written her story with the deliberate intention of highlighting the evils of social hypocrisy and although she regretted any 'pain'[66] this might have given her readers, and promised to 'endeavour to do better another time', yet, she said, 'be it understood, I shall not limit my ambition to this'. And every bit as firmly as Charlotte, she rapped the knuckles of those critics who sought to discriminate against her on account of her sex. 'If a book is a good one,' she said 'it is so whatever the sex of the author may be.' She added:

All novels are or should be written for both men and women to read, and I am at a loss to conceive how a man should permit himself to write anything that would be really disgraceful to a woman, or why a woman should be censured for writing anything that would be proper and becoming for a man;[67]

Quaintly naive as these sentiments may seem to us today, their logic was faultless, and once again we see it put to the service of an androgynous or asexual concept of the artistic function.

An essential part of Anne's purpose in *The Tenant* was to draw attention to injustices affecting both women and children arising from inequality between the sexes. In particular, she had seen at first hand something of the pernicious effect of male self-centredness and dissipation upon the lives of womenfolk. She was nevertheless criticised for making no attempt to explain the behaviour of her profligate males from 'inside'.

She puts a man on trial, but . . . not nearly enough is said in his defence. With a more mature knowledge of life Anne might have seen more deeply into the mind of even a wastrel.[68]

It is difficult, however, to imagine what 'more mature knowledge' Anne might have had than that which she acquired from the intimate and tolerant witness, lasting over some eight years, of her own brother's steadily disintegrating life. If she failed to transmit this sense of deep-sighted empathy to her portrayal of Huntingdon, it seems likely that this was because she felt that a merely surface appraisal best served to mirror the shallow nature of his personality and to point the message it contained. We note, for example, that even on his death-bed Huntingdon is shown to be capable of only one profound emotion: that of purely selfish fear. Anne's purpose, like Emily's, was clearly to emphasise that self-love, taken to its logical conclusion, breaks normal relationships with others. Feeding only on itself, it then ultimately exhausts its resources and ends in isolation and terror. '. . . if I had heard you long ago,'[69] cries the dying Huntingdon to his wife, 'Oh, God! how different it would have been!'

On the face of it, it is undoubtedly true that in the characterisation of Helen Huntingdon we have a true feminist prototype in romantic literature. As Inga-Stina Ewbank comments, 'through the very nature of its central concern, this novel is feminist in the deepest sense of the word.'[70] She adds: 'The Preface to the second edition of

The Tenant of Wildfell Hall . . . is, by implication, the bravest statement for the literary equality of the sexes that any of the Brontës ever made.' Not only is this so, but Helen Huntingdon is unique among Brontë/Eliot heroines, since, while remaining the essentially 'virtuous woman', she is capable, metaphorically speaking, of trading violence with violence. 'I was almost sick with passion,'[71] she writes when her husband's mistress, Lady Lowborough, taunts her to her face; 'I took her hand and violently dashed it from me';[72] finally, she cries, '. . . he may drink himself dead, but it is NOT my fault!'[73]

A quiet anger burns through *The Tenant of Wildfell Hall*. Furthermore, it is a very personal emotion. Anne had herself experienced many of the injustices created by a complacent and self-gratifying society; she had also seen poignantly close to her the logical effects of such a society on a character too weak to withstand its blandishments and its ultimate heartlessness. While I would argue *against* the view that *The Tenant* is inherently a feminist novel, and would claim that Anne, like Emily, was primarily concerned to show the effects of a deeper, more universal sense of social folly, yet I would agree that in exposing the potentially 'profligate'[74] nature of the society she had in mind, she also reveals it to be deeply sexist in its bland acceptance of double standards. Her portrayal of a decent woman dominated by a selfish and debauched husband underlines the point that the right to respect is properly accorded not by biology, nor by privilege, but by innate good will. In particular, she challenges the sexual arrogance that enables Huntingdon to expect virtuous obedience from his wife while excusing his own infidelity, and last but not least she claims for Helen Huntingdon the natural prerogative of a free-born human being to decide her own fate.

Perhaps the most remarkable aspect of *The Tenant* is the gloomy picture it paints of marriage itself. Almost every kind of adverse motivation is presented, from the romantic idealism of the young girl who deceives herself into seeing a philandering rake as reformative material, to the marriage marketeers governed by the blatant pursuit of social gain. Most common of all in this survey of marriage at its worst is the union which, for women, results in the benign nihilism which Gilbert Markham recognises in his own mother's life: a life which is dictated, he says, by 'what's proper to be done, and secondly, what's most agreeable to the gentlemen of the house – anything will do for the ladies'.[75] To this, Mrs Markham typically provides bland confirmation by assuring him that the most 'any woman can expect of any man'[76] is that he will be 'steady and punctual', seldom find fault 'without a reason', always do justice to his wife's 'good dinners' and 'hardly ever' spoil her cookery 'by delay'. The irony is perfect, and the scene is only spoilt by the implausibility of a young man who, like Charlotte's William Crimsworth, is forced into the role of Exemplary Male and has thus occasionally to voice such impossibly smug sentiments as the following:

> when I marry, I shall expect to find more pleasure in making my wife happy and comfortable than in being made so by her: I would rather give than receive.[77]

By contrast, however, the gross self-indulgence of Arthur Huntingdon is made to seem all the more offensive.

> his idea of a wife is a thing to love one devotedly and to stay at home – to wait upon her husband, and amuse him and minister to his comfort in every possible way, while he chooses to stay with her; and, when he is absent, to attend to his interests, domestic or otherwise, and patiently wait his return; no matter how he may be occupied in the meantime.[78]

The message is summed up in Helen's warning to her young friend, Esther Hargrave: 'Marriage *may* change your circumstances for the better, but in my private opinion, it is far more likely to produce a contrary result.'[79]

So great is the difference in this respect between Anne's two novels that we may well wonder what accounts for it, and from where, in fact, she derived her so varied and unerring pictures of marriage. As Jenni Calder points out,[80] although Agnes Grey had 'to take the governess route to a modest marriage', she had at least the 'moral example' of her parents' marriage, which had 'taught her the importance of honest love'. Although only one year separates the publication of the two novels, Anne's diary paper of July 1845[81] indicates that between the inception of *Agnes Grey* and that of *The Tenant of Wildfell Hall* something more like three to four years must have intervened. In that time, much had happened to turn 'the gentle Anne' into a compassionate but unsentimental realist, with a blend of ardour and stoicism in her make-up matched only by that of her sister, Emily. Primarily, of course, there had been the shameful

experience of her brother's dismissal from Thorp Green, resulting in
the humiliating relinquishment of her own position there. It is
virtually certain that this provided the paramount motivation for *The
Tenant*, with its emphasis on the evils of 'spoiling' in youthful
upbringing; it is equally clear, however, that the singular realism of
Anne's treatment of the 'woman' theme in both *Agnes Grey* and *The
Tenant* derived from carefully observed empirical evidence of an even
longer duration. Anne's first governess post was with the Ingham
family at Blake Hall, Mirfield, and Susan Brooke's[82] description of
the circumstances prevailing at the time is directly relevant to the
pattern of socio-sexual protest which we find in Anne's work. 'At
this period,' Susan Brooke writes, 'ladies were not supposed to
know anything about business affairs – indeed they were trained to
turn a blind eye to most masculine activities.' Men never discussed
serious matters in front of women, and the lack of parental
discipline which had troubled both Charlotte and Anne as
governesses was, she records, 'characteristic of many Yorkshire
households'. Boys, she says, 'were frequently over-indulged by
their parents and if they teased or bullied their sisters it was merely
considered a sign of manliness'. Girls, on the other hand, 'were
usually brought up to feel that they were of little value compared
with their brothers'.

Where the treatment of marriage is concerned, the Brontë sisters
together reveal some interesting comparisons. It would be
simplistic, and possibly false, to categorise Charlotte as 'pro-
marriage' and her sisters as 'against', but certainly neither Anne nor
Emily shows anything like Charlotte's consistent orientation
towards wedded bliss as the appropriate 'happy ending'. Both
Wuthering Heights and *The Tenant of Wildfell Hall* conclude on this
conventional note, it is true, but in both cases the reference,
presented in somewhat summary fashion at the end, smacks of a
kind of structural necessity, a restorative coda to a rondo of
variations on a negative theme. Neither Anne nor Emily provides
the kind of post-marital 'idyll' to which Charlotte was inclined in
each of her first three novels. Anne concedes the most in *Agnes Grey*,
and with Gilbert's brief closing picture of happy married life in *The
Tenant*; but this latter circumstance, we note, has not been arrived at
with any flattering precipitation on the bride's part. Helen indeed
suggests to Gilbert that they wait 'another year',[83] assuring him that
'we will write every day; my spirit shall be always with you; and
sometimes you shall see me with your bodily eye'. This very

un-yearning little speech is followed by some brisk bargaining between them as to the precise date of the wedding.

> '*Next* spring' [says Gilbert].
> 'No, no – next autumn, perhaps.'
> 'Summer, then.'
> 'Well, the close of summer. There now! be satisfied.'[84]

It is a far remove from one of Charlotte's romantic climaxes, with their characteristic antiphons of mastery and submission, in which the heroine waits 'with declined brow, and ringlets drooped'.[85] With Anne, as with Emily, the challenge is sustained. There is no Master/Pupil relationship in *Wuthering Heights* or *The Tenant of Wildfell Hall*. There is one feature, on the other hand, that we find to be common to *all* the Brontë heroines that sets them apart among English fictional heroines of their time – their ability to take the romantic initiative and still remain unquestionably virtuous. In the novels of Dickens, Thackeray or Trollope, such sexually-orientated boldness in women would almost certainly have been required to go hand in hand with a proportionate reduction of moral value; either such women would be seen as cunning manipulators, hiding their true colours under charming exteriors, or else gross distortions of femininity whose coarseness would stamp them as women who, if not downright 'bad', were certainly not 'good'. When Helen Graham offers the Christmas Rose to Gilbert Markham in *The Tenant of Wildfell Hall*,[86] she takes her stand beside Frances Henri, Jane Eyre, Shirley Keeldar, Lucy Snowe and both Catherine Earnshaws in a gesture that unites them all as surely the first of the truly un-Victorian heroines in mid-Victorian English literature.

In a *Leader* article, written in March 1856,[87] George Eliot expressed what would appear to have been the nub of her attitude towards more or less all forms of social radicalism. We might accordingly feel that it contained the answer which she would have wished given to modern feminists, resentful and dismayed[88] at her failure to assume the leadership of a 'revolution' which she 'lived . . . but did not write of'.[89] It was her professed belief that the basic argument contained in the *Antigone* of Sophocles – that a valid principle of action may be opposed by another equally valid – was as true by the standards of modern culture as in an ancient, 'polytheistic' world. In the *Leader* article, she wrote:

> we shall never be able to attain a great right without also doing a wrong. Reformers, martyrs, revolutionists, are never fighting against evil only; they are also placing themselves in opposition to a good – to a valid principle which cannot be infringed without harm . . . .[90]

Thus, to a friend who had urged her to comment on the suffrage question she replied, somewhat waspishly,

> I thought you understood that I have grave reasons for not speaking on certain public topics . . . . If I had taken a contrary decision, I should not have remained silent till now. My function is that of the *aesthetic*, not the doctrinal teacher . . . .[91]

According to Pinney, the anonymity of article-writing gave George Eliot a greater freedom to speak on such controversial issues as the Woman Question than was afforded her in her novels, where, in any case, her heroines were 'concerned with a much wider range of issues than the status of women'.[92] In the 'Life and Opinions of Milton',[93] for example, she 'urges her readers to reconsider Milton's "calm and dignified" arguments for divorce – a suggestion she could not have dared to make in print after she became famous'. Noting the mixture of conservatism and mild radicalism that informed her thinking on women, Pinney considers it 'not very helpful' to categorise her opinions on the subject. In the present context, however, it is interesting to observe this mixed reaction *vis-à-vis* the similar pattern of indetermination seen in Charlotte Brontë. In each case, a highly aware and original mind hesitates on the brink of total commitment. This might suggest that the restraining influence derived from mutual intellectual judgements within a shared historical experience; but we have already seen how personal and emotional considerations might be accepted as having also played a large part in the formation of attitude in Charlotte Brontë, and we can readily detect an even more cogent explanation of this sort for George Eliot's cautious response to the feminist cause. Writing on the subject to John Morley in 1867, she stated that the 'peculiarities of my own lot have caused me to have idiosyncracies rather than an average judgment'.[94] It was an admission that her social position as the common-law wife of George Henry Lewes affected her by reason of its singularity. That it also inhibited her, perhaps more profoundly than she would have cared even to think, let alone express, seems a wholly admissible assumption.

It was left to Cross to emphasise that George Eliot was 'keenly anxious to redress injustices to women',[95] but he was at pains to lay particular stress on her dislike of masculinity in women. 'She was, and as a woman she wished to be above all things feminine,' he said. In the main, Cross's emphasis on George Eliot's femininity tends to be counter-productive, because it attempts to establish something that up until then no-one had questioned – thus ensuring that it *would* be questioned thereafter. George Eliot's 'manlike qualities'[96] have accordingly been duly observed and thoroughly analysed by recent critics. Redinger, for example, noting the influence on her of her childhood 'identification with her brother',[97] writes: 'This masculine identification was to be a strong component in her psychic make-up and thus destined to play a vital role in both her personal and creative life.' Androgyny being a concept undreamt of in George Eliot's time, it was little wonder, adds Redinger, that 'her sense of identity was blunted and her sense of unworthiness augmented. Where in the great family of man–woman did she belong?'

Our own uncertainty, on the other hand, arises out of the conflict which we sense between the 'Madonna' figure[98] of the Eliot myth which arose in her lifetime and the sharp, probing mind that produced the novels. To say that she encouraged the myth would perhaps be unjust, certainly when judging her by impressions created by a biographer as anxious to 'feminise' her as was Cross. It might, however, be concluded that such an aura, elevating, almost sacrosanct, afforded her a certain blanketing protection against the outside world, and that in certain matters – of which the Woman Question was patently one – she appeared disinclined to step out into the clear and possibly harsher light of reality. With an equivocation that was consistent with the Aristotelian 'middle-way' advocated in her *Leader* article, she expressed, on the one hand, her fears that women would turn their backs on traditional female drudgery and instead attempt to do 'the highest kind of work, which ought rather to be held in sanctity as what only a few can do well',[99] and on the other, argued for 'a more thorough education' for women.[100] It is interesting, in the light of the latter statement, that her involvement in the new Girton College project never went beyond the offer of a donation. George Eliot did, however, claim a special distinction for women in literature, albeit one unlikely to have commended itself to the Brontë sisters all that strongly and to modern feminists not at all. Women, she argued, were equipped with 'a class of sensations and emotions – the maternal ones – which must remain unknown to man'.[101]

In sum, George Eliot's 'public' view would seem to have been that the concept of 'equal but different' was the true one, but that its realisation waited upon the better education and awareness of women. Pending this utopian ideal, she attacked what she called the *'mind-and-millinery* species'[102] of fashionable romantic literature written by women, not, she believed, from professional or economic necessity, but out of 'busy idleness'. Such women, she felt, shamed their sex by their literary mediocrity and moral irresponsibility. She urged critics to deal much more severely with them than had been the case, pointing out, with heavy irony, that women writers of 'excellence', such as 'Currer Bell', had been treated as 'cavalierly as if they had been men'. This comment appeared anonymously in the *Westminster Review* and would thus have appeared to contemporary readers to have been written by a man. There was therefore a certain furtive sycophancy about it that modern feminists will possibly not have cared for; however, the most that it seems fair to say about this apparent sexual 'treachery' is that it was a rather artful refinement of the use of the male pseudonym, and less blatantly sycophantic, perhaps, than Charlotte Brontë's constant reiteration of the Master/ Pupil metaphor. In both novelists, what we are seeing in gestures of this sort is, in fact, the deep insecurity of women artists who, impelled by needs greater than their sense of self-preservation, dared the censure and – worse – the ridicule of a male-dominated world.

Pinney rightly states that in the novels George Eliot dealt only 'indirectly' with the Woman Question; nevertheless, there is a contrast to be observed between the tone of this fictional treatment and the essentially cautious note of the 'public' voice. In itself, this contrast emphasises one of the obvious functions of creative art – that of releasing attitudes, impulses and desires which lie deep within the artist, but for which no outlet is granted, or is acceptable to him, in normal life. For George Eliot, such release seems to have been achieved by a process of what might be called 'inversion', which is to say that her characters suffered instead of her for acts of emotional commitment and social defiance that were very like her own. Unlike Charlotte Brontë, who longed for something to happen, and wrote it into being, George Eliot ultimately enjoyed a full experience of life, for which, in her books, she often seemed to be trying to atone. It has been suggested[103] that an element of 'confession' runs through all the Eliot novels and can be seen in 'Janet's Repentance' as 'a major and redemptive theme'. George Eliot herself once admitted, 'my own books scourge me',[104] and again and again in the characterisation and events of her novels we can see her seeking expiation for the failure of her life to measure up to the virtue which, as a woman, her society expected of her and which she herself admired. Writing of *Romola*, Ruby Redinger comments: 'if she looked into its contents, she found the saintly Romola to remind her of what she was not . . . .'[105] The same could be said of Mrs Barton, Dinah Morris, Eppie Cass, Mary Garth and Mirah Cohen, all sterling representatives of that 'loving woman's world'[106] in which noble female souls live out their lives in service to others. In her Religion of Humanity, 'the deepest human values', it has been said,[107] 'were feminine ones'. And certainly in her fiction she created – as much for herself, possibly, as her readers – the apotheosis of the Woman made for Worship in the grand Victorian tradition. *Romola*, again, is our example:

> Tito . . . felt for the first time . . . that loving awe in the presence of noble womanhood, which is perhaps something like the worship paid of old to a great nature-goddess, who was not all-knowing, but whose life and power were something deeper and more primordial than knowledge.[108]

But such nobility, George Eliot suggests, involves suffering, and again it is surely possible to see an element of self-propitiation in the unusually high incidence of female chastisement in the Eliot novels. Caterina Sarti, Janet Dempster, Hetty Sorrel, Maggie Tulliver, Mrs Transome, Dorothea Brooke, Gwendolen Harleth, each in her way flings her little challenge to the fates, and each is forced in the end to capitulate. And if Romola is the essence and symbol of feminine triumph in compromise, Maggie Tulliver is surely that of a divine despair: she who, as Patricia Beer comments, 'turns away from the love of two adult men and from any hope of future personal happiness to die, ecstatically, in the arms of a loutish cruel brother'.[109]

Although the Eliot males fare little better, their apparent freedoms being shown to be largely illusory, the difference is that, whereas the men are chiefly the instigators of their own sufferings, the women suffer doubly by being the victims also of a sexually discriminating society. From Maggie Tulliver, via Mrs Transome to Romola Bardo, a specifically female frustration forms a continuum in which at times an authorial bitterness seems but thinly veiled beneath the controlled rationalism. At first sight of the deserted Lydia Glasher, Gwendolen Harleth is made to feel not guilt, nor even pity, for the victim but instead her own inescapable involvement in a universal nightmare; '. . . as if some ghastly vision had come to her in a dream and said, "I am a woman's life"'.[110]

But mixed with George Eliot's compassion for the female condition is always that curious contempt for her own kind that inspired the denunciation of the women writers of 'Silly Novels' and the women who were unworthy to do 'the highest kind of work'. It would seem that part of the process of self-scourging was a need to find scapegoats, and in the novels these chiefly became the young, the pretty and the ultra-feminine. Thus, we have the patronising diminution of simple souls such as Caterina Sarti, Hetty Sorrel and the little Florentine *contadina*, Tessa, and even more effectively the merciless exposure of less simple lives, such as those of Rosamond Vincy and Gwendolen Harleth, where devastating contrasts could be shown between a mammoth self-concern and an extreme physical delicacy and charm.[111] There are no simple answers to such complex psychological problems, but perhaps we might assume that, for Eliot, it was easier to denounce women – as she has Felix Holt do – because 'all life is stunted to their littleness'[112] than to face the massive differences, social, intellectual and personal, that she could not but be aware separated her from the great female majority.

At the same time, this treatment of 'unworthiness' in women was an aspect of that creative androgyny which, as in Charlotte Brontë, led to flashes of deep insight into the workings of the masculine nature as well as to a considerable tolerance in the delineation of male foibles. In Charlotte Brontë, we saw these qualities at their best in the creation of Paul Emanuel in *Villette*; in George Eliot, the tolerance is perhaps most noticeable in the characterisation and treatment of those members of her 'Rogues' Gallery' in whom a fatal weakness, rather than inherent vice, was the operative element; Arthur Donnithorne and Stephen Guest come readily to mind, with

Tito Melema as perhaps a border-line case between them and the unredeemable Henleigh Mallinger Grandcourt.

On the other hand, in her attitude to marriage, George Eliot shows a profound resentment of the meanness and injustice of male authoritarianism, although her treatment differs from that of both Charlotte and Anne Brontë's inasmuch as there is a much greater and more consistent correlation of *female* power with male dominance. A classic example is the typical fluctuation of control and uncertainty that dogs all Tito's dealings with his wife.

> now, at least, he believed that he had mastered Romola by a terror which appealed to the strongest forces of her nature . . . .
> Yet Tito was not at ease . . . .[113]

Again, in *Middlemarch*, when Lydgate and Rosamond quarrel over her interference in his money affairs, Lydgate, we are told, speaks to her with 'biting severity',[114] but he is aware that 'it would assuredly have been a vain boast in him to say that he was her master'.[115] Even the repellent Grandcourt finds, in Gwendolen's mettlesome and self-centred nature, a constant provocation to dominate and control – and a frequent frustration of his hopes. The result is a challenging fight for the balance of power.

> He meant to be master of a woman who would have liked to master him, and who perhaps would have been capable of mastering another man.[116]

Another important difference here between Eliot and the Brontës is that Eliot suggests that it is only the more unpleasant type of women who will attempt to fight men on their own ground. And in the end, they will be their own destruction.

> Why could she not rebel, and defy him? She longed to do it . . . .
> Certain words were gnawing within her. 'The wrong you have done will be your own curse' . . . .[117]

Despite this – and as confirmation of George Eliot's marked ambivalence on the Woman Question – we find in the characterisation of Daniel Deronda's mother, the Princess Halm-Eberstein, what must be the nearest approach to an out-and-out female liberationist in English romantic fiction of the period. In some of the Princess's confessional speeches to her son, it is impossible not to feel that we are hearing the voice of her author.

> Every woman is supposed to have the same set of motives, or else to be a monster. I am not a monster, but I have not felt exactly what other women feel – or say they feel, for fear of being thought unlike others.[118]

Again, in the Princess's description of her life with her father, echoes of George Eliot's own early and unhappy home relations are inevitably present:

> such men turn their wives and daughters into slaves. They would rule the world if they could; but not ruling the world, they throw all the weight of their will on the necks and souls of women.[119]

Finally, of course, there is the celebrated speech in which the Princess expresses the anguish of the woman who has 'a man's force of genius' trapped within 'the slavery of being a girl'.[120] Of this, Cross wrote: 'This is a point of view that must be distinctly recognised by any one attempting to follow the development of George Eliot's character'.[121] His subsequent efforts to smother this under eulogistic tributes to her emphasis on the 'soothing, strengthening, sacred influences of the home life, the home loves, the home duties' did her a disservice, for it sought to do the very thing of which – via the Princess Halm-Eberstein – she had complained: to trap her within the slavery of being, not simply female, but no *more* than female.

The argument here has been that it is in her fiction that we see the clearest revelations of George Eliot's extremely complex attitude towards her own sex. We cannot, however, any more than with Emily Brontë, separate that attitude from those universal principles that lay at the heart of her philosophy of life. One of these was her passionate belief in the need for the renunciation of the self: a theme repeated throughout her novels and seen in such characters as Dinah Morris, the final Maggie Tulliver, Romola and Dorothea. Renunciation, says Basch, was for George Eliot 'the essence of virtue',[122] and she describes Eliot's 'lay morality'[123] as 'built of stoicism, resignation, and an ethical altruism which places a higher value on acceptance than on revolt'. It was indeed a delicate balance between a deterministic view of human life and the meliorism which

George Eliot interpreted in strictly individual terms. Thus, we might construe her ultimate response to the Woman Question as being, perhaps, along the lines that each woman must assume individually the right and responsibility to whatever action seems to her fit, whereupon concerted action – that is, of an aggressive sort – becomes both unnecessary and undesirable. She herself had so acted, and in confining her comments on the Woman Question to her books she may well have felt that the best she could do for her fellow women in the battle-field was not to make speeches, but to provide them with a map.

Certain common factors have emerged in looking at the attitudes of all four novelists on this question. Paramount among these has been that of 'conflict': the inevitable conflict of which they were aware as women in a male-dominated society; the conflict between their needs and fears as women and their sense of responsibility to the truth as authors; and perhaps most harrowing of all because the least understood, the conflict between the twin aspects of the androgynous Self, of which all, in their creative function as well as in their personal lives, appear to some extent to have been aware.

On the whole, we might feel the feminist verdict on Charlotte Brontë and George Eliot – of guilt by omission – to be ill-judged. The burden of this verdict is in the main that both authors 'opted out' of their obligation to provide clear examples of women who realised their full potential; in other words, they simply let them meet the 'right man' and get married, the only alternative being death or renunciation. Against this, it could be argued that the connection between marriage *per se* and capitulation is clearly not a necessary one. On the other hand, where the feminists are perhaps justified is in the much more essential way in which both Eliot and the Brontës fail their heroines: that is, in the consistent reduction of potentially heroic characters by the grafting on to them of uncharacteristic attitudes of almost cringing submission. This is particularly true of Charlotte's heroines, who, in varying degrees but without exception, are initially presented as brave, proud and independent, but in almost every case are ultimately made to utter the phraseology of abject surrender. They are betrayed by their author's own fears and uncertainties. Perhaps, however, it is George Eliot who will be least forgiven, for, as Jenni Calder points out, she 'diagnoses so brilliantly "the common yearning of womanhood", and then cures it, sometimes drastically, as if it were indeed a disease'.[124]

In searching for answers to this phenomenon in novelists who were in all other respects far ahead of the thinking of their time, we can only deduce that these answers lie somewhere in the area of social and psychological pressure. Where Charlotte Brontë is concerned, it has already been suggested that there could well have been a fear of appearing 'unwomanly', and thus placing herself beyond the hope of ever achieving the kind of romantic relationship for which she yearned. Eliot's emotional life had moved to what would appear to have been a satisfying plateau by the time the novels came to be written, but beyond that safe ground lay a potentially menacing outside world of social criticism. For both women, the need to keep what today we call a 'low profile' was pressing, and in the light of this it is all the more remarkable that they sometimes spoke as boldly as they did. In all four authors, for example, we see a significant stand being commonly taken on the subject of marriage – that is, in its connection with the central dynamic of *work*. As Calder observes, in George Eliot's world of the Poysers', 'marriage and family life . . . are seen as inseparable from work';[125] what is created here is a 'community' rather than just a family, and, within it, 'a positive creative force'. On a very much smaller scale, we see both Charlotte and Anne Brontë making a similar point. Both Jane Eyre and Frances Henri argue for a 'working' marriage, and Helen Huntingdon is already a woman with a career; the notion of work is integral to that of marriage. As Charlotte once wrote to her publisher's reader: 'Most desirable then it is that all, both men and women, should have the power and the will to work for themselves . . . .'[126] As for the world of Wuthering Heights, this is patently a working community: as distinct from that of Thrushcross Grange, where human beings grow weak from idleness and lack of purpose. In the mutually reformative relationship of Hareton and the younger Cathy we see the beginnings of a new order in which it is obvious that the emphasis will be on education, industry and improvement, irresistibly sweeping away the destructive forces of the past.

From such examples, it is clear that in all four novelists there existed a sense, subconscious or otherwise, of the links that lie between work and equality, sexual as well as social. Similarly, all four provide cogent examples of the debasement of marriage by its deliberate use as a means of the making or breaking of lives.

Wuthering Heights, of course, offers some of the most powerful examples of both these processes in all literature, and, in Gwendolen Harleth, George Eliot exposes the bitter irony of a woman whose marriage schemes become a whiplash to her own proud spirit. Both Charlotte and Anne Brontë uncover the venality of a society that coerces young girls into marriage with men for whom they have no respect, let alone affection.

In the end, we have to return to Emily Brontë for the most telling witness of all on the Woman Question. By ignoring the subject completely, she denied it reality. For Emily, there can be little doubt that female equality was a presupposition in general terms; in particular terms, its denial was merely one aspect of the illegitimate denial of freedom, a process which turned some individuals into tyrants and others into victims. It was Freedom, and not simply for women, to which she was deeply and passionately committed. If Emily Brontë had spoken at all on the Woman Question, she might perhaps have given us some message that would have anticipated the thought of Virginia Woolf, expressed more than eighty years later:

> One must turn back to Shakespeare then, for Shakespeare was androgynous . . . . It is fatal to be a man or woman pure and simple; one must be woman-manly or man-womanly. It is fatal for a woman to lay the least stress on any grievance; to plead even with justice any cause; in any way to speak consciously as a woman. Some collaboration has to take place in the mind between the woman and the man before the art of creation can be accomplished. Some marriage of opposites has to be consummated.[127]

Possibly, to a considerable extent, all our novelists knew this; and this, more even than the natural, inborn empathy they shared with all human beings, both male and female, more even than their fear of losing readers or the good opinion of their admirers, was what stood between them and the feminist flag.

6
Tragedy, Death and Eschatology

No study of the lives and work of nineteenth-century authors would be complete that failed to take account of their attitudes to the problems of death and human destiny. Of all the matters to exercise the Victorian imagination, none did so more powerfully than these. 'Where we have sex at every turn,' it has been said,[1] 'they had death.' Their society was 'haunted and fascinated' by it, their fiction 'filled with wasting diseases, slow-motion dying, funerals and cemeteries.'

The reasons for this excessive interest in eschatology are not entirely clear. The population of the United Kingdom was rising; people were living longer. However, infant mortality was still high,[2] and this, perhaps, was a not insignificant factor, inasmuch as few families could escape this depressing reminder of the fragility of human existence. Children themselves were early drawn into the ritual surrounding death. By the time a child reached the age of ten, writes Geoffrey Rowell,[3] 'it was likely that he would have experienced at least one death in the family, and quite possibly more'. Parents, he states, were urged 'to let children have experience of Christian death-beds', and we can imagine situations all up and down the country similar to that in which the young Branwell Brontë was shown the bodies of his two elder sisters.

Another important element, of course, was the steadily increasing scepticism about religion. While church-going continued, doubt and certainty alternated. Much emotion was generated and no little fear. There was reassurance still for those who could unquestioningly associate death with the Christian view of life, but the new mood of scientific inquiry made this progressively more difficult for an increasing number of people. Even before the challenge of Darwin, there were many for whom all that remained was a residual hope for the valuative nature and ethical purpose of human life on earth; beyond that point, far more people than ever before in the period would not have cared to commit themselves, and many were unequivocally pessimistic. Thus, while possibly no single factor adequately explains the Victorian preoccupation with death, a very significant front-runner must surely be the profound apprehension of individuals and society as a whole for whom deep psychological needs for reassurance were being assailed on all sides. The effects of this were felt not only by the waverer in his dreadful uncertainty about the end of things but also by the believer. If wrongs committed in this world had to be atoned for, what form did that atonement take? How long would it last? Was 'everlasting punishment' anything more than just a theological doctrine? Today, few would take the last question seriously; indeed, as Rowell tells us,[4] it was almost finished as a subject of debate by the end of the nineteenth century. For most of the period, however, it was the source of much anxiety, and of the kind of 'hell-fire' preaching indulged in even by such as the Reverend Patrick Brontë, tolerant Arminian as he was.

As would be expected this emotion-charged atmosphere was reflected in much of the writing of the period. Although the Evangelical distrust of fiction lasted sporadically until late in the century, there were many who began to see the novel as a potential means of moral influence. Some did so to excess. Of such, Priestley writes:[5] 'These novelists did not cast the first stone, they hurled huge rocks at their sinners.' Visions of the blinded Rochester, the drowned Grandcourt, inevitably arise, but the position here is more ambiguous than this association of ideas would suggest. Large questions underlay Brontë Christian conformity, while George Eliot's attitude was even more ambivalent. She has been linked with Trollope[6] as a writer who, believing that the novel could be 'a potential instrument for moral education', set out to achieve this via a more realistic approach to things as they were. But George Eliot's freedom from the 'Old Religion' had not been accomplished without a certain hankering after the old ideals, and thus, despite her best intentions, she occasionally fails. Two 'death-bed' scenes in particular come to mind. The end of *The Mill on the Floss* and the death of Mordecai Cohen in *Daniel Deronda* may not quite rival Dickens at his sensational best, but the difference is a fine one.

The Brontës' personal attitudes to death seem to have varied chiefly in the degree of emphasis which each sister placed upon the different strands in a basically conformist pattern of fear, hope and resignation. That Charlotte's response was principally that of fear was first noted by Mrs Gaskell; Charlotte, she said, was afraid 'not only of dead bodies',[7] but of death itself, which she dreaded because she 'did not know how long the "moment of dissolution" might really be, or how terrible'. It has been argued[8] that the deaths of Branwell, Emily and Anne were not, in fact, the paramount losses in Charlotte's life, but were the 'continuation of a psychological response she had learned earlier, when she suffered bereavement as a child'. Thus, Robert Keefe has claimed, the single most important event in her life was the death of her mother, the supporting psychological theory being that mother-loss, 'unless dealt with by adequate mother substitution, . . . may lead to pathological changes in personality development'. According to this view, mother-loss in Charlotte formed 'a complex web of feelings . . . of sorrow, loneliness, anguish, rage, and, most importantly, guilt, which she carried with her until she died', and which 'coloured all of her novels'.

Clearly, it would be unreasonable to argue that the Brontë sisters were in no way affected by the death of their mother, but before the above theory can be accepted without reservation, two crucial questions have to be answered: first, how 'adequate' a mother-substitute was Aunt Branwell? Secondly, what allowance must be made in the case of this particular family for the unusually close companionship and support which each member received from the others? As suggested earlier, Miss Branwell has perhaps been unfairly dealt with in this respect by certain critics. In fact, there would seem to be no evidence to show that she was wanting in care and concern for the family for which she had of her own good will assumed responsibility on her sister's death; nor, for that matter, is there anything to show that the children themselves thought that she was so lacking. Mrs Gaskell provides the information, presumably received direct from Charlotte, or from other sources connected with the Parsonage, that Miss Branwell was particularly fond of Anne and of her nephew, Branwell, and it is on record that the latter 'loved' her.[9] To his friend, Grundy, he wrote of her as the woman 'who has been for twenty years as my mother', and after her death he is reported as saying, 'I have now lost the guide and director of all the happy days connected with my childhood'. Even if Branwell was alone in feeling such depth of emotion for his aunt, it is noteworthy that it was to Aunt Branwell that Charlotte turned for financial help to enable her and Emily to go abroad to study, and that in this she was not disappointed. When all is said, the point about Aunt Branwell is that she was 'there', and she was caring and loyal in the most practical ways to her adopted family.

Even more important, however, is the fact that Charlotte and her sisters had each other; for, if there is one single element that distinguishes this particular family, apart from the obvious literary one, it is the degree of interrelation that existed within it. For each member, the death of the mother was compensated for by a strengthening of the unities of sistership, so that a more than adequate mother-substitution was provided, at least up until the time that the death of Anne left Charlotte and her father alone in the world. It was then, not surprisingly, that death became for her 'the King of Terrors'.[10]

Beginning therefore with Charlotte, it is my view that the awareness of motherlessness remained on a relatively objective level until the accumulation of grief, stemming from the successive deaths, all within eight months of each other, of her two remaining sisters and her only brother crystallised into a particular and personal aspect of a general and instinctive horror: the horror she had always had of mortality itself as the great mutilator and divider of human life, joy and companionship on earth. Orphanhood – one of the foremost constants in her imaginative world – is thus a symbol of something more than mere parent-loss. It stands for the whole empty experience of alienation and solitariness, and of the greatest loss of all – the internal security necessary for the development of the true, free self. This it was that Charlotte feared above all other terrors; thus, in all her work, the sustenance vital to the proper development of the self became the deep and abiding love of one human being for another.

This change of attitude in Charlotte, from the objective treatment of orphanhood to the deeply personal, can be seen, it is suggested, if we look at the differences of treatment of orphanhood and death between, on the one hand, *The Professor* and *Jane Eyre*, written while Branwell, Emily and Anne were still alive and *Shirley* and *Villette*, completed after their deaths. In the earlier novels, the status of orphanhood is dealt with fairly dispassionately. It is merely a fact of life from which more immediate facts arise, notably the necessity for each of the individuals involved to earn a livelihood. In *The Professor*, for example, so far as Crimsworth is concerned, beyond a reference to his desire to possess a portrait of his mother, no attempt is made to convey any emotional response to the condition of orphanhood.

Indeed, when the portrait is presented to him, having at the time nowhere suitable to hang it, he puts it under his bed, and that, oddly, is the last we hear of it. Again, while the death of Frances Henri's aunt does have a great significance in the novel, this is primarily as a device for an important mobilisation of the plot, inasmuch as it results in the reunion of the lovers. And it is in this essential statement about the priority of love – reiterated in all her work – that Charlotte confronts her Demon and ultimately confounds those who would see her as eternally death-haunted. As she has Crimsworth say, '. . . if we rarely taste the fulness of joy in this life, we yet more rarely savour the acid bitterness of hopeless anguish',[11] adding with a tenacity of spirit that faithfully reflects that of the inmates of Haworth Parsonage, '. . . the man of regular life and rational mind never despairs . . . he leans on Hope's anchors. . . .' Immediately after these reflections, Crimsworth finds Frances in the Protestant Cemetery of Louvain and leads her home, and this has an extra significance, because, for Crimsworth, ever conscious of the lack of a real home, it is the beginning of the trail that will eventually end in the fulfilment of the house in Daisy Lane. Charlotte closes this chapter with a lapse into a lush sentimentality that she was never henceforth to equal, but in essence it contains much that, contrary to attempts to prove otherwise,[12] was true to the basic Brontëan attitude to life: 'Hope smiles on Effort!'[13]

With *Jane Eyre*, the argument that Charlotte had a 'guilt-induced will to die'[14] and that it coloured all her novels becomes even more difficult to accept. For in this novel, the delineation of human tenacity confronting a remorseless spirit of negation is surely the most death-defying, the most life-affirming gesture that she was to make. Much more does she seem concerned here with the problems of frustration and repression than with those of death *per se*, or with guilt. Thus, the little girl, ready and willing to answer bullying violence blow for blow, develops into the young woman prepared to fight, first for her principles and then, literally, against starvation and exposure, for her life. On only two occasions could it be said that the will to die is reflected in the characterisation of Jane Eyre, and neither is particularly convincing. The first is when, still a child, she is locked in the sinister dark of the Red Room in her aunt's house, fearing it to contain the restless ghost of her uncle. But the impulse to oblivion, when it comes, consists half of terror, half of a child's bravado that longs to expend itself in paying out its tormentors. We almost expect to hear the words, 'they'll be sorry when I'm dead.'

The second occasion is when Jane flees Thornfield Hall on the morning following her abortive marriage. Tortured by pity for the man she has abandoned, she falls to the ground, temporarily overcome by weakness, fearing – hoping – that death might come. But the moment is brief. Charlotte has her say: 'I was soon up; crawling forwards on my hands and knees, and then again raised to my feet – as eager and as determined as ever to reach the road'.[15] And the journey she faces is but another phase of that quest for independent identity which, beginning at Gateshead, is continued at Lowood School and culminates at Thornfield Hall: a quest in which the deadly lures towards self-immolation come in many forms, ranging from the nobility of a Helen Burns, to the passion of a Rochester and the egotism of a St John Rivers. To survive, to live, to be herself, Jane *will* resist them all. Moreover, survival must mean more than mere existence; it must mean the enjoyment of 'being' to the fullest extent. 'I *will* be happy',[16] she tells St John Rivers, and she means in her own material world of loving and sharing, not in his restrictive sphere of detached spirituality, in which, as she has already begun to recognise, self-abnegation so easily becomes self-serving.

However, during the time that she was writing *Shirley*, Charlotte's letters to her publisher's reader, W. S. Williams,[17] show her coming agonisingly to terms wth the inevitability of the deaths of her brother and two remaining sisters. By the end of May 1849, it is all over. She writes first, a simple note, to tell him that Anne is dead, and then, on 4 June, a longer letter, in which she describes what the deaths of both her sisters have meant to her.[18] This letter is important to our understanding, not only of Charlotte's own attitude to the facts of life and death, but also to those of both Emily and Anne. Indeed, if Charlotte's view of the former as here expressed is accurate, it can be seen to amend all those impressions of Emily as a near-manic depressive, with eyes turned towards the grave, which have tended to stem from a criticism steeped in Freudian psychology. Charlotte writes:

> I let Anne go to God, and felt He had a right to her. I could hardly
> let Emily go. I wanted to hold her back then, and I want her back
> now. Anne, from her childhood, seemed preparing for an early
> death. Emily's spirit seemed strong enough to bear her to fulness
> of years. They are both gone . . . .

And yet, despite it all, she can speak of a God who is 'wise – perfect – merciful', can cling to the idea of an 'immortality' which 'guarantees' the good things of life 'from corruption', and can say: 'God has upheld me. From my heart I thank him.'[19]

These letters leave little doubt that the deaths of her sisters – especially of Emily and Anne – were the paramount tragedies in Charlotte's life. They also make it almost impossible to believe that someone who could so recoil from the acceptance of death in someone as young as Anne could herself harbour the 'will to die'. Charlotte, in fact, found this death 'sadder'[20] intrinsically than that of Emily, who she could at least persuade herself had passed 'reluctantly' from this world. Just how valid these views of Charlotte's were concerning her sisters' respective attitudes will be discussed later; it is obvious, however, that her comment upon Emily is at variance with the impressions we gain of the latter's essential philosophical position as summarised, for example, in the final verse of the poem 'No coward soul is mine' (see p. 160).[21] Apart from the probably harrowing pathological differences obtaining between the two deaths, we cannot, of course, discount the possibility that Charlotte's interpretation owed something to her own need to see in the moment of dissolution the kind of conventional reassurance which Anne could give to her, but which Emily could not.

Such comfort, via the words of the old Christian message, Anne's faith supplied and Charlotte's could respond to; but never, apparently, in her lifetime had Emily spoken directly of her religious beliefs, and in her death she remained silent. Thus left to provide her own interpretation, Charlotte would perhaps more naturally see Emily's death-struggles as conveying a reluctance to depart from the mortal world. That they might instead have represented a fierce conflict between a spirit eager to be gone and a body accustomed to resistance would possibly have raised inferences altogether too disturbing.

Such, at all events, was the catalytic background to the writing of Charlotte's final novels. As earlier indicated (see Chapter 3), there have been many criticisms of *Shirley*: that it lacks unity, that as an attempt at being a 'social' novel it is a failure, and so on. Apropos of Charlotte's attitude towards life and death, assessments of this kind about the novel's structure or intent remain insignificant beside its ultimate hypotheses, which are, firstly, that a human being, full of the yearning for life, can be brought literally to the brink of death when deprived of hope; secondly, that the most fundamental of human hopes is for the kind of relationship that bestows a sense of identity, the restoration of which renews the will to live.

Even while she was writing of these things, we can see the selfsame struggle taking place in Charlotte's own life. Right up to the time of *Villette*, her last completed novel, her experience was still essentially tragic. Death had claimed every member of her family except herself and her father; all hope of romance seemed gone and a life of loneliness to lie ahead of her. It is undeniable that at this point she struggled against what has been described as a 'numbing depression'.[22] But Robert Keefe's suggestion that this was 'the final state . . . from which she was never to recover' is hardly accurate. In fact, the end of Charlotte's life fits almost exactly that hypothesis which I have suggested she presented to us in the description of Caroline Helstone's life in *Shirley* – that via the accumulation of loss and the deprivation of hope, a human life can be brought to the edge of despair; but that the will to live is renewed by the restoration of love and companionship. For Charlotte, these events came, of course, with her marriage to her father's staid and conventional curate, Arthur Bell Nicholls. It was an event far from the fulfilment of her adolescent dreams; Nicholls was hardly the Byronic Hero, but neither was this the Charlotte of those dreams. Suffering had brought to her a maturer vision of love; and she had learnt that the death of the body could be accepted with less anguish than that of the spirit and the heart. Thus, at the onset of her last illness she could write of her husband that he was 'the best earthly comfort that ever woman had'.[23] Against this evidence, any view of Charlotte's life as fixed in a static solution of morbidity is surely insupportable. At the conclusion of *Villette*, we feel that her Demon has at last been exorcised, shown to be as fraudulent as the novel's ubiquitous 'nun'. Writing of this novel, and of its acceptance of suffering, Charles Burkhart has justifiably claimed that here Charlotte 'finally transcended herself, and touched on the universal'.[24]

When we come to Emily, it is interesting to us today to recall that her first biographer, Mary Robinson, wrote that Emily 'grew up to have no dreary thoughts'[25] of death, 'neither any dreams of a far-off heaven'.

Since then, of course, critical opinion has changed. It is curious that the sister whom Charlotte saw as 'strong' with the will to live is, of all the Brontës, the one whom critics have most associated with death. There are a number of reasons for this: the nature of the poetry, its many references to death, in particular the notion we repeatedly find there of death as a release from the imprisonment of suffering, and finally the dark, death-haunted vision of *Wuthering Heights*, in which death is almost apotheosised by being the means whereby the thwarted love of Heathcliff and Cathy is given a putative fulfilment. It has been claimed[26] that, for Emily, death was 'the true goal of life'. It was part of a process of transformation by which life was brought, via suffering, to what in her essay, 'The Butterfly', she had called a 'glorious outcome'. And Margaret Lane has supplied a valuable pointer to how this acted as a source and motivation in Emily's work. She writes: 'The whole unspoken theme of *Wuthering Heights* is somehow to do with this, and if we could clearly grasp it we would have the key to her mystery.'[27] Under 'the music,' she says, of 'everything that Emily Brontë wrote the echo of Heathcliff's leap into the dark reverberates again and again like a roll of drums.'

A more negative interpretation[28] of Emily's death-orientation draws attention to what is described as a possible 'suicidal' tendency in the lines from her poem, 'A Day Dream'[29] – 'Thou would'st rejoice for those that live/Because they live to die'. It is at least arguable, however, that these lines express hope rather than despair: the hope inspired by a belief, which Emily's work overall suggests that she had, in a kind of Platonist Reality, against which the mortal world seems a tragic distortion; for human beings, a dark-veiled experience of universal sorrow from which they must awake, via the nightmare of suffering, to knowledge of the True and Eternal. In this vision of life, the term 'suicidal' is meaningless, for death becomes the entrance to a different awareness. And this is exactly the scenario that is presented to us in the ending to *Wuthering Heights*, seen both in the mysterious references to 'change'[30] in the dying Heathcliff, and also in the reformation that takes place in the young Catherine.

Wuthering Heights, possibly more than any other novel in the English language, has baffled readers and critics alike. The latter, in an attempt to unravel its complexities, have produced a positive minefield of conflicting interpretation. It is here claimed, however, that the novel yields much clearer insights when it is looked at not simply as a work in isolation, but rather as the climax to a logical train of thought that had been gradually and perhaps more inconclusively developed throughout both the poetry and the essays of earlier days. We then see in its violent human tragedies the dramatic summary of Emily Brontë's ideas about a mortal world that, like Plato's, was essentially a corruption of reality; in other words, a kind of death in itself. We see, too, although in much more violent form, the same point as was to be made by George Eliot about the *spiritual* death that results from the malevolence of the uncontrolled human will. And this again was a theme that had appeared much earlier in Emily's work. In another of the essays of her young womanhood, Death itself had been the subject:[31] Death seeking a prime minister to oversee his empire, and dismissing the claims of Rage, Vengeance, Envy and so on, in favour of the final candidate, Intemperance, who claims as his most powerful ally, 'Civilisation'. In *Wuthering Heights*, Emily turned once again to these two influences, and, in the sustained drama of the novel, she was able the more effectively to expose what she saw as their most baneful aspects. 'Civilisation' at its most spurious is represented by the effete standards of Thrushcross Grange and the oppressive tyranny of Hindley Earnshaw. Still more importantly, the intemperance of self-will in human relations is reflected in Heathcliff and Cathy, where it takes the form of a monstrous distortion of love in which each seeks to devour the other. Such a form of love, excluding, as it does, not only all other human beings around it, but also the true interests of the life it focuses upon, can only end in death. But it is Emily's thesis that no human condition is beyond the possibility of change, and with change comes the hope of salvation. This said, no comforting death-bed conversions awaited the Victorian readers of *Wuthering Heights*, no last-minute scenes of Christian repentance. But in the agonising pre-death struggles of Heathcliff, through his strange transformation and 'ecstasy', *something* is happening: something that if we keep in mind the message of earlier expressions such as 'The Butterfly', we surmise to be about the purgation of the soul through suffering. And, in the final sequence of the 'ghosts' on the moors,[32] something, very possibly, about the salvation of sinners. It is vital that we should perceive – for it is no accident – that it is on this note of change that *Wuthering Heights* ends.

On a more concrete level, *Wuthering Heights* gives the death theme a highly contemporary application. Mrs Earnshaw dies when Cathy is little older than Emily was when she lost her own mother (although if Emily had this in mind, there seems to be no evidence that personal emotions were involved). Heathcliff, too, is orphaned at about the same age. Mr and Mrs Linton die within days of each other after 'both took the fever',[33] thus orphaning the young Edgar and Isabella, while tuberculosis removes Edgar Linton, Isabella and her son, Linton. Even the drink-induced death of Hindley Earnshaw, though almost certainly drawn from eye-witness experience of Branwell, was by no means an uncommon destiny among the spoilt sons of the better-off Victorian families. Bearing this general picture in mind, it might be felt that what Derek Traversi has called Emily's 'tendency to see human life and individual passions in the shadow of death'[34] defines her more as a *realistic* novelist than as one whom he claims to be basically influenced by the romantic tradition. Equally, her uncompromising delineations of the relationship between sin, suffering and death would seem to reflect a philosophy of causal determinism every bit as inexorable as that of George Eliot. In the tragic passion of Heathcliff and Cathy is projected an unsurpassed example of self-annihilation brought about by a blind indifference to moral law. The causal links between cruelty and revenge, and between vengeance and self-destruction are described with a pitiless logic; no horror is spared us because this is what the truth demands.

At the same time, it is this deterministic view of life that lifts some of the burden of guilt from the novel's two main characters, making them, as it were, more to be pitied than condemned. By this view, 'sin' and ignorance are the obverse of one and the same blind face, therefore we should tremble for the sinner as we sympathise with the victim. And this is the recurrent message of everything that Emily Brontë wrote – from the early poem, 'Well, some may hate and some may scorn'[35] to the long Gondal poem, written only two years before her death, 'Why ask to know the date – the clime?', with its somewhat cumbrous but pointed lines:

> I know that Justice holds in store
> Reprisals for those days of gore;
> Not for the blood but for the sin
> Of stifling mercy's voice within.[36]

It may have been true, as Mary Robinson suggested, that Emily had no notions of a 'far-off heaven', although the last paragraph of 'The Butterfly'[37] certainly suggests otherwise, with its references to a 'divine harvest' to be gathered in 'an eternal realm of happiness and glory'. The truth is that – old-fashioned, unpopular, uninteresting even as it may seem to us today – Emily Brontë was essentially, though not dogmatically, a conformist Christian. Where she 'takes off' from this position is in those mystic apprehensions that, constantly flaring and fading from within, render her work so palpably different from any other. But it is in this work, and in the strange vision that informs it, that we have as clear a clue as we need to her innermost beliefs about human life and its ultimate destiny. In the final verse of one of the last poems of her life she wrote:

> There is not room for Death
> Nor atom that his might could render void
> Since thou art Being and Breath
> And what thou art may never be destroyed.[38]

If we look at that poem as it appears in the definitive Hatfield collection, we notice that the only words capitalised are 'Death', 'Being' and 'Breath'; the word 'thou' is not. While this cannot be said to constitute proof of any kind, it does strongly suggest that, for Emily, the sense of a personal God and of some specific Heaven was less important than the idea that 'Being' and 'Breath' – both immediate concepts of Life – were all that there could ever be, since there was 'not room for Death'. Put another way, it would seem to indicate that, for Emily Brontë, death was simply the obverse view of Life; or, in Platonist terms, the end of illusion and the beginning of reality.

Charlotte's picture of Anne as the sister attuned to thoughts of death from an early age has long clouded much critical commentary upon this youngest of the Brontës. She has been seen as a free spirit dragged down by religious pietism,[39] for which some have blamed the close, cloistered influence of the church in its almost physical encroachment upon the Brontë living room. Others[40] have placed the onus upon Aunt Branwell, over whom there has been some confusion as to whether her brand of fervent Methodism was of the relatively tolerant Wesleyan order or of the harshly proscriptive Calvinist variety: a point that is not without importance if her influence upon Anne is to be seen as significant. The issue, like so many concerning the Brontës, is open to a certain amount of speculation, which has the salutary effect of sending us back to Anne herself. It is undoubtedly clear from many of her poems, such, for example, as 'The Doubter's Prayer'[41] and 'Despondency',[42] that at one period of her life Anne passed through an experience of spiritual crisis at the core of which were dark eschatological doubts. Through the pages of the *Methodist Magazine* she discovered the poetry of Cowper, whose language of manic despair seems for a time to have touched a chord in her own soul. One of her poems is dedicated to Cowper,[43] but the profound apprehensions expressed in the first two and last verses of this poem[44] are importantly countered by six middle stanzas which clearly convey Anne's own belief in the forgiveness of God and the soul's ultimate salvation.

Today, the picture of Anne that is beginning to emerge more clearly is that of the Brontë sister who, of all three, was the one with her feet most firmly planted on this earth. While Emily concerned herself with universal problems of life and death, Anne's focus was closer, narrower, more specific, more personal. She seems always to have been more anxious to see eradicated the immediate and particular ills of the here and now than to ponder their riddles *vis-à-vis* eternity. She looked long at the world around her, and, like Charlotte, but much more objectively, drew for her fictional themes upon those situations which she had witnessed or experienced personally.

It is, perhaps, surprising, but true, that one of the bravest and most important pieces of writing on the subject of death and eschatology which any of the Brontës achieved was produced by Anne. Her description of the death of the profligate and unrepentant Arthur Huntingdon in *The Tenant of Wildfell Hall* has rightly been called[45] a pioneering commitment to the doctrine of universal salvation, since it was to be five years before F. D. Maurice was deprived of his Chair at King's College, London, for proclaiming his disbelief in Everlasting Damnation and another thirty years before Dean Farrar's controversial work, *Eternal Hope*, appeared. What we hear in this scene, via the voice of Helen Huntingdon as she watches beside her dying husband, is undoubtedly a personal statement of Anne's own belief (shared in particular with her sister, Emily) in the regeneration of the human soul. She begins by pleading with her husband to pray for himself, telling him, 'no man can deliver his brother, nor make agreement unto God for him'.[46] It is a statement of that typical Brontë acceptance of individual human responsibility which all three sisters shared with George Eliot. But at the end, faced with her husband's craven collapse into self-pity, Helen says: 'How could I endure to think that that poor trembling soul was hurried away to everlasting torment?'[47] 'But thank God I have hope,' she says (the unfailing Brontë hope) 'that God who hateth nothing that He hath made *will* bless it in the end!'

Anne Brontë's answer to her own night of doubt was to cling with a fierce tenacity to the single, simple concept of a God of love and forgiveness, and she allowed no evidence of personal pain, nor of the sin or weakness of others, to cause her to abandon it. Thus, while we might conclude that Charlotte was possibly right in believing that Anne had wrestled long with thoughts of death, she was surely wrong in construing this as an indication of a readiness to die. Anne's response to the approach of her own death was to express a deep regret at leaving so many plans unfulfilled. Her calm submission at the actual moment of death was no more and no less than a further characteristic example of the courage and practicality with which she had faced everything that her twenty-nine years of life had thrown at her. Typically, she wasted no time and emotion over the inevitable. Her last words were an exhortation to Charlotte to be brave.

As suggested earlier, in the work both of the Brontës, as a group, and of George Eliot, the worst kind of death appears not so much that of the body but is rather represented by that breakdown and dissolution of the guiding spirit that, left unchecked, reduces a human life to a level lower than that of the animals. In the novels of George Eliot, one of the recurrent metaphors used to denote this was that connected with death by drowning. Examples abound: there is Adam Bede's 'poor wandering father',[48] submerged by drink long before his tragic stumble into the Willow Brook; there is Tom Tulliver, a man blind to 'the depths in life'[49] and Maggie, a woman overwhelmed by them, a woman adrift between the conflicting tides of 'passion and duty',[50] floating to a spiritual death far more terrible than that of the Flood in which she is ultimately lost; there is *Silas Marner*'s Dunstan Cass, stumbling into the stone-pit with his hands full of stolen gold;[51] *Romola*'s Tito Melema, seeking escape from his deserts in the river, only to be cast at the feet of the man whose only reason for living is to kill him;[52] and, most repellant of all, *Daniel Deronda*'s Grandcourt, who calls in vain from the sea for a life-line from the wife in whom shame and hatred have paralysed all natural feeling.[53] All these characters 'die' first from within, and all in a sense by their own hand, for all have flouted some aspect of the moral law, whose operation, for George Eliot, was as inflexibly part of cause and effect as was that of the natural world around us. The primary source of tragedy for human beings was, as she saw it, their inability to recognise this fact and to exercise a choice of action in line with a realistic assessment of the inevitable results.

In this alignment of human frailty with a causal moral law, a particular link can be seen between George Eliot and Emily Brontë, an example of which is contained in the respective characterisations and deaths of the two heroines of *Wuthering Heights* and *The Mill on the Floss*. Both Catherine Earnshaw and Maggie Tulliver are childhood victims of that typical Victorian mixture of spoiling and emotional deprivation that in the case of each of them ends in an inordinate need of emotional satisfaction. Maggie never becomes quite the emotional predator that Cathy is. Her sense of moral responsibility is far greater and she does at least struggle to resist the weaknesses within her own nature. But her failure to do so results in consequences to others every bit as cruel and shocking as those emanating from the behaviour of Catherine Earnshaw, and the inevitable ending is equally fatal for them both. Each in her way wills her own death by reason of having sacrificed all hope of a return to normal life around her. The failure of each had its root in something much more inflexible than mere moral fragility; it is something which George Eliot's friend, Charles Bray, had once defined[54] – and which she accepted: that everything in life, including the human mind, was regulated by an invariable sequence of cause and effect and that it was 'man's duty to trace out their connexion and to adapt his conduct to it'. In other words, the necessary adjustment is basically a rational one. George Eliot herself wrote that '. . . Tragedy consists in the terrible difficulty of this adjustment'.[55]

The difference between George Eliot and the Brontës here is that, as Felicia Bonaparte explains: 'Eliot perceived a tragic universe in which man is born and dies for no purpose and with little hope of joy'.[56] By her insinuation of a limited degree of 'choice' into the deterministic concept, George Eliot had to some extent mitigated the inevitable despair. But what still remained was the eternal problem of the non-believer: that individual human life is inevitably diminished by there being no sense of personal continuity. If death were to be the end of things, what meaning was there to life, and what incentive to live it according to a sense of 'duty' that had no authority other than that given it by fallible human beings? One argument has been that George Eliot took up this challenge by means of an emphasis upon the significance of the Family. Edward T. Hurley writes:[57] 'the family becomes throughout the novels the focus and bearer of continuing life'. It is, he says, 'the instrument of immortality'. He adds:

> In the earlier, more modest novels, this is simply a family that carries on the family work on the family land. In the later novels it becomes a broader social revolution, culminating in the transcendental notion of *Daniel Deronda*.

It could hardly be denied that the concept of Family was an important one in George Eliot's work, but whether the purpose was to provide a 'focus and bearer of continuing life', or whether it served as an apt piece of symbolism, a convenient paradigm for the whole great 'family' of the world, remains arguable. For the artistic expression of her Religion of Humanity, the Family offered a ready-made source of imagery for the ideals of human feeling and interrelation, but it might be concluded that since she had discarded what she saw as the mythology of transcendentalism, it was precisely the strength of her position that she offered her readers *no* solution for what she saw as the insoluble tragedy of human destiny in individual terms. In general, she declared that her aim, in the depiction of tragedy, was to 'urge the human sanctities . . . through pity and terror as well as admiration and delights';[58] in other words, via the 'collision of forces',[59] which, in the humble as in the heroic life, she saw as the 'germ of tragedy'. It was there, she wrote, 'lying in the experience of a human soul that looks out through dull grey eyes and that speaks in a voice of quite ordinary tones'.[60]

It has been said that 'it might be argued that George Eliot always evades the tragic conclusion':[61] in the sense, for example, that Maggie Tulliver is 'rescued' by death, Dorothea Brooke by marriage, Gwendolen Harleth by Deronda and Romola Bardi by Savonarola and good works. If, however, we measure these respective fates against the golden Eldorados of hope to which each of these protagonists originally felt herself beckoned, they assume their true proportions as representatives of an ineradicable tragic irony. Each, too, is all of a piece with George Eliot's view of that intrinsic fact of life that makes it tragic – that it is by its very nature *unfinished*, incomplete. Thence, as she saw it, came the lure of wishful thinking, which, defined specifically in the nature of the gambler, became for her another potent metaphor in the context of tragedy and death. This idea she personified literally in the characterisation of Gwendolen Harleth in *Daniel Deronda*, but the same device crops up in a variety of ways in many of her other novels. In *Middlemarch* alone, for instance, we see no fewer than three cases, in the happy-go-lucky Fred Vincy and his hopes of inheritance, and the tragically delusive relationships of Lydgate and Rosamond and of Dorothea and Casaubon. At the heart of all these experiences is a kind of death: the death of hopes that were false from the start by reason of a failure to face reality.

Ironically, it is this vitalising element of hope – so very persistent in the work of the Brontës – that is so often felt lacking in the tone of George Eliot's writing. An undoubted factor in this contrast between the two literary expressions was the Brontës' fidelity to their inherited Christianity; for concomitant with Christian conformity was the comforting sense of a personal relationship between creature and Creator. Instead, for George Eliot, God had become an amorphous 'Humanity', the Devil human 'Egoism', and the Holy Spirit something even more rarely seen, 'Reason'. As one commentator puts it:[62] for George Eliot, '"evil" seems to have had no metaphysical reality'; it was 'a problem to be analyzed . . . it was not a transcendent mystery'.

This, however, reminds us that in George Eliot's work it is necessary to note the distinction she makes between the outrightly transcendental and elements of metaphysical imagery which stand as poetic pointers to certain human attitudes or conditions. These pointers occur frequently throughout her novels. An example is the passage in her introduction to *Felix Holt*,[63] where she indicates a connection between sin, suffering and death in a deeply enigmatic reference to the 'thorn bushes' of the poets' 'under world'. These, she says,

> have human histories hidden in them: the power of unuttered cries dwells in the passionless-seeming branches, and the red warm blood is darkly feeding the quivering nerves of a sleepless memory through tall dreams. These things are a parable.

And the 'parable' is given a potent symbolic force in this story of a woman trapped in a living death of remorse and blighted love, existing in a desert of lonely, embittered hours in the empty silence of a once grand house. Around the house stand 'large motionless'[64] trees. Trees and bushes are significantly linked in this imagistic way with death in the Eliot novels. Hetty Sorrel (one meaning of whose name, incidentally, derives from an 'acid-leaved herb'),[65] leaves her baby under a 'nut-bush',[66] and Molly Cass dies amidst the 'furze'.[67] In *Daniel Deronda*, the word 'thorns' symbolises guilt, suffering and death in Gwendolen Harleth's 'confession' to Deronda concerning her failure to save her husband from drowning.

> Deronda could not utter one word to diminish that sacred aversion to her worst self – that thorn-pressure which must come with the crowning of the sorrowful Better, suffering because of the Worse.[68]

Despite the Christian allusions of 'crowning', however, and the 'sorrowful Better' taking on the sins of the 'Worse', the essential meaning is, as ever for George Eliot, related to a limited, causally-determined life. 'It can never be altered,'[69] is the thought in Deronda's mind; 'it remains unaltered, to alter other things'.

Only when we come to the Mordecai sequences of *Daniel Deronda* does it seem that George Eliot's attitude to the transcendental, to the numinous, undergoes some kind of change. Here, we have a theme of which a very large part is concerned with the faith of a dying Jewish leader in the transmission of the soul from one body to another and the continuation therein of a divine messianic purpose. Given what we understand her personal beliefs (or *dis*beliefs) to have been, this seems on the face of it an extraordinary path for her to have taken. It might be argued that the attraction to her was of the Jewish ideal of a 'new brotherhood'[70] on earth, which would be in line with her ideas of a Religion of Humanity. In this longing of the people of the Diaspora for 'Unity'[71] was her opportunity to express her commitment to what had always been her paramount concern – the need for human beings to cohere in a common unity of sympathy, understanding and a sense of shared moral duty. But such explanations do not wholly cover the sense she gives us in these sequences of *Deronda* of a deeply personal sympathy not merely with the Judaic cause of nationhood but also with its sense of messianic calling.

Nor are the metaphysics of *Daniel Deronda* the novel's only concessions to the unfamiliar. With the exception of the drastic causal effects of *The Mill on the Floss, Daniel Deronda* is the only Eliot novel to end with a classic 'death-bed' scene. Of the novel as a whole, Barbara Hardy[72] writes that 'George Eliot is attempting to include new aspects of life, both social and psychological, which she had only touched on in her earlier "experiments in life"'. It could be said that those 'new aspects of life' included a new vision of death such as nothing she had written before could be said remotely to have foreshadowed.

Intellectually, the differences between the respective viewpoints of the Brontë sisters, as a group, and George Eliot on the subjects of death and eschatology are those which we would expect: that is to say, the differences represented by the radical opposition between Christian orthodoxy and rational humanism. The differences of literary style, on the other hand, are in some ways more intriguing, deriving as they do not merely from diverse beliefs and temperaments, but from differing elements of personal experience. The Brontës' handling of tragedy has, for example, a noticeably 'brisker', more astringent tone than is to be found in most of the Eliot novels. It is not difficult to see why. For the sisters, suffering and death were matters too real for artifice, too dangerously close for the expansive exhortation by which George Eliot often sought to engage her readers' sympathies. They did not plead with their readers, as Eliot does in 'Amos Barton', to perceive the 'poetry and the pathos, the tragedy and the comedy'[73] of human lives. They put their faith in direct statement, and the efficacy of this technique, if such it can be called, is well conveyed in the great tragic scene of *Jane Eyre*, where Jane leaves Rochester, with all the force of her love contained in the simple statement, 'you will forget me before I forget you'.[74] By contrast, in *Middlemarch*, while we are *told* that Mr Casaubon 'was spiritually a-hungered like the rest of us',[75] we are unable to *understand* his hunger because we are never shown its precise source. We are conscious that the description of the 'small hungry shivering self'[76] that is Mr Casaubon hints at some supreme tragedy; we realise that he is emotionally arid, possibly – but only possibly – physically impotent, but the real reasons that he feels as let down in his marriage and in his life generally as does Dorothea remain undefined. It is possible to feel that perhaps one of the novel's most promising sources of tragedy remains untapped.

In looking at these differences between the Brontës and George

Eliot it is perhaps not insignificant that, for George Eliot, the deepest personal experience of tragedy and death remained ahead of her for the whole of her writing career. Not until the death of Lewes did she know the ultimate darkness of grief and despair. As a novelist, therefore, her probings of what she called 'the pains and joys of others'[77] were, for the most part, unavoidably at second-hand; she was compelled at this deepest level to draw upon the imagination to add the requisite feeling to an essentially objective view.

Nevertheless, in their treatment of the sources and patterns of tragedy and death, all four novelists worked from much the same premises towards similar conclusions. For all of them, the essential core of human tragedy was, like the 'worm' in Emily Brontë's description of 'The Butterfly', a spurious self which, either through ignorance or wilfulness, is enabled to eat away the life on which it fastens. This was the tragedy which all four novelists most deplored, this the death which all were united in identifying as life's most bitter and most destructive enemy. Only in their respective attitudes to the transcendental were they essentially divided, and in that respect it is at least a matter of speculation, perhaps, as to whether George Eliot's deeply sympathetic response to the Judaic messianic tradition in *Daniel Deronda* does not leave a tentative question in the air.

7

Conclusion

I have maintained in this work that, despite the considerable differences of personal belief and literary style that separate the Brontë sisters and George Eliot, there nevertheless exists between them a special and almost necessary kind of relationship. It can be claimed to be necessary by reason of the historical contiguity of their lives and the external influences to which they were all alike exposed. And it can be said to be special in the light of the vital contribution which these four major novelists made to the form of the English novel in its transition from the Romantic-Idealistic mode to the Realism of the early Modern.

Notwithstanding this, it must be emphasised that divisions of this sort are seldom consistent and clear-cut. The commitment to the new 'Truth', largely inspired by Thackeray and later seen to marked effect in Trollope, was, in its early stages, by no means an unadulterated quality. There lingered among many writers, notably Dickens and the Brontës, and – despite a decade's lapse – George Eliot, many of the attributes that belonged to the Romantic tradition: idealism, rebellion, nostalgia, an emphasis upon the innocence of the child, the exaltation of romantic love and of womankind, and an impulse towards the liberation of human feeling. A vigorous reliance on poetic imagery likewise remained. Despite, for example, George Eliot's stated preference for 'strong concrete language',[1] we see in her work a considerable dependence upon metaphor and symbolism to evoke or suggest powerful ideas. The distinction between her and Charlotte Brontë made by R. H. Hutton in 1860[2] – that she wrote out of '*observation*' and Charlotte from *imagination* 'out of the heart' – remains true, but seems a greatly over-simplified assessment of an author such as Eliot, whose penchant for the creation of 'noble', profoundly idealised figures was a characteristic of the Romantic imagination at its most compelling. Repeatedly throughout her work we see how she exemplifies the way in which, as Houghton points out, Romantic 'enthusiasm'[3] which extolled 'the vitality of the noble emotions' so often went hand in hand, even in the same person, with a 'contrasting mode of earnestness', with its 'concern for moral discipline and the performance of duty'.

> In a Victorian like George Eliot, brought up in Evangelicalism and yet filled with Romantic ardour, the creed of strict conduct, the renunciation of self, and a dedicated pursuit of social duty could become a sublime object of passionate devotion.[4]

And Houghton quotes her own comments on the nature of Maggie Tulliver:

> From what you know of her, you will not be surprised that she threw some exaggeration and wilfulness, some pride and impetuosity, even into her self-renunciation: her own life was still a drama for her, in which she demanded of herself that her part should be played with intensity.[5]

The Brontëan connection here hardly needs stressing. For all four novelists, a major concern was that most vital of all Romantic elements, the expression of *feeling*. With it went the urgent need of the author to create bridgeheads between people, irrespective of sex, class and race:[6] also the inclination towards a moral didacticism expressed in various forms of 'ennobling' idealisations. While Emily Brontë might on the face of it seem an exception to the latter trend, the implications of the final stages of *Wuthering Heights*, with their emphasis on character reformation, afford her a qualified candidature.

The Brontës and George Eliot were parts together of a rather special kind of mid-Victorian Romanticism which stood half-way between an ornate, Tennysonian type of idealism and a new, driving impulse towards a more 'truthful', more realistic development of the novel. The passion for truth-telling, which was to take extreme forms – in France in particular[7] – before the century was over, was seen, in the Brontës and George Eliot, as a delicate balance between the real and the ideal, between the passionate, sometimes nostalgic, desire for life-as-it-was and an equally urgent commitment to the extension of its present-day boundaries. Sometimes, truth and nostalgia would seem to merge; in *Adam Bede*, for example, George Eliot wrote of the 'rare, precious quality of truthfulness'[8] which delighted her 'in many Dutch paintings'.

I find a source of delicious sympathy in these faithful pictures of a monotonous homely existence, which has been the fate of so many more among my fellow-mortals than a life of pomp or of absolute indigence, of tragic suffering or of world-stirring actions.

And going on to extol the virtues of the homely and the real in artistic expression, she underlined her viewpoint with a question that strongly hints that in her mind were thoughts of Charlotte Brontë and Jane Eyre: 'But, bless us, things may be lovable that are not altogether handsome, I hope?' Human feeling, she said, 'does not wait for beauty – it flows with resistless force and brings beauty with it'.

This new 'commitment'[9] to an integrity of feeling in the novel has been seen by Raymond Williams to be part of a response to a world of 'desire and hunger, of rebellion and pallid convention' that was reminiscent of Blake's:

> an intensity of desire is as much a response . . . to the human crisis of that time as the more obviously recognisable political radicalism . . . . What was at issue really was relationship itself.[10]

And here, the germinal influence on the novel of the Brontë/Eliot connection is seen most clearly, for, as Williams points out, although this concern with feeling had been present, albeit in varying ways, in the major Romantic poets, such as Blake and Keats, and Shelley and Byron,[11] it had not been comparably treated in the novel, in which hitherto the tendency had been to stress love's worldly qualities. It was 'the achievement of the Brontë sisters . . . that in different ways they remade the novel so that this kind of passion could be directly communicated'. In George Eliot, it emerged in an intensity of concern for the interrelationship of individuals within the social grouping, covering a wider range, both human and geographic. Despite this apparently more 'worldly' approach, however, a compelling argument for the essentially 'poetic' nature of George Eliot's imagination has been made.[12] Part of the famous Eliot experimentalism, we might conclude, was the grand attempt to effect a union between the poetic vision and verisimilitude.

One of the effects of this was the emphasis upon the lives of 'ordinary' individuals, seen as part of the wider social *milieu*, a pattern that became increasingly apparent in George Eliot's novels from *Romola* on. In this, her realism was similar to that of Thackeray and Trollope, in that there was less concern for the complexities of plot as of those of human personality. Unlike Thackeray and Trollope, however, and more in common with Dickens, she often reflected the difficulty of harmonising realism with the portrayal of feeling. Her many idealisations, her sudden lapses into sentimentality, testify to this difficulty; for whereas Dickens found it possible to conceal much human anguish under comedy, the deep seriousness of George Eliot's art put such ploys beyond her reach. The Brontës, on the other hand, being unconfined by so great an urge towards objectivity, and choosing as their protagonists people whose lives were *not* by any means ordinary, had no such problem. For them, 'relationship' meant for the most part the 'I' – that is to say, the first person singular – sharply focused against a background of 'others', most of whom formed a group that was similarly *un*ordinary by virtue of being predominantly hostile. It is perhaps not too gross an over-simplification to say that, for the Brontës, the creative use of feeling remained to some extent a weapon in the war of rebellion between the individual and society, whereas, for George Eliot, it became increasingly an instrument of armistice, a basis for the negotiation of a new harmony and understanding between human beings.

For all that the latter position is necessarily and primarily a social one, however, the important paradox in George Eliot's novels is that the creation of a 'society' is always seen via layer upon layer of *individuation*; each life emerges from the group within its own centre of difference. It was the logical structural arrangement for a novelist for whom one of the most destructive defects of which human nature was capable was the failure of one human being to recognise the uniqueness in every other. In this failure, the problem was not, as she saw it, the egoist's *lack* of feeling, but his *misdirection* of it; the gentle Dorothea, for example, finds it 'easier'[13] to 'devote herself' to her husband than to understand him. In George Eliot's humanism, the danger posed by the ego was always that it could lead to ego-*ism*. It was a danger from which the Brontës were protected by their relatively undisturbed religious conformism, which obviated the need to deify Society in the place of God, and which meant that they could extol the importance of the individual self within the safe parameters of a morality presided over by a Higher (and Absolute) Authority. Over and above these differences, however, was a concept that all four shared: the concept of a unity that bound all human beings together in a common ontological experience. In one form or another, the effort to express this was paramount in their respective creative output.

Connected with the idea of unity is the second outstanding link between the four, referred to above – the element of moral didacticism: for here we see the Romantic influence merging not merely with Realism, but also with aspects that had a significantly *social* basis. R. W. Harris, writing of 'the emergence of radical and socialist thought'[14] in the period after the American and French revolutions, points to a reaction against 'the worship of Reason':

> a great seriousness swept over an important part of the nation, a deep concern for morality, an acute sense of guilt and sin, on both a personal and a national level, requiring a re-examination of personal and social morality, and accompanied by an urgent sense of the need for a return to religion.

The upper time limit of the period dealt with by Harris is 1830 – when the Brontë sisters and George Eliot were approaching their teens – but the *Zeitgeist* described here was not of rapid resolution. From 1831, when Carlyle lamented that 'the Time is still in pangs of travail with the New',[15] right through to mid-century and beyond, there was little change. We can thus see how credible is the idea of an affinity of thought and inspiration arching between the years that mark the boundaries of Brontë and Eliot creativity. Though in the sphere of religion, George Eliot had no rapport with Charlotte Brontë's 'Providence',[16] with Emily's 'eternal realm',[17] or Anne's 'great Redeemer',[18] yet even here, as already shown, she was in tune with the dominant spirit of their shared age to the extent that her 'New' religion retained many points of contact with the old. In *Daniel Deronda*, in particular, we saw what seemed to be some kind of experimental fusion between the two. In modern jargon, the result might be dubbed the 'Feuerbach/Luria Connection',[19] for the conception of God as 'man's self-reflexion'[20] and of man as seeking to see his soul perfected in the likeness of another[21] are not wholly dissimilar. In each idea, an assumption of unity – in the sense of the wholeness, or one-ness, of human interrelation – is fundamental.

It can be seen, too, how the notion of unity was connected in George Eliot's work with didactic elements centred on the ideal concept of Nobility. She herself resisted the didactic label, preferring the word, 'teaching',[22] yet those sections of *Deronda* that deal with the Judaic aspiration towards the renewal of national and spiritual unity bear the stamp not only of earnest proselytising but also of an idealism which, as always in the Eliot novel, took noble human shape. The charge of proselytism may seem unfair inasmuch as it is provoked by Mordecai's passionate hopes for the Hebrew nation, but it is argued that these hopes reflect too closely George Eliot's universal aspirations for humanity for there to be no personal element involved. The political and social aspects of Mordecai's dream are all of a piece with George Eliot's philosophy of life, which, conceding possibilities of human choice and potential, laid stress upon a melioristic view of society.

The way in which the Romantic ideal of nobility – especially of 'noble womanhood' – is subtly connected with George Eliot's vision of unity is via the individual will to sacrifice, even (as in Romola and Mordecai) to transcend, the self in the interests of others. It is an essentially, almost solely, social version of Romantic idealism and, as such, a reflection of that difference that every so often sets George Eliot apart from the Brontës even in matters in which they so clearly share a common aim. On the intellectual level, the links that have so often seemed most strong in the foregoing chapters have been with Emily. Although, in *Wuthering Heights*, the search for unity is far more central, more subjective and infinitely more intense than in any aspect of Eliot's work, yet the separations between the worlds of Wuthering Heights and Thrushcross Grange are seen to be in effect as much social as individual, and to point up the disastrous divisiveness of human attitudes as clearly as anything in the Eliot novels. At the same time, in the tragic distortion of individual character that is Heathcliff is found an adumbration of all George Eliot's fears concerning the moral perils of untrammelled 'egotism' as seen in the older Byronic mode. Given, however, this transformation on her part of old-style, egotistic Romanticism into heroic social awareness, it is interesting to reflect on the creation of a character such as the Princess Halm-Eberstein in *Daniel Deronda*. Here, we have a full-blooded Byronic egotist if ever there were one, and George Eliot gives to her the most impassioned speech on female emancipation in all her fiction. It is one of several instances in her work in which can be sensed a certain equivocation suggestive of some subterranean division of feeling within the authorial self.

Similar divisions have earlier been traced in Charlotte Brontë in her efforts to close the gulf between man and woman, both in her work and in her own personal life. It is in fact to the personal that we must turn for the essential explanation of this shared preoccupation with human unity: to that painful residue of early emotional insecurity and frustration that binds all four lives together. In the novels, this is worked out consistently via the anguish of the 'displaced' individual, the most powerful examples, of course, being Emily Brontë's Heathcliff and Charlotte's Jane Eyre, but Anne's heroines are similarly disadvantaged and not a book of George Eliot's exists that does not have its 'lost soul', whether of a literal or figurative kind. Typically, it is to Emily that we must turn for the last word on the unity of being. Instead of George Eliot's evolutionary journey between Maggie Tulliver's irresolute 'path of penitent sacrifice'[23] and the exaltation of Mordecai Cohen – or even the long haul between Jane Eyre and Lucy Snowe – we have just one novel which says it all. In *Wuthering Heights*, unity becomes a present reality when the spirits of Heathcliff and Cathy seek and find each other in death, and a new and better kind of love than theirs heals the scarred young lives they leave behind. Unity between human beings, and the union of souls in immortality, are seen to be instant upon the dissolution of the mortal self. As had been foreshadowed in 'The Butterfly', it is the primal Christian message, innocent of punitive doctrine: '*This* day shalt thou be with me . . . .' The italics are mine; the emphasis is Emily Brontë's.

Up to this point, most of the discussion in this concluding section has been on those attitudes and attributes which the sisters and George Eliot can be seen to have held in common. A final look at the major differences between them reveal these to be concentrated in important distinctions of style rather than of attitude or intent. The most obvious difference is that between two kinds of narrative, which might be called, respectively, the Ego-Assertive and the Ego-Repressive. The former is represented by the Brontës' autobiographical approach, with its effect on the reader of being directly involved in a process of spontaneous development. This contrasts with the Ego-Repressive style of the Eliot authorial voice, which is reflective, interpretative, and often with hortative overtones that have a distancing rather than participative effect. Paradoxically, the differences here turn upon a factor that, in principle even if not in practice, has been found to have been held by the four in common: the celebration of feeling. Writing of Charlotte Brontë, Geoffrey Tillotson comments: 'Feelings constitute the inner strength of the novels, and are the main source of that "almost preternatural power" that George Eliot responded to in *Villette*'.[24]

H. V. Routh, on the other hand, claims that George Eliot showed how the surface of things 'had been encrusted and frozen by the conventionalities of civilisation, so the feelings could not find their proper channels'.[25] Not too many would perhaps agree with him today that 'her novels have not stood the test of time',[26] or that they can be compared to 'a menagerie of performing animals'; but it might well be conceded that, although her characters 'may seem to be free . . . her creativeness is circumscribed by her exemplary sentiments'. The difficulty is intrinsic and is perhaps best illustrated by a comparison with Emily Brontë, of whom Tillotson observes:

> Like all writers, she put her whole genius into her book . . . . She was a recluse from choice, being self-sufficient. Accordingly, she did not need to make use of her fiction to unload much turmoil of private personality. It was her intellect rather than her feelings that found Lockwood and Nelly useful as a screen.[27]

And yet, despite this intellectualism, this self-sufficiency, this hard-headed objectivity, *Wuthering Heights* might well be described as Feeling in essence. A trite observation, though perhaps a not inappropriate one, is that the Brontë 'message' came from the heart, whereas George Eliot's came from the heart via the mind. She once wrote to Clifford Allbutt:

> the inspiring principle which alone gives me courage to write is, that of so presenting our human life as to help my readers in getting a clearer conception and a more active admiration of those vital elements which bind men together and give a higher worthiness to their existence . . . .[28]

It is not disputed that such aims may be proper in themselves; unless very carefully controlled in practice, however, the result could be a degree of authorial intrusion that readers – especially in a more critical age – may well resent. In her own lifetime, George Eliot achieved a success such as only Charlotte among the Brontës was to know. No doubt one reason for this, however – as it was the reason for the disapproval initially accorded all the Brontës – was the Victorian concern for moral 'earnestness'[29] and 'self-improvement', which found an answering note in George Eliot's high-toned moral stance and her emphasis on duty. An interesting modern view is supplied by Quentin Anderson, who finds 'a seeming paradox in the fact that, although admired, she is not much read'.[30] The paradox exists for Anderson because 'no novelist in English has come closer to answering a question which is very important to us: How can a social world be felt and understood?' He seems, however, to be in part providing his own answer to this paradox when he later states (in relation to *Middlemarch*) that 'George Eliot is present as the only fully realized individual in her book';[31] more significantly, that she is present as 'the Wise Woman', an image which she herself encouraged.

> She was unable, even in the years of her maturest art, to conceive of fiction as a truly independent form . . . . We must conclude, I think, that the fairy-tale triumph of Romola over the physical and moral ills of a fever-stricken village, and the fantastic errand which takes Deronda to Jerusalem . . . are not merely tributes to a Victorian taste for moral exaltation. They are attempts on the part of the writer to give herself a recognizable moral status.[32]

In itself, this is perhaps not so very different from what in an earlier chapter I suggested Charlotte Brontë was doing in her novels in order to protect her own moral image after the Heger experience. The important difference between her and George Eliot in this respect – and one which may allow the Brontë novels as a whole to move forward more felicitously than Eliot's out of their own time into ours – is that free, unannotated expression of feeling that universalises Brontë fiction. This is the quality that Derek Traversi, writing of both Charlotte and Emily, describes as 'emotional intensity, the product of a unique concentration upon fundamental passion in a state approaching essential purity'.[33] Its authenticity, recognisable to human beings anywhere, in any age, wins for it a vital participative response. In discarding the personal viewpoint, along with the personal pronoun, George Eliot sacrificed that relationship of special intimacy with the reader that she came nearest to achieving in *The Mill* and that is still an essential part of the overall Brontë appeal.

An example of what is meant, above, is afforded by Charlotte's portrayal of Mr Rochester in *Jane Eyre* after his dramatic exposure as a would-be bigamist, contrasted with George Eliot's detached analysis of the state of Mr Casaubon's heart after his marriage to Dorothea Brooke in *Middlemarch*. Both incidents are crises which profoundly affect their respective protagonists, but in *Jane Eyre* Charlotte works on two levels to give her readers the closest possible insight into the mixed reactions of anguish and resignation with which Rochester faces the fact that he is about to lose his only true love. On the first of these levels, we hear Rochester himself telling of his feelings for Jane, reasoning with her, pleading, explaining; almost, at times, threatening, in the desperate hope that, out of understanding of the 'hideous and degrading agonies'[34] of the life he has endured with his 'intemperate and unchaste' wife, Jane will relent and stay with him. He tells how his love for her has grown slowly and deeply until it became for him a 'solemn passion'.[35] Finally, when he implores, 'what shall I do, Jane? Where turn for a companion, and for some hope?'[36] we are so committed to his plight that we instinctively shrink from the rejection that we know is coming. As an example of direct communication, this could hardly be surpassed. But Charlotte uses yet another technique for eliciting our sympathy for her erring hero. This time, she works from within Jane herself.

> Oh! with agony I thought of what I left! . . . I thought of him now . . . watching the sunrise; hoping I should soon come to say I would stay with him, and be his . . . . I could yet spare him the bitter pang of bereavement . . . . Oh, that fear of his self-abandonment – far worse than my abandonment – how it goaded me![37]

And at the end, when she returns to him again, the impact of the meeting is conveyed in words that mirror both the pity and the still palpable power of this now blind and injured man: 'The caged eagle, whose gold-ringed eyes cruelty has extinguished, might look as looked that sightless Samson'.[38] Nothing is left in these incidents to speculation, to uncertainty; instead, deep emotions are made real to us via two different kinds of interior vision, the first of the subject himself, the second of the object of those emotions.

In a previous chapter, I referred to the failure of the Casaubon/Dorothea marriage in *Middlemarch* as a promising source of tragedy that remained untapped. It might be argued, perhaps, that, as this novel is not primarily a 'love story', the omission was a legitimate one on George Eliot's part. Yet the failure of this marriage is the first turning-point in Dorothea's journey towards a measure of self-knowledge, a journey which is one of the central ingredients in a novel that is all about the attainment of such knowledge. Mr

Casaubon's inaccessibility, both to Dorothea and to himself, makes him a fascinating riddle, and is indeed part of his initial lure to his bride; but we would like to probe the secrets of his psyche. Instead, we have to make do with an omniscient, yet oddly unrevealing, dissertation on the abstracts of disillusionment, and at the end we still do not really know why, in a personal sense, Mr Casaubon 'had become indifferent to the sunlight'.[39]

Of the four novelists, however, we have once more to return to Emily Brontë for that combination of immediacy and universality of feeling that, without qualification, justifies the designation of a novel as 'a truly independent form'. As Traversi writes:

> No nineteenth-century novel, indeed, is less derivative in its essential content, or answers more fully to an intimate vision . . . no other novel of the Victorian period has penetrated so far into the depths of passion . . . . The result is a unique imaginative creation which, largely ignoring the moral and social assumptions of the contemporary novel, aspires rather to the severe simplicity of ancient tragedy.[40]

To this, it might well be added that *Wuthering Heights* also looks forward to our own age in a way that makes it equally 'unique' among its contemporaries; for Emily Brontë, who, of all our four novelists, has been the most connected with the traditions of early Romanticism, was also the creator of something that has only emerged in an exact sense in the modern novel. In Heathcliff, we have English literature's first true Anti-Hero. He is not one of the semi-lovable rogues of the picaresque novel; nor does he have that fatal mark of Cain that stamps the archetype Byronic Hero. Heathcliff is blatantly and unequivocally bad, but basically because he has himself been appallingly abused, and we can sympathise with the rational impulses that make him seek his revenge. The difference between him and Charlotte's Rochester is that the latter retains Hero status by virtue of a moral reformation that we sense from the beginning to be almost inevitable. Heathcliff's end, like that of all Anti-Heroes, is dubious, but, like so many of his kind, he carries our prayers to whatever destiny awaits him. And as he goes, his mammoth stride spans both his own and the modern world.

Finally, returning to common ground, between the Brontës and George Eliot there remains one shared feature which has not yet been touched upon. The urge to lower the temperature in imaginative fiction, which, as remarked at the beginning of this chapter, deriving principally from Thackeray, was present in the best English novelists from mid-century on. But it carried a price. In Trollope, the effort to put things plainly often resulted in their being put at inelegant length, and the determination to be straightforward led to a flatness that, ironically, was diminishing of the very realism it aimed at. Dickens, the supreme 'sensationalist',[41] provided one inimitable answer; the Brontës and George Eliot left us with another. 'You can't put a great soul into a commonplace person', D. H. Lawrence once wrote,[42] and perhaps these authors, poised in that uncertain equilibrium between the Romantic past and the dangerously experimental future, felt the same to be true of the whole ambience of the imaginative fiction they felt called upon to write. Whether rational or intuitive, however, this awareness in all of them that realism, in conjunction with the 'ordinary', has its limitations was the very essence of their literary relationship. In sum, it was a relationship formed of a unique harmonisation of the Romantic and the Realistic expression in fiction. Nothing quite like it had been seen before in the English novel, for none of the Brontës, nor George Eliot, shared with Thackeray the consistent inclination to satire, nor with Dickens the intense preoccupation with social indictment; but with each other they shared the facility to combine a rational, at times almost pragmatic, attitude to life with an acute insight into the mystic and metaphysical dimensions of the human spirit.

It was once said that 'nothing is more impertinent than the talk of permanent literary fame. Every generation has to take down and dust these idols of its predecessor, and it invariably forgets to replace one or two'.[43] On the other hand, of course, succeeding generations will often reverse the process yet again, so that eventually we come to the conclusion that good writers, like old soldiers, never really die, and that the differences between them are sometimes not as great as the oscillations of critical commentary would have us believe.

Looking back on the Brontës and George Eliot over an intervening period that has seen many such changes in literary fashion, both among critics and authors themselves,[44] the picture these four novelists present is remarkably unified. Even the great gap between them of religious belief seems diminished by distance; and, touching, as they do, over a broad spectrum of aims and ideals, they seem almost to form a special kind of 'tradition' of their own. And in a sense, indeed, they do, for theirs was the 'Middle Period', of which it has been said that we feel no sense of either the preceding or the succeeding centuries.[45] Equally, the themes, techniques and aspects of characterisation which George Eliot and the Brontës offered to a world in some ways so different, yet in others not so very unlike our own, had a universality that can be seen to remain timeless.

> The novel [wrote Lawrence] is a perfect medium for revealing to us the changing rainbow of our living relationships. The novel can help us to live, as nothing else can . . . . If the novelist keeps his thumb out of the pan.[46]

None of our four novelists kept her thumb entirely out of the pan – although one came closer to doing so than any other writer of her time. But in their art they celebrated in so many different, yet affiliated, ways, the 'changing rainbow' of human relationship; and in this they consolidated a relationship one to the other which we now recognise as being both formed by, and unique to, the distinct middle period of the Victorian age.

Abbreviations

THE NOVELS

In the notes and references, abbreviations are used wherever practicable, as follows:

The Brontës

JE	*Jane Eyre*, edited by Jane Jack and Margaret Smith (Oxford: Clarendon Press, 1969).
WH	*Wuthering Heights*, edited by Hilda Marsden and Ian Jack (Oxford: Clarendon Press, 1976).
AG	*Agnes Grey*, introduction by Margaret Lane (London: Dent, Everyman's Library, 1958).
TTWH	*The Tenant of Wildfell Hall*, edited by G. D. Hargreaves; introduction by Winifred Gérin (Harmondsworth: Penguin, 1979).

George Eliot

Scenes	*Scenes of Clerical Life*, edited by David Lodge (Penguin, 1973).
AB	*Adam Bede*, edited by Stephen Gill (Penguin, 1980).
The Mill	*The Mill on the Floss*, edited by Gordon S. Haight (Oxford: Clarendon Press, 1980).
SM	*Silas Marner*, edited by Q. D. Leavis (Penguin, 1967).
FH	*Felix Holt*, edited by Peter Coveney (Penguin, 1972).
DD	*Daniel Deronda* edited by Barbara Hardy (Penguin, 1967).

Charlotte Brontë's *The Professor*, introduction by Margaret Lane (Dent, Everyman's Libary, 1969), *Shirley*, edited by Andrew and Judith Hook (Penguin, 1974) and *Villette*, edited by Mark Lilly; introduction by Tony Tanner (Penguin, 1979), and George Eliot's *Middlemarch* edited by W. J. Harvey (Penguin, 1965) and *Romola*, edited by Andrew Sanders (Penguin, 1980) are not abbreviated.

GENERAL

The following works have also been abbreviated for easy reference:

BST	*The Brontë Society Transactions*. N.B. the numbers attached to these denote the Volume and the Part to which reference is made. To identify the year of a particular *Transactions* entry, subtract ten from the final number (for example, '17:45' – Vol. 17, 1935).
Cross	*George Eliot's Life as Related in Her Letters and Journals*, Arranged and Edited by Her Husband, J. W. Cross, 3 vols (Edinburgh and London: W. Blackwood & Sons, 1885). (A 4-vol. edition of the *Life*, published by Bernard Tauchnitz of Leipzig is also occasionally used. This is identified by the description, 'Tauchnitz edn'; all other references are to the Blackwood edition.)
CUP	Cambridge University Press.
Gaskell, *Charlotte Brontë*	Elizabeth Gaskell, *The Life of Charlotte Brontë* (London: Smith, Elder, 1857; reprinted: John Murray, 1920).
Gérin, *Anne Brontë*	Winifred Gérin, *Anne Brontë* (London: Nelson, 1959).
Gérin, *Charlotte Brontë*	Winifred Gérin, *Charlotte Brontë: The Evolution of Genius* (Oxford: Clarendon Press, 1967).
Gérin, *Emily Brontë*	Winifred Gérin, *Emily Brontë: A Biography* (Oxford: Clarendon Press, 1971).
Haight, *George Eliot*	Gordon S. Haight, *George Eliot, A Biography* (Oxford: Clarendon Press, 1968).
Haight, *Letters*	*The George Eliot Letters*, edited by Gordon S. Haight, 9 vols (New Haven: Yale UP; London: Oxford University Press, 1954–1978).
H, or Hatfield	*The Complete Poems of Emily Jane Brontë*, edited from the MSS by C. W. Hatfield (New York: Columbia University Press, 1941).
OUP	Oxford University Press.
Penguin	The Penguin English Library.
Pinney	*The Essays of George Eliot*, edited by Thomas Pinney (London: Routledge & Kegan Paul, 1963).
PMLA	*Publications of the Modern Language Society of America*.

| Redinger | Ruby V. Redinger, *George Eliot: The Emergent Self* (London: Bodley Head, 1975). |
| SHB | *The Brontës: Their Lives, Friendships and Correspondence*, edited by T. J. Wise and J. A. Symington 4 vols (Oxford: Shakespeare Head Press, 1933; reprinted: Basil Blackwell, 1980). |

All other works are given complete citations on their first mention in each chapter, and thereafter appear under the author's name and a shortened version of the title.

Notes and References

PREFACE

1. The first recorded expression of such an attitude would appear to have been the statement of Mrs Margaret Oliphant in 1887, to the effect that 'any comparison' between George Eliot and Charlotte Brontë 'would be a mistake'. See 'The Old Saloon: The Literature of the Last Fifty Years', *Blackwood's Magazine*, 141 (June 1887) 757.

INTRODUCTION

1. Haight, *Letters*, II, 320; I, 355; ibid., 268; II, 87; VIII, 73; II, 92; ibid., 91.
2. Apart from the publication of her translation of Strauss's *Das Leben Jesu* in 1846, George Eliot's journalistic career did not begin in earnest until she joined John Chapman in the editing of the *Westminster Review* in 1851.
3. For Charlotte Brontë's meetings with Harriet Martineau, see Gérin, *Charlotte Brontë*, pp. 407, 415, 456. For George Eliot's visit to Miss Martineau, see Haight, *George Eliot*, pp. 123–4. For the meeting between Lewes and Charlotte Brontë, see Redinger, p. 264, and Gaskell, *Charlotte Brontë*, p. 458. For Charlotte Brontë's meetings with Thackeray, see Gérin, *Charlotte Brontë*, pp. 404, 405, 431–6, 475–6, 479. For the first meeting between George Eliot and George Henry Lewes, see Haight, *George Eliot*, p. 127.
4. John Lock and W. T. Dixon, *A Man of Sorrow: The Life, Letters and Times of the Reverend Patrick Brontë* (London: Thomas Nelson, 1965) p. 229.
5. Redinger, p. 29. See also Haight, *George Eliot*, pp. 21, 6.
6. Haight, *George Eliot*, p. 3.
7. Lock and Dixon, *A Man of Sorrow*, p. 54.
8. Redinger, p. 36.
9. Haight, *George Eliot*, p. 8.
10. A sequence of eleven sonnets, written by George Eliot during the summer of 1869, published in *The Legend of Jubal and Other Poems*, 1874. See Redinger, p. 45; also Haight, *George Eliot*, p. 5.
11. Ellen Nussey, 'Reminiscences of Charlotte Brontë', *BST*, 2:10, 71.
12. Lock and Dixon, *A Man of Sorrow*, pp. 263–4.
13. Gérin, *Charlotte Brontë*, p. 54.
14. G. M. Young, *Victorian England: Portrait of an Age* (Oxford: OUP, 1936; reprinted 1969) p. 90.
15. Haight, *George Eliot*, p. 13.
16. Ibid., p. 29.
17. Gaskell, *Charlotte Brontë*, p. 131.
18. Haight, *George Eliot*, p. 24.
19. Gérin, *Emily Brontë*, p. 30.
20. Gaskell, *Charlotte Brontë*, p. 125.

21. Clifford Whone, 'Where the Brontës Borrowed Books: The Keighley Mechanics' Institute', *BST*, 11:60, 345.
22. Ian Dewhirst, 'The Reverend Patrick Brontë and the Keighley Mechanics' Institute', *BST*, 14:75, 35–7.
23. *SHB*, III, 89.
24. Gaskell, *Charlotte Brontë*, p. 124.
25. Ibid., p. 86.
26. T. Winnifrith, *The Brontës and their Background; Romance and Reality* (London: Macmillan, 1973) p. 95.
27. Lock and Dixon, *A Man of Sorrow*, p. 165.
28. Haight, *George Eliot*, p. 8.
29. Amy Cruse, *The Englishman and His Books in the Early Nineteenth Century* (London: Harrap, 1930) p. 66.
30. Haight, *Letters*, I, 22.
31. Ibid.
32. H. 188.
33. Ibid.
34. Ibid., 176.
35. Haight, *Letters*, II, 263 (n. i).
36. Ibid., I, 268.
37. Ibid., 355.
38. Ibid., II, 87.
39. Ibid., VIII, 73.
40. Ibid., II, 92.
41. Ibid., 91.
42. *Edinburgh Review*, 91, No. 1 (January 1850), 153–73.
43. *SHB*, III, 118.
44. 'The Seton-Gordon Brontë Letters', transcribed by Arthur Pollard, *BST*, 18:92, 110.
45. Haight, *Letters*, II, 506.
46. Thackeray, 'The Last Sketch', *The Cornhill Magazine*, I (April 1860) 486.
47. Clement K. Shorter, *Charlotte Brontë and Her Circle*, 2nd edn (London: Hodder & Stoughton, 1896) pp. 420–1.
48. Harriet Martineau, *Autobiography*, with Memorials by Maria Weston Chapman, 2nd edn (London: Smith, Elder & Co., 1877) II, Sec. V, 326.
49. R. K. Webb, *Harriet Martineau: A Radical Victorian* (London: Heinemann, 1960) p. 14.
50. Ibid., p. 39.
51. Haight, *Letters*, II, 214.
52. *The Letters of Mrs. Gaskell*, ed. J. A. V. Chapple and Arthur Pollard (Manchester: Manchester University Press, 1966), p. 587.
53. Gaskell, *Letters*, pp. 247–50, 431–4.
54. Haight, *Letters*, II, 165.
55. Ibid., 263.
56. Ibid., 320.
57. Ibid., 319–20 (n. 9).
58. *Middlemarch*, Bk. Five, Ch. 49, pp. 525–8; Ch. 50, pp. 531–2.
59. Haight, *George Eliot*, p. 258.
60. Ibid., p. 532.

61. For Emily Brontë, see the three biographies by Winifred Gérin, *Emily Brontë*, pp. 40, 58, 133; *Charlotte Brontë*, p. 205; *Anne Brontë*, pp. 73–4. For George Eliot, see Redinger, pp. 87, 180, 267, 302, 442.

62. Gaskell, *Charlotte Brontë*, p. 227.

63. 'The Cat', 'A Letter from one Brother to Another' and 'The Butterfly', *BST*, 11:60, 339–42. Reprinted from *Five Essays Written in French by Emily Jane Brontë*, ed. F. E. Ratchford, trans. Lorine White Nagel (Austin: University of Texas Press, 1948).

1 THE CHILD AND YOUNG PERSON: IN LIFE AND LITERATURE

1. Peter Coveney, *The Image of Childhood: The Individual and Society: A Study of the Theme in English Literature*, Introduction by F. R. Leavis, 2nd edn (revised) (Harmondsworth: Penguin, 1967) p. 29. First pub. as *Poor Monkey: The Child in Literature* (London: Rockliff, 1957).

2. Ibid., p. 33.

3. Ibid., p. 31.

4. 'Ode: Intimations of Immortality from Recollections of Early Childhood', in T. Crehan (ed.) *The Poetry of Wordsworth* (London: University of London Press, 1965) p. 171.

5. *Plato's Theory of Knowledge*, trans. Francis Macdonald Cornford (London: Routledge & Kegan Paul, 1935; reprinted 1970) p. 2.

6. John Reed, *Victorian Conventions* (Athens: Ohio University Press, 1975) p. 253.

7. Robert Pattison, *The Child Figure in English Literature* (Athens: University of Georgia Press, 1978) p. 95.

8. Ibid., p. 96.

9. Ibid., p. 64.

10. Coveney, *The Image of Childhood*, p. 32.

11. Ibid.

12. Ibid., p. 35.

13. Ibid., p. 21.

14. Gaskell, *Charlotte Brontë*, pp. 169, 204.

15. E. A. Chadwick, *In the Footsteps of the Brontës* (London: Pitman, 1914) p. 124.

16. Lady Wilson, 'The Brontës as Governesses', *BST*, 9:49, 229. See also Gérin, *Charlotte Brontë*, pp. 104, 144–5.

17. *Villette*, Vol. Two, Ch. 9, p. 146.

18. Gérin, *Emily Brontë*, p. 131.

19. Mary Taylor.

20. *SHB*, I, 89.

21. Ibid., 90.

22. Emily Greenwood, 'Charlotte in Sunday School', *BST*, 11:56, 43.

23. *SHB*, III, 271.

24. Gaskell, *Charlotte Brontë*, pp. 221, 371, 428, 431, 521, 522; Gérin, *Charlotte Brontë*, p. 404. See also *BST*, 2:10, 71, 73. For the lure of the imaginary worlds of Angria and Gondal, see Margaret Lane, *The Drug-Like Brontë Dream* (London: John Murray, 1980) p. 18.

25. *JE*, Vol. I, Ch. 15, p. 179.
26. Ellen Nussey, 'Reminiscences', *BST*, 2:10, 71. See also Gérin, *Charlotte Brontë*, pp. 20, 25, 28, 29, 30.
27. Bernard J. Paris, *A Psychological Approach to Fiction: Studies in Thackeray, George Eliot, Dostoevsky, and Conrad* (Bloomington and London: Indiana University Press, 1974).
28. Karen Horney, *Neurosis and Human Growth* (New York: W. W. Norton, 1950).
29. Paris, *A Psychological Approach to Fiction*, p. 45 (quotation from *Neurosis and Human Growth*, p. 18).
30. Paris, *A Psychological Approach to Fiction*, p. 45.
31. Ibid., p. 45 (quotation from *Neurosis and Human Growth*, p. 18).
32. Paris, *A Psychological Approach to Fiction*, p. 54.
33. Ibid. (quotation from Karen Horney's *The Neurotic Personality of our Time* (New York: W. W. Norton, 1936), p. 84).
34. See William H. Marshall, *The World of the Victorian Novel* (South Brunswick and New York: A. S. Barnes; London: Thomas Yoseloff, 1967) pp. 154–5.
35. Gérin, *Charlotte Brontë*, pp. 141–3.
36. Angus M. Mackay, 'The Brontës at Cowan Bridge', *SHB*, I, 70–5.
37. Letters to *The Halifax Guardian* and *The Leeds Mercury*, May–August 1857; *SHB*, IV, Appendix I, 299–314.
38. Edith M. Weir, 'Cowan Bridge: New Light on Old Documents', *BST*, 11:56, 16–19.
39. *JE*, Vol. I, Ch. 5, p. 49.
40. Ibid., Ch. 7, p. 68.
41. Ibid., Vol. III, Ch. 2, p. 414.
42. *Shirley*, Ch. 20, p. 342.
43. Ibid., Ch. 18, p. 315.
44. Ibid., Ch. 12, p. 230.
45. Ibid., Ch. 13, p. 248; Ch. 14, pp. 267–8.
46. *Villette*, Vol. Three, Ch. 42, p. 594.
47. *JE*, Vol. III, Ch. 1, p. 404.
48. Examples of the use of the word 'marble' to denote rigidity and lack of feeling occur frequently in the works of the Brontës and George Eliot. See *JE*, Vol. I, Ch. 7, p. 76; Vol. III, Ch. 9, p. 524. *Villette*, Vol. Three, Ch. 30, p. 442. *TTWH*, Vol. II, Ch. 36, p. 330. *FH*, Ch. 38, p. 473; Ch. 42, p. 515; Ch. 46, p. 562. *Romola*, Bk. Three, Ch. 59, p. 571. See also Emily Brontë's poetry, H.12, 115, 151, 190.
49. *JE*, Vol. I, Ch. 9, p. 97.
50. Ibid., Vol. II, Ch. 10, p. 361.
51. Ibid., p. 355.
52. Ibid., p. 357.
53. See, for example, Asa Briggs, 'Private and Social Themes in *Shirley*', *BST*, 13:68, 203–19; also Jacob Korg, 'The Problem of Unity in *Shirley*', *Nineteenth-Century Fiction*, 12 (September 1957) 126.
54. *Villette*, Vol. One, Ch. 12, p. 175.
55. Sydney Dobell, 'Currer Bell', *BST*, 5:28, 219. (The article first appeared in *The Palladium* in 1850. Dobell was at the time under the impression that *WH* was the work of Currer Bell).

56. H.15.
57. Gaskell, *Charlotte Brontë*, p. 76.
58. Ibid., p. 58.
59. Ellen Nussey, 'Reminiscences', 75.
60. Ibid., 76.
61. Gérin, *Emily Brontë*, p. 39.
62. Laura Hinkley, *The Brontës: Charlotte and Emily* (London: Hammond, 1947) pp. 126–7.
63. Ibid., p. 129.
64. *SHB*, II, 51.
65. Ibid., 52.
66. H.112.
67. H.187.
68. 'A Letter from one Brother to Another', *BST*, 11:60, 340–1.
69. Ibid., 99–100.
70. Irving H. Buchen, 'Emily Brontë and the Metaphysics of Childhood and Love', *Nineteenth-Century Fiction*, 22 (June 1967) 66.
71. Ibid.
72. John Hewish, *Emily Brontë: A Critical and Biographical Study* (London and Basingstoke: Macmillan, 1969) p. 100.
73. *SHB*, II, 240.
74. See, for example, H.153, 186 and 187.
75. David Cecil, 'Fresh Thoughts on the Brontës', *BST*, 16:83, 172–3.
76. Dorothy van Ghent, 'On *Wuthering Heights*', *The English Novel: Form and Function* (New York: Evanston and London: Harper Torchbooks, 1961) pp. 156–66.
77. Ibid., p. 165.
78. Ibid., pp. 165–6.
79. H.153.
80. *WH*, Vol. I, Ch. 9, p. 102.
81. Ibid., Vol. II, Ch. 1, p. 198.
82. Ibid., Ch. 2, p. 204.
83. 'The Butterfly', *BST*, 11:60, 342.
84. H.112.
85. 'The Cat', *BST*, 11:60, 339–40.
86. *WH*, Vol. I, Ch. 5, pp. 51, 52.
87. H.187.
88. Ibid.
89. H.14.
90. H.99.
91. H.111.
92. 'Dr. Blondel Writes Again on Emily Brontë', *BST*, 14:73, 22.
93. *WH*, Vol. I, Ch. 9, p. 98.
94. Ibid., Ch. 7, p. 76.
95. Ibid., Vol. II, Ch. 18, pp. 381–4.
96. H.93.
97. *AG*, Ch. 14, p. 31.
98. Ibid., Introd., p. vi.
99. Gérin, *Anne Brontë*, p. 233.
100. Susan Brooke, 'Anne Brontë at Blake Hall', *BST*, 13:68, pp. 239–49.

101. *AG*, Ch. 7, p. 50.
102. Ibid., Ch. 5, pp. 36–9.
103. Ibid., Ch. 6, p. 43.
104. Ibid., Ch. 7, p. 55.
105. *TTWH*, p. 30.
106. Ibid.
107. Sir Linton Andrews, 'A Challenge By Anne Brontë', *BST*, 14:75, 28.
108. *SHB*, III, 156.
109. *TTWH*, Vol. I, Ch. 3, p. 57.
110. Ibid., p. 54.
111. Ibid., Vol. III, Ch. 49, p. 452.
112. *AB*, Bk. Third, Ch. 24, p. 315.
113. *Scenes*, ('Amos Barton', Ch. 2), p. 58.
114. Ibid.
115. *SM*, Ch. 14, p. 179.
116. Redinger, p. 29.
117. Pinney, pp. 19–21.
118. Pattison, *The Child Figure in English Literature*, p. 101.
119. Ibid.
120. Paris, *A Psychological Approach to Fiction*, p. 185.
121. F. R. Leavis, *The Great Tradition* (London: Chatto & Windus, 1948; reprinted Penguin, 1980) pp. 55–7.
122. Haight, *Letters*, III, 382.
123. Coveney, *The Image of Childhood*, p. 172.
124. *SM*, Ch. 2, p. 68.
125. Ibid., Ch. 12, p. 168.
126. Ibid., Ch. 14, p. 185.
127. Ibid., p. 190.
128. Ibid., Ch. 12, p. 165.
129. Ibid., Ch. 14, p. 179.
130. Pattison, *The Child Figure in English Literature*, p. 105.
131. *DD*, Bk. One, Ch. 4, p. 69.
132. *Middlemarch*, Bk. Two, Ch. 20, p. 226.

2 MATTERS OF BELIEF

1. Peter Gay, *Age of Enlightenment*, Great Ages of Man: A History of the World's Cultures (Amsterdam: Time-Life International (Nederland), N. V., 1969) p. 11.
2. Bulwer Lytton, *England and the English*, Standish Meacham (ed.) (Chicago and London: University of Chicago Press, 1970) pp. 318–19.
3. Annette B. Hopkins, *The Father of the Brontës* (London: OUP, 1958) p. 51. See also Lock and Dixon, *A Man of Sorrow: The Life, Letters and Times of the Rev. Patrick Brontë* (London: Nelson, 1965) pp. 213–18.
4. Lock and Dixon, *A Man of Sorrow*, p. 292.
5. Ibid., p. 293.
6. Gérin, *Charlotte Brontë*, p. 34. First-hand impressions of Aunt Branwell

were more moderate. Mrs Gaskell wrote of a 'kindly and conscientious woman . . . but with the somewhat narrow ideas natural to one who had spent nearly all her life in the same place', (*Charlotte Brontë*, pp. 60–1); and Ellen Nussey recorded her memory of a 'very lively and intelligent woman', who missed 'the gayeties [sic] of her dear native town, Penzance' ('Reminiscences of Charlotte Brontë', *BST* 2:10, 74–5).

7. Gaskell, *Charlotte Brontë*, p. 142.
8. Ibid., p. 301.
9. Walter E. Houghton, *The Victorian Frame of Mind, 1830–1870* (London: OUP, 1957, p. 321.
10. Ibid., pp. 301–2.
11. *JE*, Vol. I, Ch. 7, p. 76.
12. *Villette*, Vol. One, Ch. 14, pp. 195–6.
13. Ibid., Vol. Three, Ch. 36, p. 514.
14. Gaskell, *Charlotte Brontë*, pp. 264–6.
15. *Villette*, Vol. Three, Ch. 36, p. 507.
16. Ibid., p. 508.
17. Ibid., p. 512.
18. Ibid., pp. 516–17.
19. Ibid., p. 512.
20. Ibid., p. 514.
21. Gaskell, *Charlotte Brontë*, p. 143.
22. Clement K. Shorter, *The Brontës: Life and Letters* (London: Hodder & Stoughton, 1908) I, 339.
23. *SHB*, I, 293.
24. Clement K. Shorter, *Charlotte Brontë and Her Circle* (London: Hodder & Stoughton, 1896) pp. 117–18.
25. *SHB*, I, 267.
26. Gérin, *Charlotte Brontë*, pp. 229, 232–3, 234, 236, 245–6.
27. Gaskell, *Charlotte Brontë*, p. 622.
28. Ibid., p. 142.
29. Eanne Oram, 'Emily Brontë and F. D. Maurice: Some Parallels of Thought', *BST*, 13:67, 131–40.
30. Parallels in Plato's thought are found in the *Symposium*, 211B–212A and in the *Phaedrus*, 247C–E; see *The Spirit of Man*, trans. R. Bridges (London: Longmans, Green, 1916) p. 37, and *Plato's Thought*, trans. G. M. A. Grube (London: Methuen, 1935) p. 31, respectively. Emily Bronte's own preoccupation with life's dualities is repeatedly seen in her poetry; e.g., H.14, 44, 61 (last stanza), 99, 112, 144, 149, 157, 188. Also the 'two children' theme in H.186 and 187.
31. As envisaged in the concluding statement of 'The Butterfly', *BST*, 11:60, 341–2, the 'resurrection' of Heathcliff in *WH* and poems H.61 (last three stanzas), 134 (last three stanzas) and 191. Plato's arguments concerning the precise nature of the soul are complex, but his statements on its essential indestructability are explicit. See *Phaedo*, 100B–105E, *Body, Mind and Death*, trans. H. N. Fowler, *Problems of Philosophy*, ser., ed. Antony Flew (New York: Macmillan, 1964) pp. 55–67, and the *Republic*, 608C–612A, trans. H. D. P. Lee (Harmondsworth: Penguin, 1955) pp. 387–91.

32. See *WH*, Vol. II, Ch. 1, p. 197 (Catherine's speech); Ch. 20, p. 409 (Heathcliff's anticipation of union after death) and p. 412 (references to their discarnate spirits). Also poems, H.41, 134 (last three stanzas), 136, 144, 188, 190 (stanzas 18–23 inclusive). For parallels in Plato, see *Phaedo*, 65A–68B, Flew, pp. 42–6.

33. E.g. 'The Butterfly', *BST*, 11:60, 341, 342; also the *Republic*, Lee, pp. 265–86.

34. Leslie Stevenson, *Seven Theories of Human Nature* (New York and Oxford: OUP, 1977) p. 26.

35. 'The Cat', *BST*, 11:60, 339–40.

36. H.37.

37. H.44.

38. H.181.

39. H.191.

40. *Republic*, Lee, pp. 265–86.

41. 'The Butterfly', *BST* 11:60, 341.

42. Ibid., 342.

43. *Republic*, Lee, p. 265.

44. Mildred A. Dobson, 'Was Emily Brontë a Mystic?', *BST*, 11:58, 166–75.

45. H.188.

46. H.176.

47. H.190.

48. Review of Philip Henderson (ed.), *The Complete Poems of Emily Brontë*, *The New Statesman and Nation*, 43, No. 1096 (8 March 1952) 277. A different viewpoint on Gondal is found in Edward Chitham and Tom Winnifrith, *Brontë Facts and Brontë Problems* (London and Basingstoke: Macmillan, 1983); see p. 41, where Chitham suggests that, for Emily Brontë, Gondal was 'only a retreat from confronting life and in many cases real feeling.'

49. Romer Wilson, *All Alone: The Life and Private History of Emily Jane Brontë* (London: Chatto & Windus, 1928), pp. 270–1; Dorothy van Ghent, *The English Novel: Form and Function* (New York: Evanston and London: Harper Torchbooks, 1961) pp. 153–70 passim.

50. *WH*, Appendix I, p. 446.

51. H.11.

52. Pinney, pp. 158–89.

53. Stevenson, *Seven Theories of Human Nature*, p. 28.

54. John Hewish, *Emily Brontë: A Critical and Biographical Study* (London and Basingstoke: Macmillan, 1969) p. 113.

55. Gaskell, *Charlotte Brontë*, p. 227.

56. 'The Butterfly', *BST*, 11:60, 341.

57. Ibid., 342.

58. Ibid., 339.

59. H.123.

60. *WH*, Vol. II, Ch. 19, p. 393.

61. Ibid., p. 395; Ch. 20, p. 411.

62. 'The Butterfly', *BST*, 11:60, 342.

63. H.184.

64. H.176.

65. H.191.
66. H.134.
67. Gérin, *Anne Brontë*, p. 171.
68. 'The Brontës', *The Cornhill Magazine*, 28 (July 1873) 68.
69. Valentine Cunningham, *Everywhere Spoken Against: Dissent in the Victorian Novel* (Oxford: Clarendon Press, 1975) pp. 125–6.
70. Ibid., p. 126, quotations from G. E. Harrison, *The Clue to the Brontës* (London: Methuen, 1948) p. 168.
71. *TTWH*, Vol. III, Ch. 38, p. 353.
72. Ibid., Vol. II, Ch. 20, p. 188.
73. *Poems by the Brontë sisters: The Early work of Charlotte, Emily and Anne Brontë*, reprint of *Poems by Currer, Ellis and Acton Bell* (London: Aylott and Jones, 1846) with new introduction by M. R. D. Seaward (Wakefield: E. P. Publishing, 1978) pp. 33–4.
74. Ibid., p. 92.
75. Gérin, *Anne Brontë*, pp. 99, 100.
76. H.190.
77. George Moore, *Conversations in Ebury Street*, Ebury edn (London: Heineman, 1936), p. 219.
78. *Romola*, Bk. Three, Ch. 59, p. 578.
79. Redinger, p. 118.
80. Haight, *George Eliot*, p. 19.
81. Basil Willey, *Nineteenth Century Studies: Coleridge to Matthew Arnold*, pbk edn (Cambridge: CUP, 1980) pp. 209–10.
82. Ibid., p. 216.
83. Ibid., p. 217.
84. Haight, *George Eliot*, p. 51.
85. Cross, I, 15.
86. Pinney, p. 180.
87. Ibid.
88. *AB*, Bk. Second, Ch. 17, pp. 227–8.
89. B. M. G. Reardon, *Religious Thought in the Nineteenth Century: Illustrated from Writers of the Period* (Cambridge: CUP, 1966) pp. 83–4.
90. Pinney, pp. 187–8.
91. Ibid.
92. *Romola*, Bk. Two, Ch. 40, p. 428.
93. Haight, *Letters*, IV, 95.
94. Redinger, p. 142. See also Haight, *George Eliot*, p. 58.
95. Reardon, *Religious Thought in the Nineteenth Century*, p. 82.
96. Redinger, p. 144.
97. Reardon, *Religious Thought in the Nineteenth Century*, p. 96.
98. Ibid., p. 93.
99. Haight, *Letters*, II, 153.
100. Reardon, *Religious Thought in the Nineteenth Century*, p. 96.
101. See Robert Preyer, 'Beyond the Liberal Imagination: Vision and Unreality in "Daniel Deronda"', *Victorian Studies*, 4, 1 (September 1960) 33–54. Preyer sees an 'element of unreality' arising out of 'the problem of characters . . . saturated in nobility but possessing only average abilities'. He argues that the frustrations of such 'ardent

idealizing natures' exposes the 'limits of the doctrine of sympathy' to which George Eliot was committed (40–3), although he suggests that the achievement of such novels as *Deronda* was their 'sustained effort to show how catching virtue is' (39).

102. *Middlemarch*, Bk. One, Ch. 3, p. 47.
103. Haight, *Letters*, III, 231.
104. U. C. Knoepflmacher, *Religious Humanism and the Victorian Novel: George Eliot, Walter Pater and Samuel Butler* (Princeton: Princeton University Press, 1965) p. 7.
105. Ibid.
106. George Eliot, 'Worldliness and Other-Worldliness: the Poet Young', *Westminster Review*, January 1857, 1–42.
107. Knoepflmacher, *Religious Humanism*, p. 7 and n. 13.
108. William Baker, 'The Kabbalah, Mordecai, and George Eliot's Religion of Humanity', *The Yearbook of English Studies*, T. J. B. Spencer and R. L. Smallwood (eds), 3 (1973) 216–22.
109. Ibid., 216, and n. 2.
110. Ibid., 216–17.
111. Ibid., 217. See *DD*, Bk. Six, Ch. 41, p. 568.
112. *DD*, Bk. Four, Ch. 33, p. 431. See also Baker, *YES*, 217.
113. Baker, *YES*, 217.
114. Leon Gottfried, 'Structure and Genre in *Daniel Deronda*', in George Goodin (ed.), *The English Novel in the Nineteenth Century: Essays on the Literary Mediation of Human Values* (Urbana, Chicago, London: University of Illinois Press, 1972) p. 170.
115. *DD*, Introduction, p. 30.
116. See George Levine, 'Determinism and Responsibility in the Works of George Eliot', *PMLA*, 77 (June 1962) 268–9. Levine states that although George Eliot's philosophy was consistently determinist, this was not incompatible with 'her continuous emphasis on moral responsibility and duty' (268). She deplored as 'vicious' the necessitarianist view that man was totally subject to his 'unconscious desires and the push of external forces' (272–3). For her, every human life was 'at the centre of a vast and complex web of causes' (270); thus, since every act had its consequence, there rested on every individual the duty to act responsibly (272).
117. *The Mill*, Bk. Fourth, Ch. 3, p. 252; Bk. Seventh, Ch. 5, p. 453; *Middlemarch*, Prelude, pp. 25–6.
118. Irving H. Buchen, 'Emily Brontë and the Metaphysics of Childhood and Love', *Nineteenth-Century Fiction*, 22 (June 1967) 70n.

3 THE SELF AND THE WORLD

1. Gaskell, *Charlotte Brontë*, pp. 58–9.
2. Walter E. Houghton, *The Victorian Frame of Mind, 1830–1870* (London: OUP, 1957) pp. 3, 5.

3. Richard D. Altick, *The English Common Reader: A Social History of the Mass Reading Public, 1800–1900* (Chicago and London: University of Chicago Press, 1957) p. 8.

4. Gaskell, *Charlotte Brontë*, pp. 88–90, 356–7.

5. J. Lock and W. T. Dixon, *A Man of Sorrow: The Life, Letters and Times of the Rev. Patrick Brontë* (London: Nelson, 1965) pp. 100–15.

6. Gaskell, *Charlotte Brontë*, p. 108.

7. Ivy Holgate, 'The Structure of "Shirley"', *BST*, 14:72, 28. See also Andrew and Judith Hook, Introduction to *Shirley*, p. 30n.

8. D. Colin Dews, *A History of Methodism in Haworth from 1744* (Haworth: West Lane Methodist Church, 1981) pp. 12, 14. Dews notes that 'Haworth' at this time included the outlying communities of Oxenhope and Stanbury.

9. Altick, *The English Common Reader*, p. 84.

10. Gaskell, *Charlotte Brontë*, pp. 49, 122.

11. Brian Wilks, *The Brontës* (London: Hamlyn, 1975) p. 33.

12. Gaskell, *Charlotte Brontë*, p. 49.

13. Ibid., p. 122.

14. See Richard Offor, 'The Brontës – Their Relation to the History and Politics of their Time', *BST*, 10:53, 150–60.

15. Herbert Heaton, 'The Economic Background of "Shirley"', *BST*, 8:42, 4.

16. Holgate, 'The Structure of "Shirley"', 28–9.

17. Kathleen Tillotson, *Novels of the Eighteen-Forties* (Oxford: Clarendon Press, 1954) pp. 92, 93, 96.

18. Barbara Ward, 'Charlotte Brontë and the World of 1846', *BST*, 11:56, 10.

19. *Fraser's Magazine* 36 (December 1847) 686–95.

20. Gaskell, *Charlotte Brontë*, p. 343.

21. Ibid., p. 415.

22. Franklin Gary, 'Charlotte Brontë and George Henry Lewes', *PMLA*, 51, 518.

23. Gaskell, *Charlotte Brontë*, p. 351.

24. *Shirley*, Ch. 1, p. 39.

25. Gaskell, *Charlotte Brontë*, p. 413.

26. Herbert J. Rosengarten, 'Charlotte Brontë's *Shirley* and the *Leeds Mercury*', *Studies in English Literature, 1500–1900*, 16, 4 (Autumn 1976) 594, 596.

27. Asa Briggs, 'Private and Social Themes in *Shirley*', *BST*, 13:68, 205–6.

28. G. H. Lewes, 'Currer Bell's Shirley', *Edinburgh Review*, 91 (April 1850) 153–73.

29. Jacob Korg, 'The Problem of Unity in *Shirley*', *Nineteenth-Century Fiction*, (September 1957) 126, 130, 133, 136.

30. Nina Auerbach, 'Charlotte Brontë: The Two Countries', *University of Toronto Quarterly*, 42 (Summer 1973) 335, 342.

31. *JE*, Vol. II, Ch. 2, p. 413.

32. *Shirley*, Ch. 10, p. 190.

33. Philip Momberger, 'Self and World in the Works of Charlotte Brontë', *English Literary History*, 32 (1965) 350 (and note), 352, 353.

34. *Villette*, Introduction, pp. 9–10.

35. *Shirley*, Ch. 26, p. 438.

36. Edith M. Weir, 'Contemporary Reviews of the First Brontë Novels', *BST*, 11:57, 92.
37. Bonamy Dobrée, Introduction to *WH* (London & Glasgow: Collins, 1953; reprinted 1960) p. 10.
38. Merryn Williams, *Women in the English Novel, 1800–1900* (London: Macmillan, 1984) p. 98.
39. *WH*, p. 442 ('Editor's Preface to the New Edition').
40. Geoffrey Tillotson, *A View of Victorian Literature* (Oxford: Clarendon Press, 1978) p. 207.
41. W. H. Marshall, *The World of the Victorian Novel*, (South Brunswick and New York: A. S. Barnes, London: Thomas Yoseloff, 1967) p. 229.
42. Ibid., p. 227.
43. Mary M. Visick, *The Genesis of Wuthering Heights*, 3rd edn (Stroud: Hodgkins, 1980) p. 75.
44. H.123.
45. David Daiches, *WH* (Harmondsworth: Penguin, 1965, pbk) p. 28.
46. George Moore, *Conversations in Ebury Street*, Ebury edn (London: Heinemann, 1924; reprinted 1936) pp. 219, 220, 215.
47. Phyllis Bentley, 'The Youngest Brontë', *The Listener*, 2 June 1949, p. 94.
48. Ada Harrison and Derek Stanford, *Anne Brontë: Her Life and Work* (London: Methuen, 1959) p. 227.
49. Inga-Stina Ewbank, *Their Proper Sphere: A Study of the Brontë Sisters as Early Victorian Female Novelists* (London: Arnold, 1966) p. 58.
50. *TTWH*, Introduction, p. 7.
51. *AG*, Ch. 1, p. 3.
52. Ibid., Ch. 4, p. 29.
53. Ewbank, *Their Proper Sphere*, pp. 58–9.
54. Moore, *Conversations in Ebury Street*, pp. 215–16.
55. *SHB*, II, 52.
56. Gérin, *Anne Brontë*, p. 200.
57. Ibid., p. 308.
58. Haight, *Letters*, III, 383.
59. Mrs Oliphant, 'The Old Saloon: The Literature of the Last Fifty Years', *Blackwood's Edinburgh Magazine*, 141 (June 1887) 757. (Unsigned but identified in *Wellesley Index to Victorian Periodicals, 1824–1900*, I, 169).
60. *Middlemarch*, Bk. Two, Ch. 21, p. 243.
61. Robert Preyer, 'Beyond the Liberal Imagination: Vision and Unreality in "Daniel Deronda"', *Victorian Studies*, 4 (September 1960) 44.
62. *Middlemarch*, Bk. One, Ch. 1, p. 30.
63. Ibid., Ch. 11, p. 121.
64. *Middlemarch*, Finale, p. 893.
65. Redinger, p. 10.
66. Ibid., p. 167.
67. Gerald Bullett, *George Eliot: Her Life and Books* (London: Collins, 1947) p. 162.
68. Houghton, *The Victorian Frame of Mind*, p. 273.
69. *DD*, Bk. Eight, Ch. 61, p. 803.
70. Redinger, p. 387.
71. Pinney, 'Leaves from a Notebook', p. 440.

72. Bullett, *George Eliot: Her Life and Books*, p. 201.
73. Barbara Hardy, *The Novels of George Eliot* (London: Athlone Press, 1959) p. 61. See also 'The Old Saloon', *Blackwood's* (June 1887) 757.
74. *The Autobiography and Letters of Mrs. M. O. W. Oliphant*, edited by Mrs Harry Coghill, 2nd edn (Edinburgh and London: Blackwood, 1899) p. 210.
75. *The Mill*, Bk. Third, Ch. 1, p. 175.
76. Marshall, *The World of the Victorian Novel*, p. 146.
77. Roe Head Journal, Bonnell Collection (No. 98), Brontë Parsonage Museum; also additional entry (No. 98 (8)), 11 August 1836, beginning 'All this day'.
78. Gaskell, *Charlotte Brontë*, pp. 283, 318–19n.
79. F. R. Leavis, *The Great Tradition* (London: Chatto & Windus, 1948; reprinted Penguin, 1980) p. 92.
80. Haight, *Letters*, VI, 304.
81. *Shirley*, Introduction, p. 31.
82. *FH*, Introduction, pp. 25, 26, 22.
83. Marshall, *The World of the Victorian Novel*, p. 78.
84. 'The Statesman's Manual, or The Bible the Best Guide to Political Skill and Foresight', *A Lay Sermon* (London: Gale and Fenner, 1816) pp. 27–8.
85. *JE* (Harmondsworth: Penguin, 1966) Introduction, p. 12.

4 LOVE AND SEXUALITY

1. *FH*, Ch. 10, p. 207.
2. *Shirley*, Ch. 7, p. 123.
3. Walter E. Houghton, *The Victorian Frame of Mind, 1830–1870* (London: OUP, 1957) p. 341.
4. *SHB*, I, 143. See also I, 153.
5. Houghton, *The Victorian Frame of Mind*, pp. 353, 354–5, 347. See also Françoise Basch, *Relative Creatures: Victorian Women in Society and the Novel*, trans. Anthony Rudolf (London: Allen Lane, 1974) Ch. 4, where she discusses the attitudes to wives and mothers of novelists such as Dickens, the Brontës and George Eliot.
6. Houghton, *The Victorian Frame of Mind*, p. 381.
7. Ibid.
8. Ibid., p. 358.
9. Eva Figes, *Sex and Subterfuge: Women Writers to 1850* (London and Basingstoke: Macmillan, 1982) p. 114.
10. Ernest Raymond, 'Exiled and Harassed Anne', *BST*, 11:59, 234–5.
11. Margaret Lane, *The Drug-Like Brontë Dream* (London: John Murray, 1980) p. 61.
12. Ibid., p. 59.
13. *SHB*, IV, 43.
14. Ibid., 42.

15. Phyllis Bentley, *The Brontës and Their World* (London: Thames and Hudson, 1970) p. 24.
16. Charles Burkhart, *Charlotte Brontë: A Psychosexual Study of her Novels* (London: Gollancz, 1973) p. 61.
17. Gaskell, *Charlotte Brontë*, p. 169.
18. Ibid., p. 179.
19. Ibid., p. 193.
20. *SHB*, III, 222.
21. Ibid., 221.
22. Alan Shelston (ed.) Elizabeth Gaskell, *The Life of Charlotte Brontë* (Harmondsworth: Penguin, 1975) Introduction, p. 31.
23. 'The Recently Discovered Letters from Charlotte Brontë to Professor Constantin Heger', *BST*, 5:24, 62, 68, 73, 74, 75. (Reprinted with an Introduction by M. H. Spielmann from *The Times*, 29 July 1913.)
24. See Edward Chitham and Tom Winnifrith, *Brontë Facts and Brontë Problems* (London and Basingstoke: Macmillan, 1983) pp. 9.13. Also John Maynard, *Charlotte Brontë and Sexuality* (London: CUP, 1984) pp. 18–26. Both these recent studies claim that Charlotte's feelings for Professor Heger were explicitly sexual; Winnifrith argues that from the evidence of a hitherto unpublished poem of Charlotte's discovered in the Berg Collection in New York Public Library, it is possible to conclude that Charlotte 'probably . . . contemplated adultery', p. 12.
25. Gérin, *Charlotte Brontë*, pp. 240–1.
26. Kathleen Tillotson, *Novels of the Eighteen-Forties* (Oxford: Clarendon Press, 1954) p. 279n.
27. 'Recently Discovered Letters', *BST*, 5:24, 74.
28. Mrs Oliphant, 'The Old Saloon: The Literature of the Last Fifty Years', 757.
29. Gérin, *Charlotte Brontë*, p. 479. (Thackeray's wife, Isabella, went insane after the birth of their third child and had to be placed in private care. Gérin comments on the fortuitous connection between this fact and the circumstances of Rochester in *Jane Eyre*: p. 348).
30. *JE*, Vol. III, Ch. 9, p. 534.
31. Ibid., Vol. I, Ch. 7, p. 123.
32. Gaskell, *Charlotte Brontë*, pp. 127, 140.
33. Robert Keefe, *Charlotte Brontë's World of Death* (Austin and London: University of Texas Press, 1979) pp. xvii, 78. See also Gérin, *Charlotte Brontë*, p. 17.
34. *Villette*, Vol. I, Ch. 13, p. 183.
35. Ibid., p. 177.
36. *JE*, Vol. II, Ch. 9, p. 328.
37. Gaskell, *Charlotte Brontë*, p. 419.
38. Robert B. Heilman, 'Charlotte Brontë's "New Gothic"', in Robert C. Rathburn and Martin Steinmann, Jr. (eds), *From Jane Austen to Joseph Conrad: Essays Collected in Memory of Thomas T. Hillhouse* (Minneapolis: University of Minnesota Press, 1958) p. 118.
39. Walter Allen, *The English Novel: A Short Critical History* (Harmondsworth: Penguin, 1962) pp. 177–8.
40. *The Professor*, Ch. 20, p. 162.

41. Burkhart, *Charlotte Brontë: A Psychosexual Study of her Novels*, p. 48.
42. George Lewes, *Edinburgh Review*, XCI (January 1850) 158.
43. Gaskell, *Charlotte Brontë*, p. 229.
44. Gérin, *Charlotte Brontë*, p. 522.
45. *SHB*, II, 148.
46. Ibid., IV, 112–13.
47. Ibid., 112.
48. Ibid., 113–14.
49. Ibid., 174, 175.
50. Leslie Stevenson, *The English Novel: A Panorama* (Boston and London: Houghton Mifflin, 1960) p. 274.
51. F. R. Leavis, *The Great Tradition* (London: Chatto & Windus, 1948; reprinted Penguin, 1980) p. 39.
52. Colin Wilson, 'A Personal Response to *Wuthering Heights*', in Anne Smith (ed.), *The Art of Emily Brontë* (London: Vision Press, 1980) pbk edn, pp. 234–5.
53. *WH*, Vol. II, Ch. 1, pp. 192, 194–200.
54. Ibid., p. 198.
55. Ibid.
56. Wilson, 'A Personal Response to *Wuthering Heights*', p. 235.
57. *WH*, Vol. I, Ch. 7, p. 76.
58. Mary Visick, *The Genesis of Wuthering Heights*, 3rd edn (Stroud: Hodgkins, 1980) p. 16.
59. Irving H. Buchen, 'Emily Brontë and the Metaphysics of Childhood and Love', *Nineteenth-Century Fiction*, 22 (June 1967) 67.
60. Irving H. Buchen, 'Metaphysical and Social Evolution in *Wuthering Heights*', *The Victorian Newsletter*, 31 (Spring 1967) 18.
61. John Hewish, *Emily Brontë: A Critical and Biographical Study* (London and Basingstoke: Macmillan, 1969) p. 150. See also Herbert Dingle, 'The Origin of Heathcliff', *BST*, 16:82, 131–8; David Cecil, 'Fresh Thoughts', *BST*, 16:83, 174; Eric Solomon, 'The Incest Theme in *Wuthering Heights*', *Nineteenth-Century Fiction*, 14 (June 1959) 80–3; Joanna E. Rapf, 'The Byronic Heroine: Incest and the Creative Process', *Studies in English Literature, 1500–1900*, 21 (Autumn 1981) 4, 637–45.
62. 'What is the matter with Emily Jane? Conflicting Impulses in *Wuthering Heights*', *Nineteenth-Century Fiction*, 17 (June 1962) 12.
63. Dingle, 'The Origin of Heathcliff', *BST*, 16:82, 132.
64. *WH*, Vol. II, Ch. 1, pp. 194–200.
65. Ibid., Vol. I, Ch. 7, p. 67.
66. Ibid., Vol. II, Ch. 18, pp. 380–1.
67. Ibid., Vol. I, Ch. 7, p. 67; Ch. 8, p. 84; Ch. 12, p. 157; Vol. II, Ch. 1, pp. 194, 195, 197, 198, 199; Ch. 15, p. 350; Ch. 18, p. 372.
68. *JE*, Vol. II, Ch. 8, pp. 319, 321, 322; Ch. 9, pp. 325, 330, 332; Ch. 10, p. 351; Vol. III, Ch. 11, pp. 555, 556, 563, 573.
69. *TTWH*, Vol. I, Ch. 12, p. 121; Ch. 18, p. 173; Vol. II, Ch. 23, pp. 215, 218; Ch. 24, p. 228; Vol. III, Ch. 39, p. 363; Ch. 45, p. 411; Ch. 51, p. 469; Ch. 53, pp. 486, 487, 488.
70. *AB*, Bk. First, Ch. 12, p. 177; Ch. 13, p. 182; Bk. Fourth, Ch. 27, p. 342; Bk. Sixth, Ch. 54, p. 576.

71. *The Mill*, Bk. Fifth, Ch. 3, pp. 286–7; Bk. Sixth, Ch. 10, p. 388; Ch. 11, pp. 394–5; Ch. 13, pp. 408–9; Ch. 14, p. 419.
72. *WH*, Vol. II, Ch. 19, pp. 394–5; Ch. 20, pp. 399–411.
73. *WH*, 'Biographical Notice'.
74. *TTWH*, pp. 29–31.
75. Gérin, *Anne Brontë*, p. 200.
76. *TTWH*, p. 30.
77. Ibid., Vol. I, Ch. 3, p. 57.
78. Guy Schofield, 'The Gentle Anne', *BST*, 16:81, 6.
79. Gérin, *Anne Brontë*, pp. 142, 145.
80. *SHB*, I, 250.
81. Anne Brontë, Diary Paper, 31 July 1845, *SHB*, II, 52.
82. Schofield, 'The Gentle Anne', *BST*, 16:81, 7.
83. Winnifrith, *The Brontës and Their Background* (London and Basingstoke: Macmillan, 1983) p. 235, n. 47.
84. Gérin, *TTWH*, Introduction, p. 7. This is a reference to the fact that before the Matrimonial Causes Act of 1857 women were reluctant to seek legal separation in the event of matrimonial breakdown, because the right, *a priori*, to all property and to the custody of the children belonged to the husband. See Basch, *Relative Creatures*, Ch. 2.
85. *TTWH*, Vol. II, Ch. 25, pp. 234–5.
86. Ibid., Ch. 27, p. 248.
87. A. Craig Bell, 'Anne Brontë: A Re-Appraisal', *Quarterly Review*, 304 (July 1966) 321.
88. Redinger, p. 300.
89. Extract from the inscription in George Eliot's hand on the manuscript of *Romola* in the British Library. See Haight, *George Eliot*, p. 373.
90. Marghanita Laski, *George Eliot and Her World* (London: Thames and Hudson, 1973) pp. 11–12.
91. Haight, *George Eliot*, pp. 507, 519.
92. Redinger, p. 8.
93. Haight, *George Eliot*, p. 544.
94. Redinger, p. 59; see also Laura Comer Emery, *George Eliot's Creative Conflict: The Other Side of Silence* (Berkeley: University of California Press, 1976) pp. 1, 9–10, 16, 17, 19, 21, 35.
95. K. A. McKenzie, *Edith Simcox and George Eliot* (London: OUP, 1961) p. 97.
96. Redinger, p. 140.
97. Haight, *Letters*, I, 279.
98. Laski, *George Eliot and Her World*, p. 100.
99. *FH*, Ch. 45, p. 553.
100. Haight, *George Eliot*, p. 496.
101. Anna Theresa Kitchell, *George Lewes and George Eliot: A Review of Records* (New York: John Day, 1933) p. 289.
102. Redinger, pp. 211–12.
103. Ibid., p. 478.
104. Barbara Hardy, *The Appropriate Form: An Essay on the Novel* (London: Athlone Press, 1964) pp. 106–7.
105. *The Mill*, Bk. First, Ch. 12, pp. 177–9; Ch. 13, pp. 181–4.

106. Ibid., Bk. Fourth, Ch. 29, p. 360.
107. *DD*, Bk. One, Ch. 7, pp. 101–4.
108. Hardy, *The Appropriate Form*, pp. 108, 109.
109. Gilbert Phelps, *A Short History of English Literature* (London: Folio Society, 1962) pp. 142–3.

5 THE WOMAN QUESTION

1. 'The Feminine Potential', *Saturday Review*, 22 June 1895, pp. 824–5.
2. Gail Cunningham, *The New Woman and the Victorian Novel* (London and Basingstoke: Macmillan, 1978) p. 2.
3. Ibid.
4. Ibid., p. 7, quotation from J. S. Mill, *The Subjection of Women* (London: Everyman, 1965), p. 232.
5. Ibid.
6. Françoise Basch, *Relative Creatures: Victorian Women in Society and the Novel*, trans. Anthony Rudolf (London: Allen Lane, 1974) pp. 3–5.
7. Walter E. Houghton, *The Victorian Frame of Mind, 1830–1870* (London: OUP, 1957) p. 349. Quotation from Tennyson, *The Princess*, Pt. VIII, lines 253–60.
8. Elaine Showalter, 'The Greening of Sister George', *Nineteenth-Century Fiction*, 35 (December 1980) 292–311. See also Richard Barickman, Susan MacDonald and Myra Stark, *Corrupt Relations: Dickens, Thackeray, Collins and the Victorian Sexual System* (New York: Columbia University Press, 1982) pp. 3, 11, 15.
9. *WH*, 'Biographical Notice'.
10. Harriet Martineau, *Autobiography*, 2nd edn (London: Smith & Elder, 1877) II, V, 323.
11. See Gaskell, *Charlotte Brontë*, pp. 155–7 for the text of Southey's letter to Charlotte Brontë of March 1837. Also p. 155 n. 1.
12. Martineau, *Autobiography*, II, V, 324.
13. *SHB*, III, 31.
14. Ibid., 67.
15. Haight, *Letters*, II, 218.
16. Ibid., 292.
17. Basch, *Relative Creatures*, pp. 10, 14, 15.
18. J. A. Sutherland, *Victorian Novelists and Publishers* (London: Athlone Press, 1976) p. 208.
19. *SHB*, II, 3.
20. Gaskell, *Charlotte Brontë*, p. 156.
21. Ibid., p. 158.
22. *SHB*, I, 243.
23. Ibid., 194.
24. Ibid., II, 26.
25. Ibid., 28.
26. Ibid., III, 150.

27. Ibid., 278. (In a footnote, the editors give the Yorkshire definition of 'bend' as 'strong ox leather'.)
28. Gaskell, *Charlotte Brontë*, p. 349.
29. *SHB*, II, 216.
30. David Cecil, 'Fresh Thoughts on the Brontës', *BST*, 16:83, 175–6. See also A. Mary F. Robinson, *Emily Brontë*, John H. Ingram (ed.), Eminent Women Series (London: Allen, 1883) p. 156.
31. *SHB*, III, 11.
32. Ibid., II, 30–1.
33. Kathleen Tillotson, *Novels of the Eighteen-Forties* (Oxford: Clarendon Press, 1954) p. 303.
34. Gérin, *Charlotte Brontë*, pp. 82–90.
35. *The Professor*, Ch. 24, p. 215.
36. Ibid., Ch. 25, p. 220.
37. *JE*, Vol. II, Ch. 9, pp. 339–40.
38. Geoffrey Wagner, *Five for Freedom: A Study of Feminism in Action* (New Jersey: Allen and Unwin & Associated University Presses, 1972) pp. 125–6.
39. Helene Moglen, *Charlotte Brontë: The Self Conceived* (New York: W. W. Norton, 1976) p. 158.
40. *Shirley*, Ch. 7, p. 138.
41. Ibid., Ch. 11, p. 205.
42. Ibid., Ch. 20, p. 343.
43. Robert Keefe, *Charlotte Brontë's World of Death* (Austin and London: University of Texas Press, 1979) p. 140.
44. Frederick R. Karl, 'The Brontës: The Self Defined, Redefined and Refined', in Richard A. Levine (ed.), *The Victorian Experience: the Novelists* (Athens: Ohio University Press, 1976) pp. 121–51 passim.
45. *Shirley*, Ch. 36, p. 584.
46. Ibid., Ch. 31, p. 513.
47. Ibid., Ch. 37, p. 592.
48. Ibid., Ch. 22, p. 377.
49. Ibid., pp. 378–9.
50. *Villette*, Vol. Three, Ch. 34, p. 488.
51. Ibid., Ch. 30, p. 443.
52. Ibid.
53. Ibid., Ch. 41, p. 587.
54. Simone de Beauvoir, *The Second Sex* (London: Cape, 1968) pp. 33, 241.
55. Gaskell, *Charlotte Brontë*, p. 227.
56. C. Day Lewis, *Notable Images of Virtue: Emily Brontë, George Meredith, W. B. Yeats* (Toronto: Ryerson Press, 1954) p. 19.
57. Gérin, *Emily Brontë*, p. 64.
58. Wagner, *Five for Freedom*, p. 107.
59. Elizabeth Hardwick, *Seduction and Betrayal: Women and Literature* (London: Weidenfeld and Nicolson, 1974) p. 8.
60. Raymond Chapman, *The Victorian Debate: English Literature and Society, 1832–1901* (London: Weidenfeld and Nicolson, 1968) p. 168.
61. Gaskell, *Charlotte Brontë*, p. 130.
62. Gérin, *Emily Brontë*, pp. 114, 177.

63. Hazel Mews, *Frail Vessels: Woman's Role in Women's Novels from Fanny Burney to George Eliot* (London: Athlone Press, 1969) p. 14.

64. The title of an article by Guy Schofield in *BST*, 16:81, 1–10, derived from the description of Anne by Charlotte's publisher, George Smith (see 'Charlotte Brontë', *The Cornhill Magazine*, December 1900, 784). George Barnett Smith called her 'this gentle woman' in his article, 'The Brontës' (Cornhill, 28, July 1873, 68). See also Charlotte's description of Anne quoted by Ada Harrison and Derek Stanford in *Anne Brontë: Her Life and Work* (London: Methuen, 1959) p. 31.

65. Tom Winnifrith, *The Brontës and Their Background: Romance and Reality* (London and Basingstoke: Macmillan, 1973) pp. 116, 118, 119.

66. *TTWH*, 'Preface to the Second Edition', p. 30.

67. Ibid., p. 31.

68. Sir Linton Andrews, 'A Challenge by Anne Brontë', *BST*, 14: 75, 30.

69. *TTWH*, Vol. III, Ch. 49, p. 448.

70. Inga-Stina Ewbank, *Their Proper Sphere* (London: Arnold, 1966) p. 84.

71. *TTWH*, Vol. II, Ch. 35, p. 327.

72. Ibid., p. 324.

73. Ibid., Ch. 36, p. 330.

74. Ibid., 'Preface to the Second Edition', p. 30.

75. Ibid., Vol. I, Ch. 6, p. 78.

76. Ibid., p. 79.

77. Ibid.

78. Ibid., Vol. II, Ch. 29, pp. 256–7.

79. Ibid., Vol. III, Ch. 41, p. 380.

80. Jenni Calder, *Women and Marriage in Victorian Fiction* (London: Thames and Hudson, 1976) pp. 30–1.

81. Gérin, *Anne Brontë*, pp. 209–10.

82. Susan Brooke, 'Anne Brontë at Blake Hall', *BST*, 13:68, 239–50.

83. *TTWH*, Vol. III, Ch. 53, p. 486.

84. Ibid., p. 487.

85. *Shirley*, Ch. 36, p. 577.

86. *TTWH*, Vol. III, Ch. 53, p. 484.

87. Pinney, 'The Antigone and its Moral', p. 265.

88. See U. C. Knoepflmacher, 'George Eliot' in George H. Ford (ed.), *Victorian Fiction: A Second Guide to Research* (New York: Modern Languages Association, 1978) p. 252.

89. Showalter, 'The Greening of Sister George', 307. Quotation from Kate Millett, *Sexual Politics* (New York: Doubleday, 1970) p. 139.

90. Pinney, pp. 264–5.

91. Haight, *Letters*, VII, 44.

92. Pinney, Introduction, pp. 7–8.

93. Ibid., pp. 154–7.

94. Haight, *Letters*, IV, 364.

95. Cross, III, 308.

96. Redinger, p. 59.

97. Ibid.

98. Ibid., pp. 286–7.

99. Haight, *Letters*, IV, 425.

100. Ibid.
101. Pinney, 'Woman in France: Madame de Sable', p. 53.
102. Ibid., 'Silly Novels by Lady Novelists', pp. 301–23.
103. Redinger, p. 347.
104. Haight, *Letters*, IV, 103–4.
105. Redinger, pp. 449–51.
106. *Scenes*, 'Amos Barton', Ch. 7, p. 99.
107. Hazel Mews, *Frail Vessels*, p. 198.
108. *Romola*, Bk. One, Ch. 9, p. 145.
109. Patricia Beer, *Reader, I Married Him* (London and Basingstoke: Macmillan, 1974) p. 178.
110. *DD*, Bk. II, Ch. 14, p. 190.
111. See *Middlemarch*, Bk. Six, Ch. 58, p. 369, and *DD*, Bk. Four, Ch. 29, pp. 371–2.
112. *FH*, Ch. 10, p. 212.
113. *Romola*, Ch. 48, p. 495.
114. *Middlemarch*, Bk. Seven, Ch. 65, p. 715.
115. Ibid., p. 718.
116. *DD*, Bk. Four, Ch. 28, p. 365.
117. Ibid., Bk. Five, Ch. 36, pp. 503, 504.
118. Ibid., Bk. Seven, Ch. 51, pp. 689, 691.
119. Ibid., p. 694.
120. Ibid.
121. Cross, I, 34–5.
122. Basch, *Relative Creatures*, p. 97.
123. Ibid., p. 95.
124. Jenni Calder, *Women and Marriage*, p. 158.
125. Ibid., p. 133.
126. *SHB*, II, 220
127. Virginia Woolf, *A Room of One's Own* (London: Hogarth Press, 1929) pp. 156–7.

6 TRAGEDY, DEATH AND ESCHATOLOGY

1. J. B. Priestley, *Victoria's Heyday* (London: Heinemann, 1972; reprinted Book Club Associates, 1974) p. 56.
2. B. R. Mitchell and Phyllis Deane, *Abstracts of British Historical Statistics* (Cambridge: CUP, 1971) Table 12, p. 36. See also E. J. Hobsbawm, *Industry and Empire*, The Economic History of Britain, Vol. 3 (Harmondsworth: Penguin, 1969) p. 160.
3. Geoffrey Rowell, *Hell and the Victorians: A Study of Nineteenth-Century Theological Controversies Concerning Eternal Punishment and the Future Life* (Oxford: Clarendon Press, 1974) p. 12, 7.
4. Ibid., p. 3.
5. J. B. Priestley, *Victoria's Heyday*, p. 123.
6. Elisabeth Jay, *The Religion of the Heart: Anglican Evangelicalism and the Nineteenth-Century Novel* (Oxford: Clarendon Press, 1979) p. 196.

7. Gaskell, *Charlotte Brontë*, p. 127.

8. Keefe, *Charlotte Brontë's World of Death*, pp. xi–xiv.

9. John Lock and W. T. Dixon, *A Man of Sorrow: The Life, Letters and Times of the Rev. Patrick Brontë* (London: Nelson, 1965) pp. 307, 311.

10. *Villette*, Vol. Three, Ch. 37, p. 533.

11. *The Professor*, Ch. 19, p. 140.

12. Keefe, *Charlotte Brontë's World of Death*, p. xvi; see also Margot Peters, *Charlotte Brontë: Style in the Novel* (Madison, Wisconsin: University of Wisconsin Press, 1973) p. 128.

13. *The Professor*, Ch. 19, p. 158.

14. Keefe, *Charlotte Brontë's World of Death*, p. xvi.

15. *JE*, Vol. III, Ch. 1, p. 410.

16. Ibid., Ch. 34, p. 500.

17. *SHB*, II, 313, 320, 327, 329.

18. Ibid., 337–8.

19. Ibid., 340.

20. Ibid., 339–40.

21. H.191.

22. Keefe, *Charlotte Brontë's World of Death*, p. 156.

23. *SHB*, IV, 175.

24. Burkhart, *Charlotte Brontë: A Psychosexual Study of her Novels* (London: Gollancz, 1973) p. 121.

25. A. Mary F. Robinson, *Emily Brontë*, John H. Ingram (ed.), Eminent Women Series (London: Allen, 1883) pp. 38–9.

26. J. Hillis Miller, *The Disappearance of God: Five Nineteenth-Century Writers* (London: OUP, 1963) p. 203.

27. Margaret Lane, *The Drug-Like Brontë Dream* (London: John Murray, 1980) p. 80.

28. Elizabeth Hardwick, *Seduction and Betrayal: Women and Literature* (London: Weidenfeld & Nicolson, 1974) p. 19.

29. H.170.

30. *WH*, Vol. II, Ch. 19, pp. 394–5.

31. 'Le Palais de la Mort', *BST*, 12:64, 281–5, trans. by Margaret Lane.

32. *WH*, Vol. II, Ch. 20, p. 412.

33. Ibid., Vol. I, Ch. 9, p. 109.

34. 'The Bronte Sisters and *Wuthering Heights*', *From Dickens to Hardy*, ed. Boris Ford, The Pelican Guide to English Literature, Vol. 6 (Harmondsworth: Penguin, 1958) p. 271.

35. H.123.

36. H.192.

37. 'The Butterfly', *BST*, 11:60, 342.

38. H.191.

39. Ernest Raymond, 'Exiled and Harassed Anne', *BST*, 11:59, 225–36.

40. Gérin, *Anne Brontë*, p. 33. See also Margaret Lane's comments in the Introduction to *AG*, p. v.

41. *Poems by the Brontë Sisters* (Seaward), pp. 97–9.

42. Stevie Davies (ed.), *The Brontë Sisters: Selected Poems* (Cheadle: Fyfield Books/Carcanet Press, 1976) pp. 100–1.

43. *Poems by the Brontë Sisters*, pp. 92–4.

44. Gérin, *Anne Brontë*, p. 38. Gérin cites only the three 'doubting' verses of this poem (excluding the more optimistic sections) in her argument for a despairing Anne.
45. Ada Harrison and Derek Stanford, *Anne Brontë: Her Life and Work* (London: Methuen, 1959) p. 240. See also Gérin's introduction to *TTWH*, pp. 17–18, and n., p. 18, concerning Anne's belief in Universal Salvation.
46. *TTWH*, Vol. III, Ch. 49, p. 451.
47. Ibid.
48. *AB*, Bk. First, Ch. 4, p. 91.
49. *The Mill*, Bk. Seventh, Ch. 5, p. 458.
50. Ibid., Ch. 2, p. 437.
51. *SM*, Ch. 18, pp. 222–3.
52. *Romola*, Bk. Three, Ch. 67, pp. 637–9.
53. *DD*, Bk. Seven, Ch. 56, p. 761.
54. Charles Bray, *The Philosophy of Necessity, or the Law of Consequences as Applicable to Mental, Moral, and Social Science*, 2 vols (London: Longman, 1841) Vol. I. See p. 94.
55. 'Notes on "The Spanish Gypsy"', Cross III, 266 (Tauchnitz edn).
56. Felicia Bonaparte, *Will and Destiny: Morality and Tragedy in George Eliot's Novels* (New York: New York University Press, 1975) p. viii.
57. Edward T. Hurley, 'Death and Immortality: George Eliot's Solution', *Nineteenth-Century Fiction*, 24 (September 1969) 225, 226, 227.
58. Haight, *Letters*, IV, 301.
59. Pinney, 'Liszt, Wagner and Weimar', p. 104.
60. *Scenes*, 'Amos Barton', Ch. 5, p. 81.
61. Barbara Hardy, *The Novels of George Eliot* (London: Athlone Press, 1959) p. 63.
62. Leon Gottfried, 'Structure and Genre in *Daniel Deronda*' in George Goodin (ed.), *The English Novel in the Nineteenth Century* (Urbana, Chicago and London: University of Illinois Press, 1972) p. 173.
63. *FH*, 'Author's Introduction', p. 84, also p. 657 (n. 22).
64. Ibid., Ch. 1, p. 86.
65. *The Concise Oxford Dictionary*.
66. *AB*, Bk. Fifth, Ch. 43, p. 480.
67. *SM*, Ch. 12, p. 165.
68. *DD*, Bk. Seven, Ch. 56, p. 762.
69. Ibid.
70. Ibid., Bk. Six, Ch. 42, p. 598.
71. Ibid., p. 592
72. Ibid., Introduction, p. 8.
73. *AB*, Ch. 5, p. 81.
74. *JE*, Vol. III, Ch. 1, p. 404.
75. *Middlemarch*, Bk. Three, Ch. 29, p. 312.
76. Ibid., p. 314.
77. Cross, II, 118.

7 CONCLUSION

1. Pinney, p. 210, n.7.
2. R. H. Hutton, 'The Novels of George Eliot', *National Review*, XI (July 1860) 191–219. The article is not signed, but is identified in the *Wellesley Index*, III, 154.
3. Walter E. Houghton, *The Victorian Frame of Mind, 1830–1870* (London: OUP, 1957) p. 264.
4. Ibid., p. 273.
5. Ibid., p. 293. Quotation from *The Mill*, Vol. 2, Bk. Fourth, Ch. 3, pp. 255–6.
6. In her treatment of the Belgians in *The Professor* and *Villette*, Charlotte Brontë countered criticism with praise and showed an equally discerning eye for her own compatriots (*The Professor*, Ch. 19, p. 145; *Villette*, Vol. One, Ch. 8, p. 138, pp. 102–3). Relevant to the writing of *DD*, George Eliot expressed her disapproval of English chauvinist prejudice against foreigners (*Letters*, VI, 301–2, 304). It is also noteworthy that Heathcliff was initially distrusted because he spoke in 'some gibberish that nobody could understand' (*WH*, Vol. I, Ch. 4, p. 45).
7. Miriam Allott, *Novelists on the Novel* (London: Routledge & Kegan Paul, 1959, pbk 1973) pp. 26–7. Allott discusses the ideas of Balzac and Zola and the 'prolonged controversies over Realism and Naturalism'.
8. Ibid., p. 25. Quotation from *AB*, Bk. Second, Ch. 17, p. 223. In a letter to W. S. Williams, 14 August 1848, Charlotte Brontë also referred to 'Art' in relation to Truth. See *SHB*, II, 243.
9. Raymond Williams, *The English Novel: from Dickens to Lawrence* (London: Chatto & Windus, 1973) p. 60.
10. Ibid.
11. Ibid., p. 61.
12. Felicia Bonaparte, *The Triptych and the Cross: The Central Myths of George Eliot's Poetic Imagination* (Brighton: Harvester Press, 1979) passim.
13. *Middlemarch*, Bk. Two, Ch. 21, p. 243.
14. R. W. Harris, *Romanticism and the Social Order, 1780–1830* (London: Blandford Press, 1969) pp. 10, 11.
15. 'Characteristics', *Critical and Miscellaneous Essays* (1838) 5 vols in the Centenary Edition of Carlyle's *Works*, H. D. Traill (ed.), 30 vols (New York, 1896–1901) III, 32.
16. Barbara Hardy, *The Appropriate Form: An Essay on The Novel* (London: Athlone Press, 1964) pp. 62, 70.
17. 'The Butterfly', *BST*, 11:60, 342.
18. *Poems by the Brontë Sisters* (Seaward), p. 44.
19. Isaac ben Solomon Luria, sixteenth-century Jewish mystic, whose ideas – including that of the migration of souls – strongly influenced Jewish belief. In a note to Ch. 43 of *DD*, Barbara Hardy writes that Luria's 'theory of impregnation is precisely what Mordecai has in mind'. (*DD*, Ch. 43, pp. 899, n.1).
20. Reardon, *Religious Thought in the Nineteenth Century: Illustrated from Writers of the Period* (Cambridge: CUP, 1966) 'Feuerbach', p. 83.

21. The transmigration of souls, which constitutes the starting-point of Mordecai's vision in *DD*.
22. Redinger, p. 387. See also Miriam Allott, *Novelists on the Novel*, p. 208.
23. *The Mill*, Bk. Sixth, Ch. 14, p. 421.
24. Geoffrey Tillotson, *A View of Victorian Literature* (Oxford: Clarendon Press, 1978) p. 191. Quotation from Haight, *Letters*, II, 87.
25. H. V. Routh, *Towards the Twentieth Century: Essays in the Spiritual History of the Nineteenth* (Cambridge: CUP, 1937) p. 261.
26. Ibid., p. 276.
27. Tillotson, *A View of Victorian Literature*, p. 206.
28. Haight, *Letters*, IV, 472.
29. Houghton, *The Victorian Frame of Mind*, p. 238.
30. Quentin Anderson, 'George Eliot in *Middlemarch*', *From Dickens to Hardy*, Boris Ford (ed.), The Pelican Guide to English Literature, Vol. 6 (Harmondsworth: Penguin, 1958) p. 274.
31. Ibid., p. 287.
32. Ibid., p. 293.
33. Ibid., p. 256 ('The Brontë Sisters and *Wuthering Heights*').
34. *JE*, Vol. III, Ch. 1, p. 391.
35. Ibid., p. 502.
36. Ibid., p. 403.
37. Ibid., pp. 409–10.
38. Ibid., Ch. 11, p. 552.
39. *Middlemarch*, Bk. Two, Ch. 20, pp. 224–35.
40. Derek Traversi, The Pelican Guide to English Literature, Vol. 6, p. 261.
41. Tillotson, *A View of English Literature*, p. 154.
42. D. H. Lawrence, 'Giovanni Verga', *Phoenix* (1922). See Allott, *Novelists on the Novel*, p. 78.
43. Thomas Seccombe, 'The Place of the Brontës Among the Women Novelists of the Last Century', *BST*, 5:23, 9. Report of an address reprinted by permission of the Editor of the *Huddersfield Daily Examiner*.
44. See, for example, Neil McEwan, *The Survival of the Novel: British Fiction in the Later Twentieth Century* (London and Basingstoke: Macmillan, 1981) p. 7.
45. Charles Frederick Harrold and William D. Templeman (eds), *English Prose in the Victorian Era* (Oxford: OUP, 1972) p. xiv.
46. D. H. Lawrence, 'Morality and the Novel', published posthumously in *Calendar of Modern Letters* (December 1925). Reprinted in Arnold Kettle (ed.), *The Nineteeenth-Century Novel: Critical Essays and Documents* (London: Heinemann, in association with The Open University Press, 1972) p. 48.

Bibliography

THE NOVELS

Charlotte Brontë

The Professor (London: Dent, 1969).
Jane Eyre (Oxford: Clarendon Press, 1969; reprinted 1975).
Shirley (Harmondsworth: Penguin, 1974).
Villette (Harmondsworth: Penguin, 1979).

Emily Brontë

Wuthering Heights (Oxford: Clarendon Press, 1976).

Anne Brontë

Agnes Grey (London: Dent, 1958).
The Tenant of Wildfell Hall (Harmondsworth: Penguin, 1979).

George Eliot

Scenes of Clerical Life (Harmondsworth: Penguin, 1973).
Adam Bede (Harmondsworth: Penguin, 1980).
The Mill on the Floss (Oxford: Clarendon Press, 1980).
Silas Marner (Harmondsworth: Penguin, 1967).
Romola (Harmondsworth: Penguin, 1980).
Felix Holt (Harmondsworth: Penguin, 1972).
Middlemarch (Harmondsworth: Penguin, 1965).
Daniel Deronda (Harmondsworth: Penguin, 1967).

POETRY

The Brontës

Poems by the Brontë Sisters: The Early Work of Charlotte, Emily and Anne Brontë (Wakefield: E. P. Publishing, 1978. Reprint of *Poems by Currer, Ellis and Acton Bell*, London: Aylott and Jones, 1846), with a new introduction by M. R. D. Seaward).
Stevie Davies (ed.), *The Brontë Sisters: Selected Poems* (Cheadle: Carcanet Press, 1976).
C. W. Hatfield (ed.), *The Complete Poems of Emily Jane Brontë* (New York: Columbia University Press, 1941).

George Eliot

The Spanish Gypsy (Edinburgh and London: Blackwood, 1868).
The Legend of Jubal and Other Poems, Old and New (Edinburgh and London: Blackwood, 1874).

ESSAYS AND LETTERS

The Brontës

The French *devoirs* of Charlotte and Emily Brontë appear in the Brontë Society's *Transactions*, BST, 6:34, 11:60, 12:62, 12:64, 12:65 (Haworth: Brontë Parsonage Museum). See also F. E. Ratchford (ed.), *Five Essays Written in French by Emily Jane Brontë*, trans. L. W. Nagel (Austin: University of Texas Press, 1948).

George Eliot

Thomas Pinney (ed.), *The Essays of George Eliot* (London: Routledge & Kegan Paul, 1963).
Gordon S. Haight (ed.), *The George Eliot Letters*, 9 vols (New York: Yale University Press; London: OUP, 1954–78).

OTHER WORKS CONSULTED

The inclusion of reference details in the following list has been confined to works specifically by and about the Brontës and George Eliot. Books of general social commentary and articles from journals are omitted. Full details of all material to which reference is made are included in the notes.

Beer, Patricia, *Reader, I Married Him* (London and Basingstoke: Macmillan, 1974).
Bentley, Phyllis, *The Brontës and Their World* (London: Thames and Hudson, 1970).
Blondel, Jacques, *Emily Brontë: Expérience Spirituelle et Création Poétique* (Clermont Ferrand: Presses Universitaires de France, 1955).
Bonaparte, Felicia, *Will and Destiny: Morality and Tragedy in George Eliot's Novels* (New York: New York University Press, 1975).
————, *The Triptych and the Cross: The Central Myths of George Eliot's Poetic Imagination* (Brighton: Harvester Press, 1979).
Bullett, Gerald, *George Eliot: Her Life and Books* (London: Collins, 1947).
Burkhart, Charles, *Charlotte Brontë: A Psychosexual Study of her Novels* (London: Gollancz, 1973).

Chadwick, E. A., *In the Footsteps of the Brontës* (London: Pitman, 1914).

Chitham, Edward, *The Poems of Anne Brontë: A New Text and Commentary* (London and Basingstoke: Macmillan, 1979).

———— and Winnifrith, Tom, *Brontë Facts and Brontë Problems* (London and Basingstoke: Macmillan, 1983).

Cross, J. W. (ed.), *George Eliot's Life as Related in Her Letters and Journals*, 3 vols (Edinburgh and London: Blackwood, 1885).

————, *George Eliot's Life as Related in Her Letters and Journals*, 4 vols (Leipzig: Tauchnitz, 1885).

Emery, Laura Comer, *George Eliot's Creative Conflict: The Other Side of Silence* (Berkeley: University of California Press, 1976).

Ewbank, Inga-Stina, *Their Proper Sphere: A Study of the Brontë Sisters as Early Victorian Female Novelists* (London: Arnold, 1966).

Gaskell, Elizabeth, *The Life of Charlotte Brontë* (London: Smith, Elder, 1857; reprinted John Murray, 1920).

Gérin, Winifred, *Anne Brontë* (London: Nelson, 1959).

————, *Charlotte Brontë: The Evolution of Genius* (Oxford: Clarendon Press, 1967).

————, *Emily Brontë: A Biography* (Oxford: Clarendon Press, 1971).

Haight, Gordon S., *George Eliot: A Biography* (Oxford: Clarendon Press, 1968).

Hardy, Barbara, *The Novels of George Eliot* (London: Athlone Press, 1959).

Harrison, Ada, and Derek Stanford, *Anne Brontë: Her Life and Work* (London: Methuen, 1959).

Hewish, John, *Emily Brontë: A Critical and Biographical Study* (London and Basingstoke: Macmillan, 1969).

Hinkley, Laura L., *The Brontës: Charlotte and Emily* (London: Hammond, 1947).

Hopkins, Annette B., *The Father of the Brontës* (London: OUP, 1958).

Keefe, Robert, *Charlotte Brontë's World of Death* (Austin and London: University of Texas Press, 1979).

Kitchell, Anna Theresa, *George Lewes and George Eliot: A Review of Records* (New York: Day, 1933).

Knoepflmacher, U. C., *Religious Humanism and the Victorian Novel: George Eliot, Walter Pater and Samuel Butler* (Princeton: Princeton University Press, 1965).

Lane, Margaret, *The Drug-Like Brontë Dream* (London: John Murray, 1980).

Laski, Marghanita, *George Eliot and Her World* (London: Thames and Hudson, 1973).

Leavis, F. R., *The Great Tradition: George Eliot, Henry James, Joseph Conrad* (London: Chatto & Windus, 1948).

Lewis, C. Day., *Notable Images of Virtue: Emily Brontë, George Meredith, W. B. Yeats* (Toronto: Ryerson Press, 1954).

Lock, John, and W. T. Dixon, *A Man of Sorrow: The Life, Letters and Times of the Reverend Patrick Brontë* (London: Nelson, 1965).

Maynard, John, *Charlotte Brontë and Sexuality* (London: CUP, 1984).

McKenzie, K. A., *Edith Simcox and George Eliot* (London: OUP, 1961).

Mews, Hazel, *Frail Vessels: Woman's Role in Women's Novels from Fanny Burney to George Eliot* (London: Athlone Press, 1969).

Moglen, Helene, *Charlotte Brontë: The Self Conceived* (New York: W. W. Norton, 1976).

Moore, George, *Conversations in Ebury Street*, *Works*, Ebury edn (London: Heinemann, 1924; 1936).

Paris, Bernard J., *A Psychological Approach to Fiction: Studies in Thackeray, George Eliot, Dostoevsky, and Conrad* (Bloomington and London: Indiana University Press, 1974).

Pinion, F. B., *A George Eliot Companion: Literary Achievement and Modern Significance* (London and Basingstoke: Macmillan, 1981).

Redinger, Ruby V., *George Eliot: The Emergent Self* (London: Bodley Head, 1975).

Robinson, A. Mary F., *Emily Brontë*, John H. Ingram (ed.), Eminent Women Series (London: Allen, 1883).

Shorter, Clement K., *The Brontës: Life and Letters*, 2 vols (London: Hodder & Stoughton, 1908).

—————, *Charlotte Brontë and Her Circle*, 2nd edn (London: Hodder & Stoughton, 1896).

Smith, Anne (ed.), *The Art of Emily Brontë* (London: Vision Press, 1980).

Visick, Mary M., *The Genesis of Wuthering Heights*, 3rd edn (Stroud: Hodgkins, 1980).

Wilks, Brian, *The Brontës* (London: Hamlyn, 1975).

Wilson, Romer, *All Alone: The Life and Private History of Emily Jane Brontë* (London: Chatto & Windus, 1928).

Winnifrith, Tom, *The Brontës and their Background: Romance and Reality* (London and Basingstoke: Macmillan, 1973).

————— and Chitham, Edward, *Brontë Facts and Brontë Problems* (London and Basingstoke: Macmillan, 1983).

Wise, T. J. and Symington, J. A. (eds), *The Brontës: Their Lives, Friendships and Correspondence*, 4 vols (Oxford: Shakespeare Head Press, 1933; reprinted in 2 vols, Basil Blackwell, 1980).

Index

Abelard, Peter, 79
à Kempis, Thomas *see* Kempis, Thomas à
Allbutt, Clifford, 176
Amberley, Katherine Louise Stanley, Viscountess, 27
Anderson, Quentin, 176–7
Arnold, Matthew, 40, 62
Auerbach, Nina, 73
Augustine, St, 12–13
Austen, Jane, 95; *Sense and Sensibility*, 79

Baker, William, 62
Basch, Françoise, 117–18, 144, 197 n.5
Beauvoir, Simone de, 130
Beer, Patricia, 142
Bell, A. Craig, 108
Bentley, Phyllis, 77
Blackwood, John (publisher), 33
Blake Hall, Mirfield, 137
Blake, William, 12, 171; 'The Clod and the Pebble', 76
Bodichon, Barbara Leigh (*formerly* Smith), 111, 118
Bonaparte, Felicia, 163
Brabant, Dr Robert, 57, 109
Branwell, Elizabeth (Aunt Branwell): regime, 14; death,23; religious fervour, 39, 160; letter from CB on ambitions, 120; as mother substitute, 151–2; influence on AB, 151, 160; Mrs Gaskell and Ellen Nussey on, 190 n.6
Bray, Caroline (*née* Hennell), 56
Bray, Charles: letter from GE on *Jane Eyre*, 7; dissenting thought, 56; religious influence on GE, 56–7; GE's attachment to, 109, 112; and GE's male pseudonym, 118; on causal moral law, 163
Briggs, Asa, Baron, 72
Brontë sisters: family background, 2–3; education, 3–4, 16; early cultural influences and reading, 4–5; early religious influences, 5–6, 37–9; youthful writing, 6; search for ideal unity of self and another, 6–7; and 'mask' incident, 67; interest in political events, 68; and local social

conditions, 68–9; theme of imprisonment, 84; selflessness, 86; male pseudonyms, 117; mutual feelings, 152; and Romantic tradition, 169–70, 172, 174; and common humanity, 172–3; autobiographical approach, 175; *see also* individual sisters
Brontë, Anne: religious views, 6, 45, 50, 52–5, 65–6, 162, 173; character, 11; attitude to Branwell, 15, 21–2, 49, 53, 79, 104, 134, 136; works as governess, 27–8, 52–3, 137; attitude to children, 29–30; reaction to Aunt Branwell's evangelism, 39; heroism, 52–3, 79–80; realism, 78; social consciousness, 78–9, 115; lack of fulfilment, 84–5; emotional life, 105; and Weightman, 105–6; on love and marriage, 106, 114; character as 'little girl', 123; on women and sex equality, 133–4, 137–8, 143, 147; death, 151–2, 154–5, 162; relations with Aunt Branwell, 151, 160; attitude to death and salvation, 160–2; pragmatism, 161
WORKS: *Agnes Grey*: children in, 27–8, 30; George Moore praises, 55, 77–8; autobiographical elements in, 78, 105; inception as *Passages in the Life of an Individual*, 105; and social inequality, 78; Weightman portrayed in, 105; women and marriage in, 136–8
'Despondency' (poem), 161
'The Doubter's Prayer' (poem), 161
The Tenant of Wildfell Hall: children in, 17, 27–30, 78; aspects of Branwell in (*via* Arthur Huntington), 22; position of women in, 29, 78–9, 106–8, 131, 133–8; reception, 29, 53; on God's redemptive love, 54; social themes, 78–9; masculinity in, 96; sexual contacts in, 102; and truth-telling, 104–5; 1848 Preface, 104, 134; Bell describes as masterpiece, 108; death in, 161
'Vanitas Vanitatum, Omnia Vanitas' (poem), 54

213

Index